Nutrition, Additive & Flavor Standards

Revised Edition

VOLUME 1

The L.J. Minor Foodservice Standards Series

Nutrition, Additive & Flavor Standards

Revised Edition

LEWIS J. MINOR

School of Hotel, Restaurant and Institutional Management
Michigan State University
East Lansing, Michigan

avi

AVI PUBLISHING COMPANY, INC.
Westport, Connecticut

THE AVI PUBLISHING COMPANY, INC.
250 Post Road East
P.O. Box 831
Westport, Connecticut 06881

Library of Congress Cataloging-in-Publication Data

Minor, Lewis J.
Nutrition, additive, and flavor standards.

(The L.J. Minor foodservice standards series ; v. 1)
Rev. ed. of: Nutritional standards. c1983.
Bibliography: p.
Includes index.
1. Food--Standards. 2. Food industry and trade--Standards. 3. Food service. 4. Nutrition.
I. Minor, Lewis J. Nutritional standards. II. Title.
III. Series.
TX537.M55 1985 641.1 85-22873
ISBN 0-87055-520-0

ISBN 0-87055-520-0
Printed in the United States of America
ABCDE 4321098765

To hotel, restaurant, and institutional management students, managers, chefs, dietitians, engineers, manufacturers, distributors, planners, and operators who strive to achieve high quality foodservice standards by developing and marketing very modern lines that give relevance to our complex industry.

And to my devoted wife, Ruth

Contents

Preface

Mankind's primary requisites include air, water, and food, as well as fuel (warmth), clothing, and shelter. Without these essentials human beings cannot exist.

This book is aimed at helping to explain the basic factors that influence the wholesomeness, nutritive value, flavor, color, texture, appearance, and preservation of food products. Just as important, it also provides guidelines used to set quality standards for institutional and commercial dietary services.

The study of food science and nutrition is critical to our ability to provide healthy diets to future generations. Food is a complex subject, and proper focus embraces the physical, chemical, biological, and social sciences. Fortunately, as great scientists are choosing careers in food science, the development of flavorful and nutritious foods together with processes for preserving these products are fulfilling our current needs and providing great promise for the future. Concomitantly, the safety of our food supply is being monitored with ever-increasing care and accuracy.

The reader will have to decide about the acceptability of governmental agency and food industry policies that affect the environment and the availability of a safe and abundant supply of good, wholesome, and economical food.

My sincere thanks to my colleagues and friends Dr. Lendal Kotschevar, School of Hotel, Restaurant and Institutional Management, Florida International University, for assisting with the development of the chapter on nutrition; to Dr. Jack Ninemeier, Michigan State University, and Dr. Ronald F. Cichy, School of Hotel and Restaurant Management, University of Denver, for editing various stages of manuscript; and to Michael L. Minor and others for assistance with illustrations.

Lewis J. Minor

Introduction

The L. J. Minor Foodservice Standards Series is a concerted attempt to identify quality parameters according to which quantity foodservices should operate. Although sources of standards may vary—they emanate from professional, consumer, governmental, and other concerns—they all have several things in common:

- Foodservice standards identify goals and represent performance indicators that can and should be utilized to structure and evaluate operational performance.
- Foodservice standards provide a foundation of information that students of hospitality must acquire in order to improve our industry as they become its leaders.
- Exemplary standards of excellence must be known in order to be utilized. Each of us has a desire to do the best we can in the activities with which we are involved. Standards become the guidelines for personal assessment; they suggest how things should be when we consider the effectiveness of our own actions.

The foodservice industry is vast and complex; the scope of the activities and job-related knowledge required to operate within it is very broad. Each book in this series is developed to focus concern for identification and application of standards upon one important but, by itself, small aspect of the entire domain of regulated standards. This is done with the hope that each book will be considered in company with others in the series. The result can be a synergistic effect that will make a difference in the way our industry evolves.

Lewis J. Minor

The L. J. Minor
FOODSERVICE STANDARDS SERIES

Lewis J. Minor, Editor

School of Hotel, Restaurant and
Institutional Management
Michigan State University
East Lansing, Michigan

Volume 1. NUTRITION, ADDITIVE AND FLAVOR STANDARDS, Revised Edition
Lewis J. Minor

Volume 2. SANITATION, SAFETY AND ENVIRONMENTAL STANDARDS
Lewis J. Minor

Volume 3. BASIC ACCOUNTING STANDARDS
Jack D. Ninemeier and Raymond S. Schmidgall

Volume 4. EMPLOYEE MANAGEMENT STANDARDS
Robert W. McIntosh

Volume 5. STANDARDS FOR FATS AND OILS
Harry W. Lawson

Volume 6. COLLEGE AND UNIVERSITY FOODSERVICE MANAGEMENT STANDARDS
Peter J. Eckel, Jr.

1 Introduction to the Study of Food

Why is a basic knowledge of food, the culinary arts and the science of preserving foods important to foodservice managers? The answer lies in the fact that mankind must eat in order to live, work, and play. However, besides fulfilling physiological needs, food also fulfills psychological and social purposes when quality standards are attained to a minimum required level as perceived by the individual. Our ethnic backgrounds, ancestry, childhood food experiences, travel, and social activities all tend to influence whether we like or dislike specific foods.

It is essential for a manager to understand the dietary preferences of clientele served by the foodservice operation. Food acceptance is determined by such factors as age, socioeconomic background, travel experiences, family size and makeup, and activity patterns. These are, of course, different for each individual.

In addition, the foodservice manager must keep abreast of general economic changes in society. People are often more concerned about the high cost of food than that of other products, and food cost ranks above many other issues. A review of consumer concerns about some economic and social problems is noted in Table 1.

Today cooking at home involves use of more fresh meats, produce, and cheeses; it involves fewer frozen dinners and other convenience food items. There has been an increase in the number of meals eaten away from home, in part because menu prices in foodservice operations are frequently less

TABLE 1. Consumer Concerns About Economic and Social Problems

Problem	Percentage of public expressing concern
High cost of food	70
Crime and violence	67
Inflation	62
High cost of medical care	60
High cost of gasoline	53
Corruption in government	53
Drug addiction	52

Source: *Forbes Magazine*, March 15, 1976.

than increased supermarket food prices. (Often commercial foodservice operators do not pass on all increased costs to their customers but rather suffer reduced profit margins.)

New cooking schools have begun operation in New York, Philadelphia, Boston, Chicago, and other cities. More men are discovering the kitchen and find the glamour of food preparation to be a challenge to their creative talents. Cooking may be first an art and then a science, but it is beauty in appearance and maximum flavor that makes food a social pastime unequaled in culture and pleasure. Growing antipathy toward synthetic ingredients and menu dishonesty is causing a renaissance in cookery.

LIGHTER EATING

The mechanical world of today has lightened the work load of individuals, which has greatly reduced the caloric needs of men and women. Inevitably, meal patterns established in the past and currently retained are causing widespread obesity.

Eating between meals also causes dietary problems. Food is everywhere. Vending machines, coffee and doughnut shops, fast food outlets, restaurants, bars, hotels, schools, and hospitals provide snacks and meals away from home. Microwave ovens at home encourage "warmer-uppers" whenever TV ads suggest eating. In general, we eat too much food and exercise inadequately.

Research indicates that eating less but more often would reduce the load on our digestive systems by providing nourishment without fatty tissue buildup and cholesterol plaque deposit. The need to change our dietary habits is creating a foodservice revolution that is really a nutritional necessity. Foodservice managers must be sensitive to these changes and develop strategies to cope with them. A constant awareness of customer attitudes and needs is the key to continuing success.

Low Temperature Cooking

Charcoal broiling, a cooking process that has been popular for many years, has been found to be dangerous because smoke introduces carcinogens into the food. As this cooking method is replaced with low temperature cooking procedures, energy conservation will result. Even more important health improvements will be attained from the retention of nutritional elements because of reduced cooking temperatures. Equipment manufacturers are already preparing for this change. Foodservice managers are again confronted with the need to keep pace by changing with the times.

Vegetarianism

Vegetarian diets modified with dairy and poultry products provide adequate nutrition and are increasing in popularity. Man's preference for meat will not change suddenly, but in new generations there may be a trend away from the meat-and-potato preference of yesteryear. Fresh fruits, not preserved with sulfite and benzoate, are always in demand; and their availability may also increase as a result of customer dislike of food additives.

Wine and Cheese

The growing popularity of both wine and cheese in the United States has created new foodservice merchandising opportunities. Knowledge concerning these products of fermentation depends on exposure to the numerous varieties available.

Coffee Brewing

Coffee brewing based on special blends and added flavoring is another phase of the foodservice art that requires special knowledge and exposure. Beans from Arabia, Java, South America, and other localities, when blended, roasted, stored, and ground in a prescribed manner, can provide countless variations in flavor. A wise foodservice manager knows that customers will choose a coffee suited to their taste that is properly prepared and served.

Soups and Salads

With lighter eating the demand for soups and salads will increase. The soup can vary from low calorie consommes or thin soups to meal-equivalent *pot au feu* soups and heavy cream soups or bisques. Salads may likewise be varied through a variety of recipes as desired. The first concern of the manager should always be customer satisfaction. High quality standards will be rewarded with steady patronage.

THE COOKING AND CATERING ARTS

A manager who knows food and recognizes the importance of cooks and the kitchen has an advantage over one who lacks this training and experience. Some individuals who aspire to become foodservice managers may begin their training by attending a commercial cooking school to learn cooking, baking, decorating, garde manger, ice carving, and other skills that one finds in a full-service catering operation. Special training in dining room service may be included along with complete knowledge of how menus are planned (daily and for special functions) in a manner that coordinates the entire activity with the available personnel and equipment. A combination of this background with management training adds a dimension to the ability of the person that could provide a distinct advantage.

FOODSERVICE SYSTEMS

Many new systems have been introduced into foodservice during the past decade. Included are the Scramble system for cafeteria service that eliminates lineups and saves time for customers; the Ready Foods system of MacLennon for on-premises preparation and freezing that provides a broad menu spectrum; The Chill System (Cry-O-Vac Division, W.R. Grace & Co.) for retention of freshness for weeks without freezing; the Chef-Ready system that utilizes a myriad of manufactured frozen or canned menu items to be warmed up, garnished, and served; the Central-Kitchen system for freshly prepared food distribution to satellite outlets; and the Neff and Kupperbusch continuous Cooking Streets for fresh and/or frozen volume food preparation. These systems or combinations of them have been developed and used successfully to save labor and capital investment costs for facilities.

Change

Change is the key word that best exemplifies the foodservice industry of today. We are witnessing a veritable revolution in products, equipment, service, and customer demand. Our future is only as secure as the effectiveness of the training of our youth and their dedication to industry improvement.

CERTIFICATION OF COOKS AND EXECUTIVE CHEFS

Estimates by the U.S. Department of Labor and the American Culinary Federation (ACF) forecast that an average of 200,000 cooks per year are needed in the United States for the next five years. Through efforts of the ACF, with the help of General John D. McLaughlin (U.S. Army, Retired) of the L. J. Minor Corporation, a certification program for cooks was approved by the U.S. Department of Labor in 1977. From 1977 to 1979, the apprentice first-time program was conducted throughout the United States by the American Culinary Federation with seed money furnished by the U.S. Department of Labor National Apprentice Program. Altogether, several thousand cook apprentices have been or are being trained in this program.

General McLaughlin also succeeded in obtaining a change in the occupational rating of executive chefs by the U.S. Department of Labor. The result is that, rather than being classed as domestics (0–3) as they had been for decades, executive chefs are now included as professionals with engineers and architects in a (0–1) classification by the U.S. government.

These historic developments should result in better food for the consumers of the nation. An auxiliary benefit will be to provide more professional kitchen personnel who will cooperate with managers, food scientists, and dietitians in helping to develop improved and more efficient food production and foodservice systems in the United States.

2 Food Product Standards

Standards are essential in the marketing of foods, as with all products in the marketplace. A higher standard denotes a different value than a lower one with respect to quality.

Standards relate to the quantity, weight, quality, and value of a food product. Standards for food products must be established by the top management of the foodservice firm. These standards are based on the desires and wants of the target markets of the firm.

Once established, standards must be communicated to lower levels in the organization. Standards are targets or levels the firm hopes to attain. In order to realize high standards in food production and service, a foodservice firm must maintain similar high standards when selecting and procuring its food products from suppliers.

EGG PRODUCT STANDARDS

Egg grades are based on U.S. Department of Agriculture (USDA) standards, which should indicate high quality.

Egg quality is measured by certain standard tests. For instance, a freshly laid egg will give a higher Haugh test value for the thickness of the white measured with a micrometer than one that has been stored. The air cell is also used to measure egg quality. For Grade AA eggs, it is ⅛ inch; for Grade

A, 3/16 inch; for Grade B, 3/8 inch; and for Grade C no limit is set. Haugh units usually will have a good correlation with USDA grades.

$$\text{Haugh units} = 100 \log \left[\frac{H - \sqrt{g}\ 30W\ 0.37 - 100}{100} + 1.9 \right]$$

where H is the height of albumen in millimeters, W is the weight of egg in grams, and g is the gravitational constant.

Eggs are also graded for size: jumbo, which weigh 30 ounces per dozen; extra large, 27 ounces per dozen; large, 24 ounces per dozen; medium, 21 ounces per dozen; small, 18 ounces per dozen; and peewee, 15 ounces per dozen.

Higher grade eggs are used for poaching, frying, and boiling. Grade B eggs are suitable for cooking and baking.

Processed Eggs

Processed eggs are sold as liquid-bulk or frozen whole eggs, yolks, and whites in 30 lb and 10 lb cans. All processed eggs must be pasteurized prior to freezing or drying in accordance with food laws.

Frozen Whole Eggs

Frozen whole eggs are available in 5 lb containers packed 4 containers to a case.

Freeze-Dried Scrambled Egg Mix

Freeze-dried scrambled egg mix is sold in 20 oz No. 10 cans packed 6 cans to a case. Low-fat milk solids, salt, and butter are listed on the label ingredient statement. Although an average quality scrambled egg may be produced using this mix, it cannot compare with those made by the kettle-cook and chill process for scrambled eggs by Cry-O-Vac.

Dried Eggs

Dried eggs are sold as whole eggs, yolks, or whites packed six 3 lb cans per case or in 50 lb pails. Bakeries use most of this product.

POULTRY STANDARDS

Factors that provide the basis for poultry quality standards are covering, fleshing, exposed flesh, discolorations, and the like that determine the grade of the bird. U.S. consumer grades for poultry are U.S. Grade A, U.S. Grade B, and U.S. Grade C. Procurement grades place greater emphasis on yield than on appearance. They are U.S. Procurement Grade I and U.S. Procurement Grade II. The latter is used primarily for the institutional trade. U.S. poultry grades apply to chicken, turkey, duck, goose, and guinea.

Birds that are well-fleshed, meaty, fully furnished, and attractive are graded USDA Grade A. A broken wing, broken skin, or other blemish may cause a bird to receive a Grade B rating, although these birds are just as wholesome and nutritious as Grade A birds.

FISH STANDARDS

Fresh fish is vastly superior to frozen, even when Individually Quick Frozen (IQF), and the discerning customer can quickly recognize the difference in quality.

Salmon is now being flown in fresh from Alaska daily during the fishing season. Salmon quality in descending order is red or sockeye, chinook or king, medium red, silver or coho, pink, chum, and heta. Tuna is canned from six species—albacore white meat, blackfin, bluefin, skippack, yellowfin, and little tuna. Lobster and shrimp come to market mainly fresh and frozen. Crab is frozen or canned. Frozen fried fish sticks and all other inspected fish and shellfish products are inspected and carry the seal of the United States Department of the Interior (USDI).

MEAT STANDARDS

Beef Grades

Beef quality grades include prime, choice, good, standard, commercial, utility, and canner and cutter. Foodservices seldom use prime, as it is too fatty, and usually choose choice or good grades for roasting and commercial or utility grades for hamburger. Yield grades of 1 to 5 identify differences between beef carcasses with respect to usable meat. Yield Grade 1 pertains to the highest and yield Grade 5 to the lowest yield of cuts. A yield of 82% or higher based on carcass weight may be expected from Grade 1 and 64% or lower from Grade 5.

Four factors determine the cutability of a beef carcass: (1) the external fat thickness over the ribeye muscle; (2) the amount of kidney, pelvic, and heart fat; (3) the area of the ribeye muscle; and (4) the carcass weight.

Veal and Calf Grades

Veal and calf USDA grades are prime, choice, good, standard, utility, and cull.

Lamb and Mutton Grades

Lamb and mutton USDA grades are prime, choice, good, utility, and cull.

Pork Grades

Pork USDA grades are U.S. No. 1, No. 2, No. 3, No. 4, and U.S. utility.

MILK, MILK PRODUCTS, AND MILK SUBSTITUTES STANDARDS

Dairy products generally account for 10–16% of the raw food costs in foodservice operations. In comparison, meats, poultry, and fish constitute about 60% of the raw food costs.

Milk

Milk must be pasteurized to inactivate pathogenic bacteria. The 1965 U.S. Public Health Ordinance was adopted by 40 states and establishes the guidelines for pasteurizing milk labeled Grade A under the USDA approved seal. The milk fat content in whole milk is usually 3.5%. In homogenized milk the fat globules are broken into tiny particles and dispersed. Skim milk has most of the milk fat removed. Low-fat and 2% milk have a heavier consistency and richer taste than skim milk. Vitamins and minerals may be added to modify or fortify skim milk.

Milk Products and Milk Substitutes

Light cream (18–20% milk fat) is used to make sour cream or cultured sour cream. Yogurt is made from concentrated or partly skimmed whole milk and may be fruit flavored. Half-and-half contains 10–12% milk fat and is a mixture of milk and cream. Non-dairy whiteners are made from corn syrup solids, vegetable shortening, emulsifiers, and other ingredients. Their caloric content is 20–25% less than that of half-and-half (10 to 12 calories per teaspoon versus 15 calories per tablespoon) when used in coffee. However, the flavors are not comparable, and a wide edge in consumer preference for natural milk products was indicated by taste panel results from tests conducted at Purdue University in 1980 under the direction of Brother Herman Zaccarelli.

Whipped Cream and Toppings

Cream containing 30–35% butterfat is used for whipping. A fat content of below 30% will not produce a stable foam without the addition of ½ teaspoon of gelatin stabilizer per pint of liquid. Evaporated and nonfat dry milk whipped toppings require special techniques which may be used by foodservices. Evaporated milk is chilled to 32°F (0°C) or lower before whipping in a chilled bowl and with a chilled beater. It is then stabilized by folding in 2 tablespoons of lemon juice or vinegar per 8 oz of milk. Powdered sugar may be added. Nonfat dry milk is whipped using ½ cup cold water to ½ cup dry milk. It is whipped to soft peaks and 2 tablespoons of lemon juice are added while whipping is completed. Two to four tablespoons of sugar are then added.

Ice Cream and Ice Milk Products

Ice cream is a pasteurized blend of milk, cream, sugar, stabilizer, and flavoring. Plain ice cream must have a minimum of 10% butterfat, and chocolate or variety ice creams must contain a minimum of 8% butterfat according to standards set by federal law. They must have a minimum weight of 4½ lb/gal. One-half cup supplies about 125 calories. Note: Parfait ice creams contain egg yolks. Ice milk contains 3.9–6% butterfat. Its nonfat milk content is higher, and fat content is lower than that of ice cream. One-half cup supplies about 100 calories. Sherbet is made from milk that has been flavored with natural fruit juices or synthetic flavors and may contain egg white. Water-ice is made from water and sugar flavored with fruit juices or other flavors.

Butter and Margarine

Butter quality standards may be verified by checking the USDA grade seal on the package. Margarine also carries the U.S. grade mark whenever it is shipped interstate in accord with federal law. A flavor rating system is used in grading butter. Grade AA, score of 93, is the top U.S. grade. Grade A carries a score of 92, Grade B is scored 90, and Grade C is rated at 89 points. A government grade cannot be given to butter scoring below 89. Scoring includes 5 points for the package, 5 for color, 10 for salt or no salt, 5 for melting quality, 30 for body and texture, and 45 points for flavor.

Butter flavor defects are aged, alkaline, cheesy, coarse or coarse-acid, cooked, feed, fishy, flat, fruity, heated cream, malty, metallic, musty, neutralizer, obnoxious weed, old cream, onion and garlic, rancid (lipase), scorched, scorched-neutralizer, smothered, sour, stale cream, storage, tallowy, utensil, vegetable, weedy, woody, and yeasty.

Margarine is mainly produced from hydrogenated soybean oil with vitamins A and D, salt, dry milk solids, artificial coloring, and preservatives added. Other oils including corn oil and safflower oil may be used. Margarine must have 80% fat. Butter is always preferred to margarine in baking and cooking whenever high quality standards are desired, because of the superior flavor value of butter. Nutritionally the two products are considered equal, although recent research reports show that butter is more digestible than margarine.

Cheese and Cheese Products

Cheese may be ripened including soft cheese (such as camembert) containing 40–50% water; semi-hard cheese (such as brick or blue-veined Roquefort) containing 38–45% water; and hard cheese (such as cheddar or swiss) containing 30–40% water or not ripened, such as cottage and neufchatel containing 45–75% water.

Cheddar and swiss cheese are graded. Cheddar may be rated U.S. Grade AA, A, B, or C; a scoring system has been developed for American cheddar cheese. Color is a maximum of 10 points with a normal range of score being 9 to 10; finish and appearance is a maximum of 15 points with the normal range of score being 14 to 15 points; body and texture is a maximum of 30 points with normal scores of 25 to 30 points; flavor is a maximum of 45 points with a normal range of 31 to 40 points. Swiss cheese includes U.S. Grade A, B, C, or D.

Quality-control programs and a Quality Approved rating are available for process cheese and cottage cheese. Process cheese is made by shredding natural cheeses (for example, cheddar), heating in steam-jacketed cookers at high temperatures, and emulsifying the homogeneous mass by adding and mixing-in suitable emulsification salts and air cooling. About 53% of domestic natural ripened cheese is made into process products. U.S. Federal Standards of Identity require that process cheese contain no more than 3% emulsifying salts, not more than 40% moisture, and no less than 50% fat on the dry basis (FDB). Various standards are set by different countries.

Emulsifying salts are not permitted in pasteurized blended cheese, which is produced by blending batches of young and aged cheese. Cream and neufchatel cheeses may be used in pasteurizing blended cheese. Pasteurized process cheese food contains more moisture and less fat, requires higher cooking temperatures, and has lower pH than pasteurized process cheese. Optional ingredients include skim milk, whey, milk, cream, albumin, skim milk cheese, and organic acids. U.S. Federal Standards of Identity require that process cheese food contain not more than 44% moisture and not less than 23% milk fat.

Velveeta by Kraft is an example of a pasteurized processed cheese spread. More moisture may be incorporated in a processed cheese spread than in a process cheese or cheese food, and gums may be added to facilitate water retention in the spread. Federal standards of identity require that cheese spreads contain not less than 44% or more than 60% moisture and not less than 20% milk fat.

FRUIT AND VEGETABLE STANDARDS

Fruits and vegetables may be marketed either fresh or processed (canned, frozen, or dried). Quality variations include turgor (water and inflated plant cells) and texture, structure, and color, flavor, and appearance. These differences affect value, price, and quality standards.

Federal grades for fruits and vegetables are based on color, size and uniformity. Fancy canned or frozen fruits are usually packed in extra heavy syrup. Fancy vegetables include small young peas and baby limas or green beans. Federal grades are the following:

1. Fancy or Grade A consists of top quality fruits and vegetables of uniform size and color.
2. Choice or Grade B are good quality but less uniform or desirable in size than Fancy. Fruits are usually in heavy syrup.
3. Standard or Grade C are wholesome but show more variation in color and size. Fruits are often more mature and may be of better flavor than Fancy. Standard canned and frozen fruits are usually packed in light syrup. Water packed fruits used in pie making and for low-carbohydrate diets are usually Standard Grade.

Standards are based on the minimum quality attributes below which the food may not fall unless appropriately labeled. Excessively discolored peas, canned tomatoes lacking in red color, and canned or frozen peaches that are unevenly peeled and not well trimmed must be so labeled in bold letters as follows, where appropriate:

BELOW STANDARD IN QUALITY
EXCESSIVE DISCOLORED PEAS

BELOW STANDARD IN QUALITY
GOOD FOOD–NOT HIGH GRADE

BELOW STANDARD IN QUALITY
NOT WELL-PEELED UNEVENLY TRIMMED

When containers are below standard in fill they must be plainly labeled:

BELOW STANDARD IN FILL

For most fresh fruits and vegetables, USDA uses U.S. grade standards to describe quality differences. The grade shield may or may not appear on the package. Ripened fruit is softer in texture, juicier, and tastier, providing far more eating pleasure and better quality juice than immature fruit. Canning and freezing require firmer fruit, and consequently these products have considerably lower flavor values.

Buy fresh fruit in season and obtain only the best available. Do not overbuy or acquire more than can be used or kept for a short time without spoilage. Superficial blemishes do not harm fruit and may save money. For example, discoloration on grapefruit skin or lack of color on apples and peaches may not detract from flavor.

Frozen fruits and vegetables are sometimes packed and labeled Fancy or Grade A without the U.S. shield. These must be equivalent in value though they are not officially graded and inspected. This quality of produce must be reasonably free from surface defects, extraneous material, and insects.

A trustworthy distributor will take care of foodservice needs and fulfill quality standard desires while saving time and money. However, if unsatisfactory fresh fruits or vegetables are delivered, the produce should be returned for credit or replacement with the desired quality of product. When receiving frozen food, make sure that the distributor delivers hard-frozen containers that are not stained. Container surfaces discolored from staining have probably been defrosted at some stage of distribution or storage. Care in receiving food will forestall problems that otherwise occur when food items are prepared with low quality ingredients that should have been rejected upon delivery. Labels show the product name, brand, style of cut, packing medium used, weight, and name and address of the packer or distributor. Smart operators know and buy only the best foods available, which save labor and earn customer acceptance of the menu.

Dried fruit should be in well-sealed, clean, dry containers. Dried apples, apricots, peaches, and pears should be bright in color, firm, and pliable. Specify the package type preferred. For example, polyethylene bags, plastic containers, and coated cartons give greater protection to dried fruits than do plain cardboard containers. Prunes and raisins come in moisturized and low-moisture nuggets. Choose what is best for the necessary menu applications and buy the best brand available.

Defects in potatoes include gouges or bruises, green color from sun exposure, and internal decay. These deficiencies affect both yield and labor cost as well as customer acceptance. Grade and size should appear on the bag or box together with net weight, brand and name and address of the packer. Potatoes should be stored at 50°F, and the grade specified should represent the state of the potatoes at the time of delivery.

Processed potatoes include frozen french fried in many sizes and shapes; frozen unfried; patties and puffs from mashed potatoes; ready-to-cook patties; whole, sliced, dried, or shredded potatoes; and canned, small, whole potatoes in salt brine. Dehydrated potatoes are available in flakes and granules of various mesh sizes for mashed potatoes and soup. Dried milk solids may be added. Labels show the produce name, weight, packer, brand, added ingredients, directions for use and yield. As with all other products the use in the menu dictates whether a food product must be purchased and, if so, the specifications which must be met.

Purchasing Decisions for Fruits and Vegetables

Fruit and vegetable packers want to sell their old packs quickly when fruits in season are being canned. Old packs may be good buys, but prolonged storage is injurious to food flavor. Menu needs must dictate the fresh, canned, frozen, and dried items to be purchased. Fruits packed in heavy syrup cost more than those in light syrup, and diet packs are more expensive than fruits canned in syrup. Juice-packed fruits are important for carbohydrate-restricted diets.

Factors affecting price and usage of canned and frozen vegetables include the form and style of vegetable (such as whole, sliced, or cut) and what special seasonings, sauces, or flavorings have been used. Fancy cuts used in hot vegetables and salads are more attractive but also more expensive. Short-cut green beans, diced carrots, and tomato pieces cost less and may be used in soups and stews.

Container Size

Selection of the container size is in conformity with the number of servings needed. Cans that are too small require extra labor to open them; if too large, create leftovers and additional expense.

Fruit and Vegetable Quality Comparisons

Color, flavor, texture, and uniformity of size are compared with price and yield. Drained weight values help in ascertaining yield.

Drained weight is determined by emptying contents of the container upon a U.S. Standard No. 8 circular sieve of proper diameter to distribute the product uniformly over the sieve. Without shifting the product, incline the sieve at an angle of 17° to 20° to facilitate drainage and allow to drain for 2 min. Then weigh the drained product. Drained weight is checked after 30 days storage following the canning of the product.

Menu Uses for the Food

Buying decisions are based on requirements imposed by the menu. For example, tender asparagus tips are preferred to cuts in soft diets, cuts are useful for soups, and stalks are ideal for salads, steaming, or serving plain or on toast. Tomatoes for spaghetti sauce and other cooking need not be whole. For salads the small cherry tomato may prove advantageous. Pies and puddings can be made with less-expensive water-packed peaches. Fancy and Choice packs may be used for serving as halves or in Peach Melba. Chunks and pieces of pineapple are ideal for garnishing gelatin and other desserts; slices are served with cottage cheese (broken slices may be used). Number 10 cans may contain 28, 50, or 64 slices. Meal planning requires a knowledge of how many slices are contained in each size of can.

Receiving and Storage of Fruits and Vegetables

Canned foods should be examined for swells and dents. If these are noted, the containers should be returned to the purveyor. The storage area should be dry and free of waste and steam pipes, cookers, and damp floors. It should be well ventilated and the temperature maintained at 50°–70°F (10°–21°C).

Fresh fruit should be sorted prior to storage, and moldy or decayed pieces must be discarded. Immature fruit should be set aside to ripen until it is ready to eat if this type of fruit will ripen off the plant. Pears, bananas, and avocados should be ripened at room temperature before storing or using. Temperature and humidity control are essential for the correct storage of fruits and vegetables. Plastic bags containing fruit must be perforated to allow moisture to escape and gas exchange to occur. Ripe bananas may be held a day or two by covering and storing them in the warmest part of the refrigerator at about 50°F (10°C).

Most fresh vegetables can be stored 2–3 days. Root vegetables are an exception; these may be stored from one to several weeks. Frozen fruits and vegetables may be held for about one year with negligible quality change by holding them at 0°F (–18°C).

CEREAL PRODUCT STANDARDS

Cereals may be either ready-to-eat or ready-to-cook. Some of the cereals that formerly required cooking are now instant and can be prepared by simply adding hot water, whereas others have their cooking time reduced to 1–5 min.

Cereal products are chosen mainly by brand name, as few federal standards exist for cereals; it is necessary to develop specifications for the specific foodservice operation. Portion cost is an important consideration because ready-to-eat cereals are often about four times as costly as those that need cooking. No more than one month's supply of cereals should be kept, as weevils and other insects may infest the cereals.

Flour

Flour is classified by use.

1. All-purpose flour is made from blends of wheat that are lower in protein content than some other flours. All-purpose flour is used for pastries, cookies, and cakes.
2. Bread flours are milled from hard spring and winter wheat blends and are either bleached or unbleached. Their protein content is in the range of 9–10%, compared to 7–8% for all-purpose flours.
3. Cake flours are milled from soft wheats and have low protein content in the 4–5% range. Uses include cake mixes in which the cake flour is blended with shortening, baking powder, sugar, and dry milk. Liquid (and occasionally eggs) are combined with the mix to make a batter.
4. Instantized flour used for all-purpose applications is made by exposing the starch granules to hot water or steam in order to gelatinize the individual starch particles. This facilitates blending with liquid but requires changes in formulas and baking procedures to obtain good quality finished products.
5. Pastry flours are low in protein (about 5%) but are not as finely milled as cake flours. They are used for pastry and biscuit making.

Wheat

Common types of wheat include the following.

1. Durum wheats are used for semolina that is converted to macaroni, spaghetti, and other pasta; they have protein contents higher than 10%.
2. Hard wheats include hard winter and hard spring wheats and are used for making bakery, bread, and all-purpose flours.
3. Soft wheats are used for pastry, cake, all-purpose, and biscuit flours.

Other flours and cereals include the following.

1. Buckwheat flour is finely ground and sifted buckwheat meal.
2. Oatmeal is flakes that are rolled from oats with the hull removed. These are termed groats. Quick-cooking oats are prepared by cutting and rolling the groats into thin, small flakes. Oatmeal is used as a cereal and in cooking and baking.

3. Potato flour is made from cooked dried and ground potatoes and used in baking and cooking.

4. Rye flour is sifted rye meal produced in white, medium, and dark grades.

5. Soy flour is combined with wheat flour in bread making; full-fat and low-fat soy flours are available.

6. Soy-grits are made from coarse ground soy press cake into a low-fat product.

Corn

Commonly used corn products include the following:

1. Corn meal is a cleaned and ground white or yellow corn; it contains not more than 15% moisture in addition to small amounts of fat and crude fiber. Enriched corn meal contains added vitamins and minerals.

2. Corn flour is milled and sifted white or yellow corn. Corn grits or hominy grits are names given to corn flour that has had the bran and germ removed. Grits have a coarser grind than does corn meal.

3. Hominy is corn with the bran and hull removed. Pearl hominy has the hull mechanically removed. Rye hominy has the hull removed chemically. Broken grains are called hominy grits.

4. Cornstarch is prepared from the endosperm of the grain by separating it from the gluten and germ. It is widely used in cooking both to make sauces and gravies and as a thickener. Products stabilized with pearl cornstarch cannot be successfully frozen as they will undergo syneresis (water separation). Pie fillings made with ordinary cornstarch are gummy and opaque because of the presence of amylose, which is the straight-chain glucose polymer.

5. Waxy maize is ideal for pie fillings and sauces. Products thickened with waxy maize may be frozen successfully but will not withstand prolonged storage; syneresis will occur with prolonged storage. Derivatized waxy maize produced by dual chemical treatment has greater freeze-stability than does ordinary waxy maize. However, the flavor is adversely affected by this process. Sauces and gravies stabilized with waxy rice starch have the greatest stability toward freezing. Starches that are manufactured for food uses must be processed in a manner that maintains microbial counts as low as possible in accord with federal standards.

6. Corn cereals are prepared from corn grits cooked with malt, sugar, and salt and dried. They can be toasted in flakes or puffed and enriched with vitamins and minerals.

Rice

Rice is the white endosperm of the rice grain. Brown rice is rice with nothing but the hull removed. Rice is available in long, medium, and short grain varieties. Enriched rice contains a portion of the kernels enriched with the B-complex vitamins and iron. Precooked rice consists of long grains that have been cooked, rinsed, and dried by a patented process. Parboiled rice has been steeped in hot water, drained, steamed under pressure, and dried before hulling and milling. Parboiling pre-gelatinizes the starch to make the grains translucent and brown and improves the nutritional value by causing minerals and vitamins in the exterior portion to move into the interior of the kernel. The keeping quality of parboiled rice is also better.

Other types of rice products include the following:

1. Rice bran consists of bran, germ, and hulls and is a brown powder having a mild sweet taste.
2. Wild rice is a long brownish grain of a seedlike water plant that is hulled but not milled.
3. Rice flour is a starchy white flour milled from white rice.
4. Waxy rice flour is almost 100% amylopectin (the branched glucose polymer) and imparts great freeze-thaw stability to frozen sauces and gravies.

Macaroni

Macaroni is another type of cereal product. High quality macaroni is flinty, hard and brittle. Poor macaroni products will not break evenly. The finished products should be smooth and free of broken pieces. Government standards of identity for macaroni permit the addition 0.5–2% egg white, salt, onions, celery, and bay leaf in addition to water and flour. Egg noodles must contain not less than 5.5% whole egg solids or egg yolk.

LEAVENERS

Leavening agents are or produce gases in dough or batter to make it lighter and more porous during resting, proofing, and baking. Textures of leavened products depend upon the proper choice and use of leavening agent. Air, water vapor and carbon dioxide are all used as leavening agents. One volume of water yields 1600 volumes of steam. Air is incorporated into batter or dough by mixing, beating, kneading or folding, creaming, and sifting. Leavening action with air is the result of air expansion during heating.

Carbon dioxide is produced either chemically from baking powders or biologically through the fermentation of sugars by yeast. Breads and cakes are leavened with baking soda (sodium bicarbonate) and yeast action on sugar.

Baking powders are mixtures of dry acids or acid salts and baking soda. USDA regulations require that baking powders release at least 12% carbon dioxide. Tartrate, phosphate, and sodium aluminum sulfate (SAS) phosphate powders are available. The latter is double acting and reacts with both cold and heat. Tartrate powder is fast acting and works mainly in a cold mix. Phosphate powders are intermediate, and SAS phosphates work the least well in cold mixtures. Yeast-produced carbon dioxide requires a fermentation period prior to baking; chemical leaveners do not.

SUGARS

Sugar sweeteners are naturally produced from sugar cane, sugar beets, cornstarch, maple sap, and milk. Types include white sugar, brown sugar, and syrups. Varieties of white sugars include the following:

1. Granulated sugar for general use may be branded granulated, fine granulated, or extra fine granulated with no definite variation in crystal size. A convenient bag weighs 25 lb; it handles and stores more easily than do 100 lb bags. Superfine granulated sugar is screened for use in cakes, mixed drinks, and other applications for which rapid solubility is desired.
2. Powdered or confectioners sugar is crushed and screened for use in dusting pastries, doughnuts, waffles, and the like and for applications in frostings and icings. Cornstarch is added to prevent caking.
3. Sugar cubes contain a small amount of releasing agent (for example, calcium stearate) used to prevent sticking to the cubing machine. Sugar tablets likewise require such an agent for their manufacture.
4. Corn sugar is dried corn syrup consisting mainly of dextrose but including other saccharides (sugar derivatives).
5. Lactose is the disaccharide of glucose and galactose made from milk whey. It is much less sweet than glucose, fructose, or sucrose. Its use in food manufacture is limited by its high cost and limited sweetness. Lactose is used in pharmaceuticals and some dietary products.

Brown sugar is a second type of popular sugar product. It contains some of the molasses from the mother liquor from which refined granulated sugar is crystallized and removed.

Light brown sugar is lighter in flavor and color than the dark brown because it contains less mother liquor. Brown sugar is used in baked beans, cookies, baked goods, and confections. Caking used to be a problem with brown sugar because the product is hygroscopic, that is, it takes on moisture from the atmosphere. Recently a drying agent has been successfully incorporated that prevents caking. The additive has received FDA (Food and Drug Administration) approval.

Syrups are a third popular type of sugar product. Molasses (the mother liquor from which sugar is made) retains some sweetness and has a characteristic flavor that can be used in syrups and cooked foods to add color and taste.

Maple syrup is derived from the sap of hard maple trees by cooking and concentrating by reverse osmosis. It must weigh at least 11 lb per gallon and contain no more than 35% water. Corn syrup is derived from cornstarch by acid or enzyme hydrolysis and is rated in terms of sweetness by dextrose-equivalent (DE). Acid conversion yields syrups in the 40–50 DE range. Enzyme conversion may result in much sweeter syrups that have a DE as high as 95. Light corn syrup is made by clarifying and decoloring darker corn syrup. Its flavor is mild, and it is used in confections, baking, and ice cream manufacture. Dark corn syrup is a mixture of corn syrup and refiners syrup obtained from refining cane or beet sugar. Its main use is in blended table syrups. Refiners syrup is made up of sucrose and partially inverted sucrose. Inversion is the result of acid or enzyme action on sucrose that results in a 50:50 mixture of glucose and fructose. The latter products are reducing sugars. Their presence in the syrup will result in non-enzymatic browning whenever proteins, amino acids, or amines contact them. Refiners syrup must not contain more than 28% moisture and is primarily used to flavor corn syrup. High fructose corn syrup (HFCS) can effectively replace sucrose.

Sorghum syrup is concentrated juice from sorghum. It contains less than 30% water and 6.25% ash (minerals) as calculated on a dry basis. Honey is produced by bees from sugars extracted from flowers. Naturally concentrated, it contains about 20% moisture when extracted from the comb. Composed primarily of fructose and glucose, honey is named after the primary source of the nectar, for example, clover or orange blossom.

Jellies, Jams, and Preserves

Jellies, jams, and preserves are made according to FDA standards of identity. They must contain not less than 45 parts of fruit to 55 parts of sweeteners by weight. Dietary products and others not conforming to this standard must be called imitation.

Nonnutritive Sweeteners

These products include cyclamate, cyclamate–saccharin, saccharin, and a new product, aspartame (a trade name for a dipeptide derivative of the amino acids, aspartic acid, and phenylalanine).

The latter product has no aftertaste as does saccharin and has from 100 to 200 times the sweetness of sucrose.

The FDA, by special act of Congress, still temporarily permits the use of saccharin with a label warning of cancer-causing potential, but all combinations with cyclamate must be labeled as drugs. Aspartame has been cleared and approved for use by the FDA after several years of animal feeding experiments conducted to prove its safety for food use.

MISCELLANEOUS FOODS

Quality and descriptive standards for selected miscellaneous food items include the following.

1. Aspics are jellies made from meat, poultry, or fish and bones by hot water extraction followed by clarification. Grease is removed, and the extract is strained repeatedly through cloth until it becomes quite transparent. Gelatin may be added for further gel strength when necessary, and wine may be used to flavor the aspic. A finished apsic will have an amber color and may be used as a garnish in cold cookery.
2. Dry bread crumbs may be rolled for use in stuffings, as buttered crumbs, and for coating fried foods. Soft bread crumbs from 2- to 4-day-old bread are used for bread pudding, timbales, stuffings, and croutons.
3. Catsup is made from tomato concentrate, vinegar, onions, salt, sugar, and spices. Chili sauce is made from whole, peeled tomatoes and tomato concentrate. It contains a higher level of sugar and onion than catsup.
4. Chocolate is made from ground cacao beans that have been roasted and shelled. Sweet chocolate is chocolate that is blended with sugar, cocoa butter, vanilla, and other flavoring. It is used in confections and baked items. Semisweet chocolate is slightly sweetened and is used as pieces or nibs for chocolate chip cookies and as a garnish for desserts. Unsweetened chocolate is pure baking or cooking chocolate without sweeteners or flavors.
5. Cocoa is ground chocolate having part of the cocoa butter removed. It contains between 10 and 22% cocoa fat. Breakfast cocoa contains at least 22% cocoa fat. Dutch process cocoa is cocoa that has been alkaline-modified in accord with government standards. Instant cocoa is cocoa with an emulsifying agent.
6. Coconut is the meat from the coconut. It is cut or shredded.
7. Coffee is a blend of green coffee beans that is roasted and ground prior to brewing. Flavor strength varies with the degree of roasting. Roasted beans are best stored in a freezer to retain the volatile oils. In Louisiana, chicory-flavored coffee is preferred. Instant coffee is a spray- or freeze-dried extract brewed from roasted ground coffee. Decaffeinated coffee is made by

extracting the green beans with a chlorinated organic solvent to remove the caffeine by means of a steaming and macerating procedure.

8. Fruit pectin is made by refining pectin from plant processing waste as a by-product. Grading of pectin refers to gel strength. One pound of a 100-grade pectin will form a standard gel with a mixture of 100 lb of sugar. Liquid pectins come in commercial grades of 5.0 or 5.5 and powdered pectin grades are 150 or 200.

9. Gelatin is obtained by lime treatment of collagen by soaking, followed by hot water extraction after the lime has been washed out and the pH adjusted to 5–8. An acid process may also be used, but it is not commercially favored. Gelatin is the only relatively pure protein widely used in foods. It is used as a gelling agent; as a whipping agent in foams; and as a clarifying agent in beers, wines, and fruit juices. It is also used to increase viscosity and to control ice crystal growth in frozen desserts (particularly ice cream). Gelatin is used as a coating dip for hot foods presented cold in culinary competition. Fruit-flavored gelatin is one of our favorite dessert items. Clear gelatin is an important ingredient of vegetable salad gels.

10. Vegetable gums include (a) gum arabic used for gum drop manufacture and as an emulsifier to prevent sugar crystallization; (b) gum tragacanth used for its thickening power and as a suspending agent; (c) gum karaya used as a stabilizer in cheese spreads, french dressings, sherbets, ground meats, and meringues; (d) locust-bean gum used in ice creams, cheese products, and sausages; (e) guar gum used to replace the more costly locust bean gum; (f) agar from seaweeds, a heat resistant gel-forming agent used for its gelling, emulsifying, and stabilizing properties; (g) carrageenan is a gum from red agar (Irish Moss) used to suspend cocoa in chocolate milk and in many other dairy products including cheese and ice cream; (h) algin from kelp is also used in dairy products; (i) carboxymethylcellulose (CMC) is a synthetic gum used to impart smoothness and workability to gels and to improve their freeze-thaw stability; and (j) Xanthan gum is a microbial product. It is used in dressings and ice cream to add viscosity and smoothness.

11. Mayonnaise is an emulsion of oil in vinegar stabilized by egg yolk lecithin or soybean lecithin. Lemon juice may be used as a vinegar replacement. Commercial mayonnaise contains at least 65% vegetable oil. Salad dressing resembles mayonnaise but has cooked starch paste or some gum in place of part of the oil and egg. Salad dressings contains 30% vegetable oil. French dressings are egg-free emulsions containing vegetable gums or pectins, tomato paste for color and emulsifying, paprika for color, and 30% vegetable oil. Low calorie dressings have fruit or vegetable bases, very little oil, and artificial sweetener.

12. Mustard derived from black or yellow mustard seed is passed through a colloid mill and homogenized into a paste with water and vinegar. Spices, sugar, and salt—and occasionally wine—are added for flavoring.

13. Nuts are dry fruits inside a woody shell. Filberts, hazelnuts, walnuts, almonds, pecans, and brazil nuts grow on trees. Nuts are sold in the shell or in shelled form. Shelled nuts are available chopped, ground, blanched, halved, slivered, plain, toasted, and salted. Peanuts, which are not nuts, are produced by leguminous plants and grow on vines like peas. Peanut butter is made by grinding blanched or unblanced peanuts. An emulsifier and antioxidant may be added to retard separation and rancidity.

14. Olives are the edible fruit of the olive tree. They are canned, green fermented, green brined, or processed for oil. A treatment must be given to the olives to remove the bitterness of the fruit. Ripe olives are packed in salt with or without spices and are pitted, or pitted and stuffed with celery, onions, pimiento, almonds or capers. Greek or Italian olives are dried or salt-cured. U.S. grades for ripe and green olives are Grade A (Fancy), Grade B (Choice), Grade C (Standard), and Substandard. Olives come in 9 sizes ranging from small (No. 1) to super colossal (No. 9).

15. Soups may be clear, thick, thin, or creamed. Many are served either hot or cold. Consomme is a clarified extract from meat, poultry, fish, or vegetables. Cream soups are bisques. Chowders are thick soups prepared from meat, poultry, fish, or shellfish and garnished with vegetables.

16. Food bases are concentrated extracts obtained from meats, fish, poultry, shellfish, or vegetables. Combined with seasonings, they provide a ready stock by adding hot water or may be used to flavor entrees. Chicken, beef, ham, turkey, espagnole, lobster, shrimp, fish, clam, mushroom, onion, garlic and consomme bases are available. These are made from high quality ingredients. The principal ingredient in each base is in conformity with the name of the product. These products enable foodservices to establish and maintain high flavor standards while eliminating much of the labor, energy, and space formerly needed in the kitchen.

17. Spices are natural products with high aromatic concentration obtained from the dried seeds, buds, fruits, flowers, bark, and roots of plants. Pepper is a dried berry; ginger is a root; cinnamon is a bark; saffron is a flower. Herbs are plant leaves and occasionally plant flowers and include tarragon, parsley, rosemary, thyme, sage, bay, savory, and oregano.

Essential oils and pungent substances give spices and herbs their characteristic flavors. Ground spices and herbs seldom hold their essence for longer than a year when properly stored. Oleoresins are obtained from spices and herbs by solvent extraction (percolation) with hexane followed by distillation of the solvent. To obtain the spice or herb equivalent, these extracts may be blended with salt, dextrose, or sugar to obtain a flavor level equal to that found in the spice or herb. Longer shelf-life and freedom from insect infestation are two of the advantages in using oleoresins.

18. Tapioca is derived from cassava root. Pearl tapioca pellets become transluscent after cooking in water. Quick-cooking tapioca is made by grinding and flaking pearl tapioca.

19. Tea is the leaves of an evergreen tree or shrub indigenous to China, India, and Japan. Black tea is made by fermenting dried-rolled green tea leaves and then firing (heating) them. Green tea is made in the same way without the fermentation step. Oolong tea is partially fermented. Flavored teas are made by adding aromatic substances to the leaves.

20. Cider vinegar is made from fermented apple juice. Malt vinegar is made from barley malt or cereals by fermentation. Wine vinegar is made from fermented wine. Grain vinegar is made by fermenting dilute distilled alcohol or by adding acetic acid to the water. Vinegar acidities range between 4 and 6% acetic acid (40–60 grain).

REFERENCES

AMERICAN HOME ECONOMICS ASSOCIATION. 1971. Handbook of Food Preparation, Washington, D.C., pp. 1–116.

CHARLEY, H. 1970. Food Science. The Ronald Press Company, New York.

DAY, A. and STUCKEY, L. 1964. The Spice Cookbook. David White Co., New York.

ESCOFFIER, A. 1969. The Escoffier Cookbook. Crown Publishers, Inc., New York.

FAIRBROOK, P. 1979. College and University Food Service Manual. Coleman Publishers, Stockton, California.

GERRARD, J.W. 1980. Food Allergy: New Perspectives. Charles Thomas, Springfield, Illinois.

JUDGE, E.E. and SONS, INC. 1978. The Almanac of the Canning, Freezing, Preserving Industries. Edward E. Judge and Sons, Inc. Westminister, Maryland.

KOSIKOWSKI, V. 1978. Cheese and Fermented Milk Foods, Second Edition. F.V. Kosikowski and Associates, Brookendale, New York.

MANUFACTURING CHEMISTS ASSOCIATION, INC. 1971. Food Additives. Washington, D.C.

MILLER, J.B. 1972. Food Allergy: Provocative Testing and Neutralization. Charles Thomas, Springfield, Illinois.

MINOR, L.J. 1972. Today's food production systems. Cornell Hotel, Restaurant and Administration Quarterly *13*(1), 43.

NATIONAL INSTITUTE FOR THE FOOD SERVICE INDUSTRY. 1974. Applied Foodservice Sanitation. National Institute for the Foodservice Industry. Chicago, Illinois.

NATIONAL RESEARCH COUNCIL. 1977. World Food and Nutrition Study (The Potential Contributions of Research). NAS, Washington, D.C.

NATIONAL SANITATION FOUNDATION. 1978. Food Service Equipment Standards. Ann Arbor, Michigan.

NELSON, J.A. and TROUT, F.M. 1964. Judging Dairy Products. Olsen Publishing Co., Milwaukee, Wisconsin.

PAGE, E.B. and KINGSFORD, P.W. 1971. The Master Chefs (a History of Haute Cuisine). Edward Arnold, Ltd., London.

PAUL, C. and PALMER, H.A. 1972. Food Theory and Applications. John Wiley & Sons, Inc., New York.

RANDOLPH, T.G. 1956. Specific adaptation syndrome. J. Lab. Clin. Med. *48*:934.

REA, W.J., BELL, J.R., SUITS, C.W. AND SMILEY, R.E. 1975. Food and chemical susceptibility after environmental chemical overexposure: case histories. Ann. Allergy *41*, 101.

RONAN, B. 1973. A cooking street—is it a possible food production system? J. Am. Diet. Assoc. *63*, 4, 417.

ROSS, L.N. and McHENRY, R.M. 1971. Food Purchasing: Study Course. Iowa University Press, Ames, Iowa.

SANDERS, H.J. 1966. Food additivies. Chem. Eng. News *44*(42), 100.

SMITH, L.L. and MINOR, L.J. 1974. Food Service Science. AVI Publishing Company, Inc., Westport, Connecticut.

TRESSLER, D.K., VANARSDEL, W.B. and COPLEY, M.J. 1968. The Freezing Preservation of Foods. AVI Publishing Company, Inc., Westport, Connecticut.

3 Food Additives Standards

INTRODUCTION

Mankind's first food challenge was learning to forage or hunt for a food supply. After that succeeded it became necessary to preserve food: methods included using the sun to dry it, fire to smoke it, chemicals (salt, sulfur, acid) to preserve it, and cold, fermentation, and other procedures to extend its storage life. Each process was developed through trial-and-error experimentation.

During the nineteenth century, organic chemistry was developed in Germany. With a population density much higher than that of Canada or the United States, food needs of Germany could be met only by a highly efficient agrarian development. To this end the famous chemist Baron von Liebig proved that there is no difference between the effectiveness of chemicals obtained from manure and their man-made replacements.

This landmark discovery enabled Germany to increase crop yields far beyond those of neighboring countries. The development of ammonia production from atmospheric nitrogen by Fritz von Haber spurred this development. Concomitantly German scientists found that the organic salt of benzoic acid (sodium benzoate) was useful in preserving many foods. Their rationale was the same as that for the use of fertilizer. Why use smoke to preserve food when the active ingredient can be produced in pure or standardized form? This discovery increased the application of this preservative, which has endured to this time.

FOOD ANALYSIS

As food requirements increased in the developed countries of the world, scientists worked to keep pace by analyzing foods for their chemical constituents. This led to the discoveries of amino acids, vitamins, hormones, nucleic acids, enzymes and other proteins, fatty acids, organic acids and their salts, and many other chemicals in our foods.

Nutrient Losses

Experiments by nutritionists using analytical methods showed that some of the most essential chemical compounds found in our foods are not fulfilling the requirements of the body. Studies revealed that these physiologically active food chemicals are being lost in early harvesting, shipment, storage, processing, and final preparation procedures.

Nutrient Replacement (Fortification)

To assure that these unavoidably lost nutrients could be put back into our food, these complex compounds including vitamins, amino acids, nucleic acids, and others have been taken from foods rich in them, synthesized, concentrated in yeast cells and then extracted, or produced by using enzymes acting on a suitable substrate to help in raising nutritional standards.

This plan of supplying man with his nutritional needs has been extended to include food chemicals that compensate for losses in color and flavor, taste, and other factors that detract from food acceptance and enjoyment. Texture, consistency, freeze–thaw durability, oxygen stability, and appearance of foods are also improved by the addition of chemicals that improve quality standards in our food products.

Applications of food chemicals made or extracted by man from foods have been extended to include new complete foods including whipped topping, gelatin desserts, fruit-flavored beverages, coffee whiteners, and meat analogs. In most instances, (1) the chemical added was already a natural constituent of the food to which it is added; (2) the amount used is monitored for safety; and (3) the physiological effect in the body of the food chemical is identical to that experienced with the unfortified food product. However, the quality standard of food is improved by fortification; and (4) no chemical may be used that is not on the GRAS (generally regarded as safe) list used by the FDA to assure safety.

Chemicals present in our natural foods are not listed for the consumer. If the FDA did require labeling of natural foods we would be surprised at the natural ingredients, for many of them are toxic and could not qualify for the GRAS list. However, at the levels we ingest them they present small risk in contrast to the nutritional benefits we receive by eating the foods. Table 1 lists some natural foods and a few of their chemical constituents. As food science advances, many additional compounds present in our food will be found and structurally identified.

Nitrites and nitrates used to cure meats have been found to form carcinogenic nitrosamines. We get nitrates, which are converted to nitrites in our bodies, from vegetables such as spinach, beets, radishes, eggplant, celery, lettuce, collards, and turnip greens. Concentrations of nitrate in these vegetables is as high as 3000 parts per million (ppm). Human saliva also contains 6 ppm of nitrites. Under some conditions nitrites are toxic.

Mushrooms of the death angel variety contain a toxic chemical causing degeneration of the liver, kidney, heart, and muscles.

Aflatoxin is a powerful carcinogen generated by the mold *Aspergillus flavus* and may be present in peanut butter and in nuts of all kinds. We control it by maintaining the proper equilibrium humidity in the food.

A highly poisonous gourmet menu is given in Table 2.

Racial differences in tolerance to food toxicants is extensive. Our bodies possess a detoxifying system that adapts to our environmental needs.

TABLE 1. Partial Listing of Natural Food Chemicals Found in Three Food Items

Food	Chemical constituents
Milk	Milk sugar (lactose) Proteins (several kinds of casein and lactalbumin) Minerals (mainly calcium and phosphorous) Butterfat (about 20 fatty acids, water, vitamins) More than 140 chemicals.
Apple	33 identified alcohols 23 identified aldehydes and ketones 16 acids 62 esters
Beefsteak	Creatine phosphatase Phosphofructokinase Aldolase Myosin Myoglobin Glutamic acid Nucleic acids Phospholipids Actin Cathepsins Glutathione Glyceraldehyde–phosphate Dephosphorylase

TABLE 2. A Natural Food "Gourmet Menu"

Food	Possible Toxic agent
Appetizers	
Japanese turtle soup	Tetrodotoxin, 0.024 oz (0.7 g): numb lips, tongue, toes; chills, dizziness and itchiness, vomiting, loss of speech, paralysis, and kills 160 lb man in a few hours.
Alaska butter clams	Saxitoxin, a neurotoxin (paralytic shellfish poison), deadly.
Main course	
smoked Lake Michigan whitefish	Botulism, microbial toxin (deadly): nausea and vomiting followed by muscular paralysis, double vision, drooping eyelids, dilated pupils, lassitude, fatigue, dizziness, difficulty in swallowing, tongue and throat inflamed, weakened neck muscles, death by respiratory paralysis or cardiac arrest.
cabbage salad	Goitrogen, goitrin (0.5 ppm): causes goiter
sauteed Mexican mushrooms	Hallucinatory effect
Dessert	
rhubarb and rice pudding	Oxalic acid poisoning from rhubarb; aflatoxin, carcinogen in rice
Beverages	
tea	Caffeine, causes bladder cancer
wine (hot) mulled with nutmeg	Histamine, causes headache, from wine; narcosis from nutmeg
absinthe liqueur	Thyrone, causes brain lesions

Source: National Academy of Sciences 1973.

Undoubtedly, tolerance to smoke toxicants varies widely from chain-smokers to nonsmokers. Alcohol tolerance is much higher in heavy than in nondrinkers.

Food-borne allergens are the cause of much discomfort and may cause lung damage if not controlled by diet combined with treatment by an allergy specialist.

Some people are sensitive to oranges from Florida but not from California and vice versa. Celery from Oregon causes no allergenic response in some persons, but Michigan celery cannot be eaten by these same individuals without histamine buildup and hives. In others the reverse is true.

Milk causes some persons to choke, to cough up large amounts of sputum, and to experience constipation and other discomfort. Sensitivities to bananas, grains, especially wheat, chocolate, cinnamon, cola, tea, coffee, cocoa, corn, eggs, garlic, onion, peas and beans, nuts, oatmeal, strawberries, and other foods have been reported.

ALLERGENIC TENDENCIES

Scientists studying food allergies could not find any food to which some person was not allergic with the exception of refined sugar. Then a person was found who claimed to be allergic to this food item; the researchers did not believe it. Their doubt was based on the precept that all allergenic substances are proteins or protein derivatives. Finally they put a ton of sugar into solution and filtered the solution. On the filter pad they found a monomolecular layer of a gray substance that upon analysis proved to be protein. This individual was so supersensitive that even trace amounts of allergens had an effect.

We may conclude from this experiment that any food, under certain conditions, may trigger an allergenic response characterized by headache, vomiting, nausea, stomach pain, swelling, hives, diarrhea, and occasionally sudden death. Symptoms are often misleading, masquerading as gall bladder trouble, heart disease, syphilitic rash, or ulcers.

Cerebral Allergies

Physical and mental symptoms including tensions, fainting spells, extreme fatigue, anxiety, panic, and even blacking out and colitis have been traced to allergic responses to foods. Study of cerebral allergies in schizophrenic patients gave startling results. Studies by Miller (1972), Randolph (1956), and Rea *et al.* (1975) independently showed that food, food odors, and chemicals can cause migraine in sensitive patients. The symptoms clear following avoidance or immunotherapy. General malaise, dizziness, fatigue, paralysis, seizures, hyperactivity, depression, and paranoia may also occur. Symptoms may be removed by eliminating the causative foods and chemicals from the diet and environment (Gerrard 1980).

Masked Food Allergy

In addition to these immmediate reactions there is a response called masked food allergy. After eating an individual feels well, but hours later, as the effect of food wears off, experiences a hangover. This can result in depression, fatigue, headache and, in severe cases, the stupor of catatonia (a complete loss of voluntary motion) and hallucinations. These negative reactions may be stopped temporarily by consuming more of the same food (Gonzalez 1977).

Enzyme System Depletion

Repeated exposure to a food depletes the enzyme systems needed to digest the food, which can cause poisonous by-products to enter the bloodstream. Then hives build up on the brain. Doctors use a special rotation diet to counter this problem. No food is eaten more often than once every 4 days. This prevents new allergies by limiting the stress on our digestive-enzyme systems. High levels of vitamins C, E, A, and B_6 decrease or block allergic reactions. A carefully administered vitamin-fortified diet can build resistance to cerebral allergies.

Food Additives and Hyperactivity

Food scientists have created a fantastic world of colors, according to Graham (1976), who refers us to *Why Your Child Is Hyperactive* (Feingold, 1975), which lists 10 symptoms of hyperkinesis that he attributes to natural salicylates in foods, food additives in general, and colors and flavors in particular. These symptoms are "(1) marked hypersensitivity and fidgetiness; (2) hyperactivity; (3) compulsive aggression; (4) the child is excitable and impulsive; (5) very low tolerance for frustration; (6) short attention span; (7) unable to concentrate; (8) exceptionally clumsy; (9) normal or high I.Q. but, paradoxically, often fails in school; and (10) boys are involved in a ratio of about 9 to 1 over girls, and rarely more than one child in a family is affected."

Diet for Hyperactive Children

The diet recommended by Feingold for hyperactive children is free of salicylates and food additives. He notes that hyperactive children improve markedly on this diet and claims a 50% success rate. As a result of his studies between 1965 and 1976, Dr. Feingold recommends three actions by the FDA:

1. A complete label disclosure of all flavors and colors in foods should be required.
2. A broad FDA-sponsored education on the hazards of food additives is in order. (The FDA refused to do this without proof).
3. A symbol to represent foods free of synthetic flavors and colors should be required.

Research on the behavioral aspects of food additives was started by the Nutrition Foundation in 1975. Preliminary results reported in 1976 among 6- to 12-year-olds using parental observations were as follows: mothers reported 38% improved, 16% worse, and 45% no change; fathers reported 46% improved, 10% worse, and 45% no change.

Butylated hydroxytoluene (BHT) and monosodium glutamate (MSG) are being tested for possible neurological effects.

CONSUMER PROTECTION

Consumer protection of our food supply is the responsibility of the food industry, which operates under federal, state, and local regulations. Our modern food laws are based on the Federal Food Drug and Cosmetic Act of 1938 and three amendments to the act including: (1) the Miller Pesticide Amendment, 1954; (2) the Food Additive Amendment, 1958; and (3) the Color Additives Amendment, 1960.

1958 Food Additives Amendment

Five important provisions of the 1958 Food Additives Amendment are the following:

1. Additives are defined in the Amendment.
2. The burden of proof to prove safety is now shifted from the FDA to industry.
3. The Delaney clause excluded carcinogens regardless of their concentration.
4. The GRAS list is established.
5. The GMP (good manufacturing practice) sanitation and high quality control standards in food plants are established.

Changes in food regulations occur at regular intervals.

The Delaney clause states, "No additive shall be deemed safe if it is found to induce cancer when ingested by man or animal, or if it is found after tests which are appropriate for the evaluation of the safety of food additives to induce cancer in man or animals. . . ."

Zero tolerance for carcinogenic substances is required under regulations established by the Delaney clause. At the time of its passage analytical procedures could detect parts per million of chemicals present in a given food, and this amount was viewed as practically zero (smaller quantities, e.g., parts per billion, ppb, if present, were not detectable). Now instrumentation such as gas chromatography and spectrometry can detect levels of ppb and even parts per trillion (ppt) in some cases.

Thus, appropriate tests written into the clause at that time are no longer applicable, as chemicals are detectable at levels thousands of times lower than before. There has to be a definite tolerance level in human exposure to carcinogenic substances. Otherwise we would die as a result of exposure to toxic tobacco volatiles, industrial air pollution, water contaminants resulting from chlorination, automobile exhaust fumes, etc.

WHAT ARE FOOD ADDITIVES?

The Food Protection Committee of the Food and Nutrition Board, National Academy of Sciences–National Research Council (NAS/NRC) defines a food additive as "a substance or mixture of substances other than a basic foodstuff, which is present in a food as a result of an aspect of production, processing, storage or packaging" (Food Protection Committee 1965).

Intentional Additives

By broadest definition a food additive is any substance that becomes part of a food product when added either intentionally or incidentally. Today, about 3000 substances are intentionally added to foods for a defined purpose. To be approved, a food additive must be both safe and useful.

Incidental Additives

About 10,000 compounds or combinations of compounds occur in foods as a result of processing, storage, or packaging. Infinitesimal amounts of pesticides used to treat crops, drugs fed to animals, and chemicals that migrate from plastic or paper packaging materials are examples of incidental additives.

SOURCES OF FOOD ADDITIVES

Food additives may come from foods and can be synthesized chemically or produced by biological processes.

Additives from foods include lecithin from soybeans, color from turmeric, hydrolyzed vegetable proteins derived from grains, starch from grains and tubers, gums (plant exudates), gums (seaweed extracts), sugar from sugar cane, lactose from milk, casein from milk, gelatin from animals, and many others.

Synthetic Additives

Use of synthetic food additives has increased since the turn of the century. For example, the advent of the gas chromatograph in tandem with a time-in-flight mass spectrometer has dramatically improved techniques for identifying natural flavors. Synthesizing the chemicals found in natural flavors or flavor volatiles has brought about constant improvements in synthetic flavors built to match their natural counterparts. Advantages of synthetics over natural flavors are that they can be standardized and have longer shelf-life stability than natural flavors possess.

Citrus flavors are readily oxidized and turn rancid quickly unless terpenes are removed by concentrating severalfold. This is a costly process. Accordingly the man-made lemon, lime, orange, grapefruit, tangerine, and tangelo flavors are better and less expensive. Remember, though, their makeup is the same; the identical chemicals that are the active ingredients in the natural fruits are used in development of the man-made flavorings.

Biological Additives

A few examples of biologically produced food additives include xanthan gum, monosodium glutamate, and yeast.

WHY USE ADDITIVES?

Additives must be both safe and useful, according to the Food Additives Amendment of 1958. Their use has greatly improved marketability while improving quality standards in our food supplies. Production is not the limiting factor in food availability. Transportation is. Food must be kept wholesome and palatable during the entire marketing procedure. Food additives and improved packaging are helping in this task.

Each additive has its own function, as shown in Table 3. There are many reasons that food additives are used, including the following:

preservation—to improve shelf-life
disease prevention—to improve nutrition
fortification—nutritional enrichment
flavoring—to improve flavor acceptance
seasoning
emulsification—to stabilize emulsions
acidulation—to control acidity
alkalization—to control alkalinity
buffering—to control pH
leavening—to improve baked goods
maturing and bleaching—to improve flour
sequestering—setting trace minerals apart
moistening—humectancy, keeping food moist
conditioning—prevent caking of sugar and salt

TABLE 3. Functional Classification of Food Additives

Class	Principal function	Examples	Used in
Acidulants	To impart acidity or to compensate for deficiency in natural acidity	Acetic, citric, malic, phosphoric acids	Jellies, jams, preserves, soft drinks, confections
Aerating agents	To charge with gas or to displace air	a. Carbon dioxide b. Nitrogen c. Nitrous oxide	a. Carbonated beverages b. Oxidizable oils, milk powder c. Pressure-dispensed creams, etc.
Anticaking agents and desiccants	To prevent lumping or caking	Calcium phosphate Magnesium carboate, calcium or magnesium stearate Silica gel, talc, starch	Table salt, confectioners sugar Malted milk powder, onion or garlic salt, meat-curing mixes
Antioxidants	To retard oxidative deterioration, rancidity in fats and oils or off-flavor in frozen foods, flavoring oils, beverages, etc.	a. Sulfur dioxide, sulfites b. Ascorbic and isoascorbic acid and their sodium salts; ascorbyl palmitate c. Nordihydroguaiaretic acid: propyl gallate; butylated hydroxy toluene and butylated hydroxyanisole d. Lecithin, tocopherols	a. Wine and beer; sugar syrups cut, peeled, or dried fruits and vegetables b,d. Cooked, cured, comminuted meat products; frozen fish dip; beer; flavoring oils and emulsions; confectionery c,d. Lard, vegetable oils, hydrogenated shortenings; crackers, biscuits, breakfast cereals; dry cake or soup mixes
Bleaching agents	To remove or lighten (especially carotenoid) color of certain natural products	a. Oxides of nitrogen, chlorine, chlorine dioxide, nitrosyl chloride b. Benzoyl peroxide c. Ammonium persulfate	a,b,c. Wheat flour b. Cheese (blue or gorgonzola) made from cow's milk
Buffering agents	To adjust and stabilize pH	a. Sodium acetate, citrate, phosphates, pyrophosphates b. Acetic, citric, lactic acids	a. Jellies, jams, preserves; soft drinks; confectionery Prepared cereals and farinaceous products, meal cures, evaporated milk b. Processed cheese, pickles, and brines, canned vegetables, confections

(Continued)

TABLE 3. *(Continued)*

Class	Principal function	Examples	Used in
Clarifying agents	To remove or prevent turbidity	Pectinases, proteinases (papain, bromelin, fungal enzyme preparations) Tannin, gelatin, albumin, methylcellulose	Fruit juices, vinegar, wine, beer, soft drinks
Clouding agents	To impart turbidity and prevent "ringing"	Brominated vegetable oils	Cloudy citrus-flavored drinks
Coating agents	To impart surface glaze; to facilitate removal of baked products from pans or confectionery from slabs	a. Shellac, beeswax, paraffin, gum benzoin b. Carnauba wax c. Silicone, mineral oil	a, b. Chocolates and confectionery b. Oranges c. Coating baking pans or as slab dressing
Coloring agents	To impart color or to adjust for natural variations in color	Annato, caramel, carmine, carotene, saffron, turmeric Certified food colors (FD&C coal-tar colors) Carbon black, titanium oxide	Soft drinks, confectionery icings, jellies, baked goods, fillings, cake mixes, cereal, popcorn, packed fruits, margarine, cheese, butter
Color stabilizers	To prevent fading, browning, or other discoloration	a. Sulfur dioxide and sulfites b. Sodium nitrite and nitrate c. Ascorbic and isoascorbic acids d. Citric acid	a,c. Cut, peeled, dried, or processed fruit and vegetables b,c. Cured meat products (to convert myoglobin to nitric oxide myoglobin c,d. Heat-processed (canned) vegetables
Conditioners (yeast foods)	To improve elasticity and stability of doughs and facilitate mechanical baking of products of uniform quality	Mixtures of potassium bromate and iodate; calcium peroxide; ammonium chloride, sulfate and phosphates; calcium carbonate, lactate, sulfate, and phosphates; sodium chloride	Bread, rolls, cakes, and other yeast-fermented baked goods

Emulsifying agents (surfactants)	To facilitate and stabilize oil-in-water (or water-in-oil) dispersions	Mono- and diglycerides of fatty acids; acetyl tartaric, sulfoacetate and monosodium phosphate derivatives of mono- and diglycerides; glyceryl lactopalmitate; sorbitan, polyoxyethylene, and polyoxyethylene sorbitan derivatives of fatty acids	Lard, margarine, shortenings; ice cream, frozen desserts; chocolate, confectionery; bread, baked goods, cake mixes; flavor emulsions and concentrates; vitamin concentrates
Enzymes	To hydrolyze proteins, carbohydrates, hemicelluloses, etc.	a. Proteases of plant (papain, bromelin, ficin), animal (pepsin, trypsin, pancreatin), or microbiological (fungal or bacterial) origin b. Amylase, invertase c. Pectinase d. Glucose oxidase e. Carotenase	a. Meat tenderization a,c. Clarification of fruit juices and beverages b. Manufacture of invert sugar, preparation of cocoa syrups d. Prevention of browning (sugar-amino acid reaction) e. Bleaching flour
Flavoring agents	To impart or enhance flavor or aroma	a. Natural extracts, essential oils, and oleoresins b. Alcohols, aldehydes, ketones, ethers, and esters c. Monosodium glutamate, pyroligneous acid	a,b. Soft drinks, confectionery, chewing gum, gelatin desserts, ice cream, frozen desserts, baked goods, icings c. Meat products and sauces
Foam regulators	To stabilize or depress foam	a. Dextrin, peptones, cellulose gums b. Silicone (dimethyl polysiloxane)	a. Beer, root beer, and other beverages that produce a head when dispensed b. To prevent foaming during boiling of syrups and jellies, fermentation of wine, or bottling of fruit juices, beverages, etc.
Growth stimulators	To promote more rapid growth of poultry and livestock	Antibiotics (chlor- and oxytetracyclines), stilbesterol, phenylarsonic acid	Broiler and turkey rations, cattle and hog feed
Humectants	To absorb or retain moisture	Glycerol, propylene glycol, sorbitol	Dried fruits, confectionery, shredded coconut

(Continued)

TABLE 3. *(Continued)*

Class	Principal function	Examples	Used in
Hydrolytic agents	To effect hydrolytic cleavage of proteins, carbohydrates, and cellulosic material	Hydrochloric acid, potassium acid tartrate	Manufacture of gelatin, protein hydrolyzates, sodium glutamate, invert sugar, corn syrup, etc.
Leavening agents	To render batters or doughs light and porous, as by fermentation	Sodium bicarbonate (and to a lesser extent calcium or ammonium carbonates) plus an acid (alum, monocalcium phosphate, sodium acid pyrophosphate, potassium acid tartrate), or acid-producing compound (glucono-Δ-lactone)	Self-rising flour, cake mixes, cakes, biscuits, crackers
Maturing agents	To age (oxidize) wheat flour so as to yield more elastic, stable, and uniform doughs	Chlorine dioxide, chlorine, and nitrosyl chloride; potassium bromate	Wheat flour, bromated flour
Neutralizers	To correct excessive natural acidity or to neutralize acids used in processing	Sodium, calcium, or magnesium hydroxides or carbonates; calcium or magnesium oxide	Sour cream, butter, and other dairy products; canned olives, tomato soup Wine
Nutrients	To restore nutritional values lost in processing or to supplement natural content of nutrients	Mineral nutrients: reduced iron and iron compounds (sulfate, phosphates); calcium carbonate and phosphates; potassium iodide; sodium fluoride and silico-fluoride Vitamins: vitamin A acetate and palmitate, β-carotene, thiamine, riboflavin, niacin, ergocalciferol (vitamin D_2) cholescalciferol (vitamin D_3), pyridoxine hydrochloride, calcium pantothenate, α-tocopherol Amino acids: lysine, methionine	Enriched flour, bread, and cereal products; vitamin B_1 milk and other fortified dairy products; iodized salt, fluoridated water supplies

Preservatives	To prevent infection or inhibit spoilage due to bacteria, yeast, molds, or other microorganisms	a. Chlorine, hypochlorites b. Benzoic acid and sodium venzoate c. Sorbic acid and sorbates d. Calcium propionate, sodium diacetate e. Chlor- and oxytetracycline	a. Water supplies b. Fruit jellies, jams, preserves, pickles, relishes, margarine, soft drinks c. Cheese wraps, pie fillings, fruit syrups d. Bread (rope inhibitors) e. Dressed poultry, frozen fish
Sequestrants	To trap metals (especially iron and copper) that adversely affect color, clarity, flavor, or stability	a. Citric acid and citrates, including monoisopropyl or stearyl citrate b. Phosphoric acid and phosphates c. Calcium and sodium salts of ethylenediamine tetraacetic acid	a. Frozen fruit, soup base, margarine oil b. Processed cheese, evaporated milk, rendered fat and oils c. Wines, vinegar, soft drinks
Sweetening agents (artificial)	To impart sweetness in place of sugars	Saccharin Cyclohexysulfamates (calcium or sodium salts	Low-calorie or diabetic foods, such as beverages, canned fruits, desserts, etc.
Texturizing agents	To impart firmness or improve texture in processed foods	a. Alums b. Calcium chloride, citrate, carbonate, phosphate (monobasic), or sulfate c. Magnesium chloride	a. Pickled cucumbers b. Processed cheese, canned potatoes, or tomatoes c. Canned peas
Thickening agents	To impart body or thickness to fluids or emulsions	Glycerol, sorbitol, gelatin Pectin, vegetable gums (alginates, carragheen, karaya) Cellulose gums (carboxymethyl cellulose)	Processed cheese, salad dressings; ice cream and frozen desserts Chocolate-flavored milk and syrups Confectionery and icings, low-calorie (nonsugar) beverages and canned fruits Pressure-dispensed creams

From McGraw-Hill Encyclopedia of Science and Technology (1960).

firming—to improve pickles and tomatoes
adding yeast foods—to improve bread, beer, and wine
clarifying—to improve beverages, vinegar
curing—to improve color and shelf-life in meats
foaming—to produce foam in whipped topping
anti-foaming—to improve deep fat frying
adding nonnutritive sweeteners—for caloric reduction
dissolving—to provide solvents for colors and flavors

This list represents just a few of the many uses for food additives.

HOW MUCH ADDITIVE CAN BE USED IN A FOOD?

Amounts of additives that can be added to a food vary with the additive and its use. For example, sugar and salt may be used at relatively high concentrations, whereas monosodium glutamate and 5′ nucleotides would be at considerably lower levels and synthetic flavors and colors would be at still lower concentrations.

Under FDA restrictions the quantity cannot exceed the amount necessary for the food additive to perform its function. When used at the maximum level allowed, a food additive must have a safety margin of 100 to 1, based upon animal feeding tests.

Examples of permissible use levels are given in Table 4.

TABLE 4. Additive Concentrations Allowable under FDA Standards GRAS Listing[1]

Additive	Amount allowed
Sodium or calcium propionate	0.03 oz/lb (1.87 g/kg) of bread
Butylated hydroxy toluene (BHT)	50 ppm[2] in dry cereal
Butylated hydroxy anisole (BHA)	50 ppm in dry cereal
Monosodium glutamate	0.04 oz/lb (2.42 g/kg) food
Sodium benzoate	0.016 oz/lb (1 g/kg) food
Vanilla extract	54 ppm in syrups
Oil of wintergreen	44 ppm in ice cream
Oil of lemon	9 ppm in sherbets
1,2-Butanedithiol	0.2 ppm in meat products
m-Cresol	0.5 ppm in soups
2,6-Dimenthylpyridine	10.0 ppm in snack foods
Ethyl maltol	152 ppm in baked goods

Sources: 1. Oser and Ford 1978
2. Fenaroli 1975

[1]GRAS = Generally Recognized as Safe
[2]ppm = parts per million

STANDARDS FOR LEVELS OF ADDITIVE USE

Sugar (sucrose), salt (sodium chloride), and corn sweeteners (corn syrups, dextrose, and fructose) account for 93% by weight of all food additives used in the United States. Thirty more additives account for the next 5.5%. These include yeast, citric acid, baking soda, vegetable colors (including red from beets), mustard, pepper, and carbonated gas used in soda pop. All the remaining chemicals on the GRAS list used as either direct or indirect food additives make up the remaining 1.5%. In 1978, the FDA, USDA, and Federal Trade Commission (FTC) studied consumer usage of label information and the need for further information on labels. The only information missing on current labels that consumers would like to see (as many people work to avoid these additives) is sugar content, with starch a distant second. (see Table 5).

According to the Presidental Science Advisory Committee, Americans eat from a high of 102 lb per person per year of table sugar to 15 lb of salt, 13 lb of dextrose, and 9.3 lb of the remaining food additives. On an average we use less than 0.08 oz (2.3 g) of each of about 1900 different additives. Actually, the use level of half of these 1900 totals less than 0.00026 oz (7.3 mg) per year.

TABLE 5. Ingredients Consumers Most Often Avoid[1]

Ingredient avoided	Percentage of consumer avoidance
One or more of the types listed	54.1
Sugar (excessive)	26.7
Salt (excessive)	14.2
Preservatives	11.5
Fat (excessive)	6.3
Artificial colors	5.5
Lard or animal shortening	3.6
Bleached or white flour	3.1
Artificial flavors	2.6
Artificial sweeteners	2.5

Source: Consumer Food Labeling Survey 1978 and FDA, USDA, and FTC.

[1]Consumers have the most difficulty with technical and chemical terms.

USE OF INTENTIONAL ADDITIVES

A listing of the top-selling additives used in U.S. foods in 1978 is shown in Table 6. Market growth is projected from about 1.3 billion dollars in

1978 to 4.5 billion dollars in 1990. Total growth based on this estimate would be 10.3% per year, with 3.8% being real growth and 6.5% per year allowed for inflation. A comparison of growth in end use, based on millions of pounds, is shown in Table 6 for four special end-uses.

An additive is intentionally used in foods for one or more of four purposes:

1. To maintain or improve nutritional value. Many foods are fortified with vitamins and minerals that might otherwise be lacking in a diet or that

TABLE 6. Amounts of Food Additive Shipments, 1978 and Projected for 1990, and Estimated Growth Rate

	Shipments (millions of $)		Annual growth rate (%)
	1978	1990	
By additive type:			
flavoring agents	172.7	705	12.4
flavor enhancers	66.2	290	13.1
enzymes	114.9	370	10.2
acidulants	113.9	370	10.3
nonnutritive sweeteners	23.7	95	12.3
antioxidants	54.5	130	7.5
vitamin supplements	35.0	145	12.6
surfactants	145.0	435	9.6
preservatives	62.0	185	9.5
coloring agents	43.1	135	10.0
nonspecialty additives	432.5	1585	11.4
Total	1263.5	4445	11.1
By end use:			
meat, poultry, seafood	168.2	793	13.8
dairy products	146.3	483	10.5
baked goods	123.4	390	10.1
soft drinks	114.0	397	11.0
cereals and grain products	49.1	164	10.6
processed fruits and vegetables	56.8	193	10.7
alcoholic beverages	25.6	81	10.1
sauces, dressings, oils	205.0	662	10.3
other prepared foods	375.1	1282	10.8
By end use:			
dairy products	112.8	164	
baked goods	179.8	256	
soft drinks	111.2	197	
sauces, dressings, oils	155.9	243	
Total	559.7	841	

From Pomerantz 1980.

have been destroyed or lost in processing. Common nutritional additives include vitamin D in milk, vitamin A in margarine, vitamin C in fruit drinks, and iodine in table salt. Breads and cereals are enriched with B vitamins lost or destroyed during milling and processing of grains. Nutrient fortification with vitamins or minerals has helped eradicate once-common deficiency diseases such as rickets, scurvy, pellagra, and goiter.

2. To maintain freshness. Foods last as long as they do on the shelf or in the refrigerator because of additives that retard spoilage, preserve natural color and flavor, and keep fats and oils from turning rancid. Preservatives such as sodium nitrates and nitrites, for example, protect cured meats, fish, and poultry from contamination by the bacterially produced toxin responsible for botulism (an often fatal food poisoning illness). Ascorbic acid (vitamin C) keeps uncooked peaches from turning brown. Antioxidants such as BHA (butylated hydroxyanisole) and BHT (butylated hydroxytoluene) help prevent changes in color, flavor, or texture that occur when foods are exposed to air.

3. To help in processing or preparation. A wide variety of compounds are used to give body and texture to foods, evenly distribute particles of one liquid in another, affect cooking or baking results, control acidity or alkalinity, retain moisture, and prevent caking or lumping. Chemicals called emulsifiers give products such as peanut butter and mayonnaise a consistent texture and prevent them from separating into an oily layer at the top of the jar and a dry layer at the bottom. Thickeners create smoothness and prevent ice crystals from forming in frozen foods such as ice cream. Humectants are used to keep moisture in foods like shredded coconut. Leavening agents such as yeasts and baking powder are essential to make baked goods rise.

4. To make food more appealing. The most widely used additives are those intended to make food look and taste better. These include coloring agents, natural and synthetic flavors, flavor enhancers such as MSG (monosodium glutamate), and maltol and sweeteners. The characteristic flavor of strawberry ice cream, for example, may come from real strawberries or from a chemical flavoring. As consumers associate strawberries with a reddish color, strawberry ice cream is tinted pink. These uses are the most controversial; industry says the public prefers foods that are colored and flavored while many consumers and consumer advocates believe that too many colors and flavors are used.

Many intentional additives are used in processed foods. A listing of these chemicals is included in Table 7.

TABLE 7. Intentional Additives Used in Processed Foods

Group I: Preservatives	
Additive	**Usage**
Sodium diacetate	Inhibit molds and rope in baked goods
Sodium benzoate	Preservative, fruit jelly
Benzoic acid	Preserves, jams, oleomargarine, soft drinks, salt cold fish, maraschino cherries, mincemeat
Calcium hypochlorite	Germicide and sterilizing agent. Used in sterilization of fruits by washing
Sodium hypochlorite	Preservative. Curd washing of cottage cheese
Chlortetracycline	Preservative (antiobiotic). Used in cooling dip for uncooked poultry
Hydrogen peroxide	Preservative. Bactericide for milk and cheese
Polymixin B	Antibiotic. Used as bactericide in yeast culture for beer. Conc. = 0.05 ppm
Calcium propionate	Mold and rope inhibitor
Sodium propionate	Mold and rope inhibitor
Sodium chloride	Preservative and pickling agent. Preservative for meats, vegetables, butter, prevention of browning in cut fruit
Sorbic acid	Fungistat. Chocolate syrups, soda fountain syrups, fresh fruit cocktail, salads (potato, macaroni, cole slaw, gelatin), cheesecake, pie fillings, cake

Group II: Antioxidants	
Additive	**Usage**
Sodium ascorbate	Antioxidant. Used in preparation of cooked, cured, comminuted meat food products. Concentrated milk products
Ascorbic acid (Vitamin C)	Antioxidant. Canned mushrooms. Used in preparation of cooked, cured comminuted meat food products. Frozen fruit, beer and ale, apple juice, candy
Butylated hydroxyanisole. Di-tertiary-butyl-paracresol (BHA)	Lard, vegetable oils, cookies, soup base, pie crust mix, potato chips, beverage bases
Propyl gallate	Lard, prepared breakfast cereal, chicken soup base
Gum guaiac	Not to exceed 0.1%—used in rendered animal fat or combination of such fat and vegetable fat
Nordihydroguaiaretic acid (NDGA)	Prepared pie crust mix, candy, lard, butter, ice cream, pressure-dispensed whipped cream
Lecithin	Breads, rolls, buns, etc. May be used in conjunction with the shortening. Oleomargarine, sweet chocolate, milk chocolate
Oat gum	Butter, cream, fluid milk, candy
Sodium sulfite	Preservative, antioxidant, anti-browning agent
Potassium bisulfite	Preservative, antioxidant, anti-browning agent. Ale, beer, wine
Sodium bisulfite	Preservative, antioxidant, anti-browning agent. Ale, beer, wine, fruit pie mix
Potassium metabisulfite	Preservative, antioxidant. Uses listed for sulfite bisulfite
Sulfur dioxide	Antioxidant, preservative, anti-browning agent. *See* sodium sulfite. Wine, corn syrup, dried fruits, imitation jelly
Sodium thiosulfate	Used to protect sliced potatoes and uncooked french fries from browning. Stabilizer for potassium iodide in iodized salt
Tocopherol (Vitamin E)	Antioxidant. Essential oils, candy

TABLE 7. *(Continued)*

Group III: Sequestrants	
Additive	Usage
Calcium chloride	Stabilizing agent. Evaporated milk
Calcium citrate	Plasticizer for cheese spread; emulsifier salt
Monoisopropyl citrate	Sequestrant, antioxidant
Potassium citrate	Emulsifier salt
Sodium citrate	Emulsifier salt, stabilizer. Evaporated milk, cream (prevent "cream plug"), ice cream emulsifier, processed cheese
Citric acid	Sequestrant, antioxidant, dispersing agent. Oleomargarine. Added to rendered animal fat or a combination of such fat and vegetable fat. Lard, frozen peaches, grape wine, pie crust mix, prepared breakfast cereal, soup base, antioxidant salt
Sodium metaphosphate	Emulsifier, sequestering agent, texturizer. Prevent scale formation and corrosion in potable water supplies; addition not in excess of 10 ppm
Sodium phosphate	Emulsifier salt
Monosodium, disodium, and Trisodium orthophosphate	Emulsifier salts. Disodium orthophosphate also texturizer
Sodium pyrophosphate	Emulsifier salt, texturizer. Cold water pudding
Phosphoric acid	Sequestering agent
Sorbitol	Sequestrant. Vegetable oils
Sodium tartrate	Emulsifier salt. Pasteurized process cheese
Sodium potassium tartrate	Emulsifier salt
Stearyl citrate	Metal scavenger, antioxidant. Oleomargarine
Group IV: Surfactants	
Additive	Usage
Dimethyl polysiloxane	Antifoaming agent. Permitted in soups in an amount not in excess of 10 ppm. Chewing gum bases, molasses, soft drinks, fruit juices
Mono- and Diglycerides	Emulsifying agents, bakery products, sweet chocolate, milk chocolate, ice cream, frozen custard, fruit sherbet, oleomargarine
Glycerides, monosodium phosphate derivatives of mono- and di-.	Emulsifiers. Oleomargarine
Glycerides, acetyl tartaric acid esters of mono- and di-.	Emulsifying agent. Bakery products
Lecithin	Emulsifier. Sweet chocolate, milk chocolate. Bakery products, added to rendered animal fat
Monoglycerides: Polyoxyethylene esters of Sorbitan, Laurate, Oleate, Palmitate, Stearate	Emulsifiers. These are strictly limited by law and cannot be used in bakery goods and ice creams
Group V: Nonnutritive Sweeteners	
Additive	Usage
Calcium cyclamate, sodium cyclamate	Sweetening agents
Saccharin, calcium saccharin, sodium saccharin	Sweetening agents

(Continued)

TABLE 7. *(Continued)*

Group VI: Stabilizers, Thickeners	
Additive	**Usage**
Agar-agar	Thickening agent, stabilizer. Ice cream, frozen custard, sherbets, ices
Sodium alginate	Stabilizer, water retainer. Pasteurized process cheese, cream cheese, ice cream, frozen custard, salad dressing
Alginic acid	Stabilizer
Carragheen (Irish moss derivative)	Stabilizer, emulsifier. Pasteurized process cheese spread, french dressing
Methyl cellulose (cellulose gum)	Thickening agent, stabilizer. Body agent for beverages & canned fruits sweetened with nonnutritive sweeteners. Thickener for kosher food products, binder in nonwheat baked goods for non-allergenic diets, beer foam stabilizer, low calorie dietetic products
Sodium carboxymethyl cellulose	Stabilizer. Pasteurized process cheese spread
Dextrin	Foam stabilizer for beer
Gelatin	Thickener, stabilizer. Cream cheese, ice cream, base for fruit gelatins and puddings, chocolate milk, cream, confectionery ingredients
Gum acacia (gum arabic)	Thickener, stabilizer. Ice cream, frozen custard, fruit sherbets, french dressing, salad dressing, bottled soft drinks
Carob bean gum (locust gum)	Thickener, stabilizer. Cream cheese, Neufchatel cheese
Gum tragacanth	Thickener, stabilizer. Fruit jelly, ornamental icings, confections
Pectin	Stabilizer, thickener. Fruit sherbet, water ices, fruit jelly, preserves, jams
Peptones	Foam stabilizer for beer

Group VII: Bleaching and Maturing Agents	
Additive	**Usage**
Potassium bromate	Maturing agent, dough conditioner. Bread, rolls, buns
Sodium p-toluene sulfo-chloramine	Water purifying agent; deodorant. Used to remove onion and weed odor in cheese
Chlorine	Flour bleaching, aging and oxidizing agent
Chlorine dioxide	Flour bleach, oxidizing agent
Potassium iodate	Dough conditioner, oxidizing agent
Hydrogen peroxide	Bleaching, oxidizing agent. Bleach for tripe, butter, treatment of eggs before drying

Group VIII: Food Colors	
Additive	**Usage**
Annatto	Vegetable dye. Used for dairy products (butter, cheese, cottage cheese), coloring meat product casings, margarine
Caramel	Soft drinks
Carotene	Vegetable dye. Butter, margarine, shortening
Chlorophyllins	Vegetable dye. Chewing gum, lozenges, confections
Cochineal	Vegetable dye. Meat products
FD&C Green No. 3	Fast Green FCF. Mint-flavored jelly
FD&C Red No. 3	Erythrosine. Canned fruit cocktail, cherry pie mix
FD&C Yellow No. 3	Yellow AB. Margarine, corn oil for popcorn, yellow cake mix, processed cheese
FD&C Yellow No. 4	Yellow OB. Margarine, popcorn oil, butter, cheese and other dairy products

TABLE 7. *(Continued)*

FD&C Yellow No. 4	Yellow OB. Margarine, popcorn oil, butter, cheese and other dairy products
Methyl violet	Marking ink. Branding meats
Saffron	Vegetable dye. Meat products
Titanium oxide	Colorant. White pigment for candy. Gums, marking ink for confectionery
Turmeric	Vegetable dye. Meat products

Group IX: Buffers, Acids, Alkalies

Additive	Usage
Acetic acid	Acid
Aluminum ammonium sulfate	Acid. Milling, baking and cereal industries
Aluminum potassium sulfate	Acid. Baking powder ingredient
Aluminum sodium sulfate	Acid. Acidulant in baking powder
Ammonium bicarbonate	Alkali. Leavening agent in the production of thin, baked goods
Ammonium phosphate, mono- and disbasic	Buffers. Leavening agent for cookies and crackers
Calcium carbonate	Alkali. Neutralizer in dairy industry. To reduce excessive acidity in wine; confections
Calcium chloride	Confections
Calcium citrate	Buffer. Confections
Calcium gluconate	Buffer. Confections
Calcium hydroxide	Alkali. Used to stabilize the potassium iodide of iodized salt. Sour cream butter neutralizer
Calcium lactate	Buffer. Constituent of some baking powders. Confections
Calcium phosphate, monobasic	Buffer. Self-rising flour, self-rising white and yellow corn meals
Calcium phosphate, tribasic	Buffer. Used for pH adjustment in frozen dairy products
Citric acid	Acid. Cheese products, mayonnaise, jelly, preserves, canned vegetables, fresh beef blood
Fumaric acid	Acid. Leavening agent. Dry acid for dessert powders
Glucono-Δ-lactone	Acid. Leavening agent
Hydrochloric acid	Acid. Used in manufacture of sodium glutamate, gelatin
Lactic acid	Acidulant, flavoring, preservative
Magnesium carbonate	Alkali
Malic acid	Acid
Phosphoric acid	Acid
Potassium acid tartrate	Acid. Buffer. Acid constituent of some baking powders
Potassium bicarbonate	Alkali
Potassium citrate	Buffer, confections
Potassium hydroxide	Alkali. Peeling agent for tubers and fruits
Sodium acetate	Buffer. Corn syrup, table syrup, breakfast cereal, butter salt
Sodium acid pyrophosphate	Buffer. Used as a slow-acting acid constituent of a leavening mixture for self-rising and prepared cake, doughnut, waffle and other types of flour and mixes
Sodium bicarbonate	Alkali
Sodium carbonate	Alkali. Neutralizer for butter, cream, fluid milk, ice cream. Processing of olives before canning
Sodium citrate	Buffer. Used to control acidity and retain carbonation in beverages
Sodium hydroxide	Alkali. Glazing agent for pretzels, peeling agent for tubers and fruits
Sodium metasilicate	Alkali. Used as peeling solution for peaches
Sodium phosphate, monobasic	Buffer. Puffed breakfast cereal

(Continued)

TABLE 7. *(Continued)*

Group IX: Buffers, Acids, Alkalies	
Additive	Usage
Sodium phosphate, dibasic	Buffer. Used to adjust acidity of various foods
Sodium phosphate, tribasic	Buffer, Prepared cereals
Sodium potassium phosphate	Buffer. Used in confections
Sodium sesquicarbonate	Neutralizer. Sour cream prior to butter manufacture
Sulfuric acid	Acid. Adjustment of pH in brewing industry
Tartaric acid	Acid. Dried egg whites, confections

Group X: Nutrient Supplements	
Additive	Usage
Ascorbic acid	Fruit juices, carbonated beverages
Calcium carbonate	Enriched flour
Calcium phosphate	*See* calcium carbonate
Carotene	Optional ingredient as Vitamin A source in margarine 5000 to 13000 USP units per pound
Copper gluconate	Source of copper in dietary supplements
Ferric phosphate	See Iron
Hydrofluosilicic acid, Sodium fluoride, Sodium silico-fluoride	Fluoridation of water
Cuprous iodide	Used in table salt as source of dietary iodine
Potassium iodide, 3-5 diiodo-salicylic acid	Used in table salt as source of dietary iodine
Iron	Enriched flours
L-Lysine monohydro chloride	Fortification of specialty bread and cereal mixes
Nicacin	Enriched flour
Calcium pantothenate	Dietary supplement, member of Vitamin B complex
Sodium phosphate, mono-, di-, and tri-basic	Constituent of formulated mineral supplements for cereal products, particularly farina
Potassium chloride	Substitute for sodium chloride in low-sodium dietary foods
Pyridoxine hydro chloride	Dietary supplement, member of Vit. B. complex, Evaporated milk—base food for infants
Riboflavin, Riboflavin-5-phosphate, sodium	Enriched flours, dry baby cereals, poultry stuffing, peanut butter
Thiamine hydrochloride	Enriched flours
Tocopherol (Vitamin E)	Dietary supplement
Vitamin A	Mellorine (vegetable-fat imitation ice cream), skim milk, dietary infant formula
Vitamin B_{12}	Dietary supplement (anti-pernicious anemia factor)
Vitamin D_2	Enriched flours, evaporated milk

Group XI: Flavoring Agents Aromatic Chemicals, Essential Oils, Spices	
Additive	Usage
Acetaldehyde	Black walnut flavor. Candy, baked goods
Acetanisol	Nutty flavor
Acetic acid	Rum flavor. Drinks, baked goods
Acetoin	Butter flavor. Baked goods
Acetophenone	Cherry flavor. Candy
Para-methoxyacetophenone	Vanilla-like flavor, substitute for coumarin
Acetyl propionate	Butter flavor. Baked goods

TABLE 7. *(Continued)*

Acetyl valeryl	Strawberry flavor. Hard candy
Alcohol C-8	Citrus flavor
Allyl capreate	Pineapple flavor. Beverages, candy, ice cream
Allyl cinnamate	Pineapple flavor. Soft drinks
Allyl isothiocyanante	Mustard flavor. Sauces
Allyl isovalerate	Apple flavor. Miscellaneous
Ammonium valerate	Imitation Black Walnut flavor. Ice Cream
Amyl acetate	Banana Flavor, fruit flavors. Beverages, candy, ice cream, baked goods
Amyl alcohol	Whiskey flavor. Baked goods, candy
Amyl butyrate	Banana flavor, fruit flavors. Beverages, candy, ice cream, baked goods
Amyl cinnamic aldehyde	Strawberry flavor. Hard candy
Amyl formate	Raspberry flavor. Beverages
Amyl isovalerate	Peach flavor, fruit flavor. Beverages, candy
Amyl oenanthate	Coconut flavor. Baked goods
Anethole	Root beer and anise flavors. Beverages, candy, baked goods
Angelica	Essential oil. Liqueurs
Anisaldehyde	Cherry and vanilla flavors. Candy, baked goods
Anise	Essential oil, licorice flavor. Candy
Asafoetida	Onion flavor. Meats
Balsam, Peru gum	Vanilla flavor. Ice cream, candy
Basil	Essential oil. Cordial
Benzaldehyde	Cherry and Almond flavors. Beverages, candy, ice cream, baked goods
Benzoin gum	Vanilla flavor. Ice cream
Benzyl acetate	Strawberry flavor, fruit flavor. Beverages, candy, ice cream, baked goods
Benzyl benzoate	Raspberry flavor. Gelatin desserts, candy
Benzyl valerate	Strawberry flavor. Candy
Butyl acetate	Raspberry and fruit flavors. Gelatin desserts, candy
Butyl butyrate	Fruit flavor. Candy, baked goods
Butyric acid	Butter flavor. Baked goods
Capric aldehyde	Citrus flavor. Beverages, candy, gelatin dessert
Caproic acid	Cheese flavor. Baked goods
Capryl aldehyde	Citrus flavor. Beverages
Carvone	Caraway, dill flavor; spearmint oil. Beverages, candy, baked goods
Cinnamaldehyde	Cinnamon flavor, cola flavor. Beverages, candy, ice cream, baked goods
Cinnamyl anthranilate	Grape flavor. Beverages, candy
Butyraldehyde	Nut flavor. Ice cream, candy
Citral	Lemon flavor. Beverages, candy, ice cream, baked goods
Citronellol	Rose flavor. Candy, baked goods
Cumin aldehyde	Mint flavor
Cyclohexyl acetate	Orange flavor. Soft drinks, candy
Diacetyl	Butter flavor. Butter, margarine, buttermilk, cottage cheese, baked goods
Diallyl sulfide	Garlic flavor. Meat sauces
Ethone	Vanilla flavor. Candy, baked goods
Ethyl acetate	Pineapple flavor. Beverages, candy, ice cream, gelatin, baked goods
Ethyl acetoacetate	Apple flavor. Soft drinks, gelatin desserts
Ethyl butyrate	Strawberry flavor, fruit flavor. Beverages, candy, ice cream, baked goods

(Continued)

TABLE 7. *(Continued)*

Group XI: Flavoring Agents Aromatic Chemicals, Essential Oils, Spices	
Additive	Usage
Ethyl caprylate	Cognac. Miscellaneous
Ethyl formate	Rum flavor, strawberry flavor. Beverages, candy, ice cream, baked goods
Ethyl lactate	Grape flavor. Beverages, candy, gum
Ethyl nitrite	Strawberry flavor. Hard candy
Ethyl phenylacetate	Honey flavor. Miscellaneous
Ethyl propionate	Grape flavor. Beverages
Ethyl salicylate	Strawberry flavor. Candy, gelatin desserts
Ethyl valerate	Fruity flavor. Beverages, candy, ice cream
Ethyl vanillin	Vanilla flavor. Beverages, ice cream, baked goods
Furfural	Butterscotch flavor. Candy and pudding
Monosodium glutamate	Flavor enhancer. Meat, poultry, and fish products. Vegetables, soups, salad dressings, pickles
Hexanol	Apple flavor. Soft drinks, gelatin desserts
N-Hexyl butyrate	Apple flavor, pear flavor. Beverages, baking
Isoamyl alcohol	Fruity flavor
Isobutyl acetate	Strawberry flavor. Miscellaneous
Isobutyl caproate	Raisin flavor. Bakery products
Menthol	Mint flavor. Candy, baked goods
Menthone	Mint flavor.
Methyl cyclopentanone	Maple flavor. Candy
Methyl heptenone	Fruity flavor
Methyl nonyl ketone	Orange flavor. Candy, soft drinks
Methyl salicylate	Root beer and wintergreen flavors. Beverages, candy, ice cream
Nonyl aldehyde	Citrus flavor. Beverages, candy
Octyl acetate	Brandy flavor. Candy
Phenylacetic acid	Honey flavor
Propyl butyrate	Fruity flavor
Pyroligneous acid	Smoke flavor. Salt, cheese
Quinine sulfate	Flavoring agent. Quinine water
Rhubarb, extract	Vermouth. Alcoholic drinks
Valeric acid	Butter flavor. Baked goods
Vanillin	Vanilla flavor. Beverages, ice cream, baked goods, chocolate milk

Group XII: Miscellaneous Yeast Foods, Firming Agents, Texturizers, Etc.	
Additive	Usage
Aluminum sulfate	Firming Agent. Pickles, sweet and dill
Aluminum potassium sulfate	Firming Agent, carrier for bleaching agent. Pickles, sweet and dill. Carrier for benzoyl peroxide in bleached flours and cheeses
Ammonium chloride	Yeast food, dough conditioner. Bread, rolls, buns
Ammonium sulfate	Yeast food, dough conditioner. Yeast food in production of champagne and other sparkling wines
Beeswax	Candy glaze and polish
Brominated vegetable oils	Clouding agent. Used largely in soft drinks
Caffeine	Stimulant. Cola beverages
Calcium carbonate	Yeast food, firming agent, carrier. used in candies; in hard candies to prevent sticking: in fudge to promote creaming

TABLE 7. *(Continued)*

Calcium chloride	Firming agent. Used to firm sliced apples and other fruit
Calcium citrate	Firming agent
Calcium gluconate	Firming agent. Firming tomatoes, apple slices
Calcium hydroxide	Firming agent. Firming various fruit products
Calcium phosphate, mono- di- and tribasic	Yeast food, dough conditioner, firming agent, anti-caking
Calcium sulfate	Yeast food, dough conditioner, firming agent
Carbon dioxide	Pressure-dispensing agent (pressure-dispensed whipped cream)
Carnauba	Candy glaze and polish
Sodium citrate	Nutrient for culture media. Cultured buttermilk
Citric acid	Nutrient for culture. Cultured buttermilk
Glycerol	Humectant, solvent, body agent, plasticizer for edible coatings. Humectant in marshmallows, pastilles, and jelly-like candies. Solvent for colors and flavors.
Gum benzoin	Candy glaze and polish
Calcium lactate	Yeast food, dough conditioner. Bread, rolls, buns
Magnesium carbonate	Drying agent, color retention agent, bleach ingredient, anti-caking agent, carrier
Magnesium chloride	Color retention agent, firming agent. Canned peas.
Magnesium hydroxide	Drying agent and color retention agent. Used for improved gel curd formation in cheese manufacture
Magnesium sulfate	Water corrective. Used in brewing
Mannitol	Anti-sticking agent, chewing gum. Texturizing agent, candy
Mineral oil	Candy polish
Potassium nitrate	Color fixative
Sodium nitrite	Color fixative. Bacon, bologna, frankfurters, deviled ham, meat spreads, potted meats, spiced ham, Vienna sausage, uncooked smoked ham
Potassium nitrite	Color fixative
Nitrous oxide	Whipping agent. (Pressure-dispensed whipped cream)
Paraffin	Candy glaze and polish
Petrolatum	Candy polish
Ammonium phosphate, mono- and dibasic	Yeast food, dough conditioner
Potassium phosphate, mono- and dibasic	Yeast food. Used in brewing industry
Potassium chloride	Yeast food, used in brewing industry.
Potassium sulfate	Water corrective. Used in brewing
Propylene glycol	Solvent, wetting agent, humectant. Confections, chocolate products, ice cream emulsifiers, shredded coconut
Shellac	Candy glaze and polish
Calcium silicate	Anti-caking agent. Table salt, meat dry-curing mixtures
Sorbitol	Humectant, texturizing agent. Candy, soft type, shredded coconut, dietetic fruit packs and soft drinks
Calcium Stearate	Anti-caking agent. Onion and garlic salts
Magnesium Stearate	Anti-caking agent. Onion and garlic salts, meat dry-curing mixtures
Talc	Anti-caking agent. Added to vitamin supplements to render free-flowing
Tannic Acid	Clarifying agent. Brewing and wine industry
Urea	Yeast food. Wine production

Source: The Condensed Chemical Dictionary.

ADDITIVE CONTROL BY LEGISLATION

Food additives are more strictly regulated now than at any other time in history. Despite our nostalgia for the good old days, eating was not especially safe at the turn of the century. Then it was difficult to protect foods from spoiling. Likewise, manufacturers freely used pigments containing such toxic metals as lead, copper, and arsenic to color candy, pickles, and other foods, created strawberry jam with only coloring, flavoring, and grass seed, and perhaps stretched ground black pepper with bits of charcoal.

The 1906 Food and Drugs Act and the more comprehensive Food, Drug, and Cosmetic Act of 1938 gave the Government authority to remove adulterated and obviously poisonous foods from the market. But it was not until the Food Additives Amendment was enacted in 1958 and the Color Additive Amendments in 1960 that the nation had laws specifically regulating food additives. In those amendments, the lawmakers shifted the burden from the government of proving a food additive unsafe to the manufacturer, who must prove that it is safe. The amendments authorized the FDA to regulate additives only on the basis of safety. The agency has no power to limit the number of additives approved or to judge whether a particular food color, thickener, or sweetener is really needed.

Additives Approval Tests

An approval process may take up to several years. Manufacturers first must subject a proposed new additive to a battery of chemical tests to determine whether it does what is intended and to assure that it can be analyzed and measured in the finished food product. Then the additive must be fed in large doses over an extended period to at least two species of animals (usually a species of rodent and dogs). These feeding studies are designed to determine whether the substance causes cancer, birth defects, or other injury to the animals.

Manufacturers submit the results of all these tests to FDA. If the agency indicates that the additive is safe, it establishes regulations governing how the substance can be used in food. A basic rule is a 100-fold margin of safety for anything added to food. This means that the manufacturer may use only 1/100th the maximum amount of an additive that has been found not to produce any harmful effects in test animals.

NATURAL VERSUS MAN-MADE FOODS

Natural foods as nature provides them for us undergo many changes as they move from the farm to the market to the consumer. Flavor, color, nutrition, appearance, and other quality standard factors are altered between the farm and table.

Let us consider the comparative merits of natural foods and man-made replacements. First of all, natural, no additives does not mean no chemicals. Natural grape flavor contains more than 19 chemicals (by analysis). Synthetic grape flavor consists of only 5 of the principal chemicals contained in natural grape flavor.

Dr. Julius Coon, Professor of Pharmacology, Thomas Jefferson University, reported in an NAS study that

> viewing all chemicals that are present in our food supply—the natural components, agricultural chemicals, food additives and natural and man-made contaminants in perspective—it is clear that the greatest area of the unknown involves the natural and normal components of our food.
>
> There is no scientific reason to believe that naturally occurring substances in foods are more or less safe than man-made substances.

Whether citric and ascorbic acids are extracted from oranges, purified and crystallized into white water-soluble crystals, or synthesized they are the very same compounds. They have identical melting points, solubilities, indexes of refraction, pH's, tastes, and so on. When fed to test animals their efficacies are identical. Vitamin C (ascorbic acid) from natural sources will not prevent scurvy any more effectively than the synthetic vitamin C or vice versa. There is one noteworthy difference; the relative cost of production. Once the plant has been put on-stream, the synthetic vitamin C will prove far more economical to produce than the natural product.

Imitation Foods

Each year imitation foods are getting a bigger share of the total food dollar. Fructose from corn is sweeter than cane or beet sugar (sucrose) and costs about one-third as much. It can take care of about two-thirds of our total sugar requirement. Artificial nonfat dry milk made from soy, corn syrup, and whey costs about half as much as the natural product. Its use in soft ice cream, bread, and processed meat is increasing.

Sales of engineered foods totaled $13 billion in 1973, and total consumption should double by 1980, according to the USDA.

Health Foods "Rip-off"

So-called natural or health foods cost consumers double what is paid in the supermarket for the same item. Dr. Emil Mrak, world authority on agriculture, refers to scientific experiments carried out at Michigan State University, at Cornell, and in England for 25 years in which no differences were found between organic (health) foods and foods treated with commercial fertilizers (Stephenson 1978).

ROLE OF GOVERNMENT

The role of government in regulating food production has been greatly expanded since 1958. Its power is so great under the 1958 law (which includes the Delaney clause noted earlier) that it could ban any chemical. The key is the media. Any chemical can be tried and condemned by the news media before it is proven to be carcinogenic. We must find the key to establishing fair and realistic tolerance levels for the continued use and further development of food additives.

Cranberries: The Media Scare of 1959

The first great consumer scare occurred in the fall of 1959. Traces of a weed killer, aminotriazole, was detected by food safety inspectors in a shipment of cranberries from the Pacific Northwest. When fed to rats in massive doses a few months earlier, the chemical caused cancer. (To get cancer on that basis a person would have to eat 15,000 pounds of cranberry sauce per day for many years.)

An Associated Press correspondent wrote an article on cranberry poisoning; several congressmen then pressured the FDA to ban fresh cranberries. This action ruined the cranberry growers who had already harvested the crop. Stores that had fresh cranberries to sell were unable to sell them.

Cyclamate Ban

When HEW Secretary Robert Finch decided to ban cyclamates in 1969, his decision was based on a single experiment using mixtures of cyclamate, saccharin, and cholesterol. These mixtures, with variations in concentration and in blends of the substances, were fed to white Swiss mice. Tumors grew in the bladders of 8 of 240 animals tested. These eight were the ones fed at the highest levels at the equivalent of 350 bottles of diet soda per day.

By making this decision Mr. Finch ignored completely 18 years of prior research and numerous animal feeding experiments that gave far different results. Not one single experiment showed tumors or any evidence of cancer. This evaluation of cyclamate safety had been done as the law requires by the manufacturer, Abbot Laboratories, and had led to approval of their use by the FDA. When asked why he banned cyclamates, Mr. Finch indicated that the Delaney clause required him to do so.

This experience with the cyclamate ban caused President Nixon to direct the FDA to start a review of all food chemicals on the GRAS list, including salt and sugar. This GRAS review is still in progress. Its cost will undoubtedly exceed 500 million dollars. Most important, now all foods are suspect.

Bans Caused by Politics and Inappropriate Testing

In the event that the same precepts are followed in judging other food additives as in the banning of cyclamates, the entire GRAS list and in fact the whole food industry are in jeopardy. Unfortunately, cancer was induced in the test animals by using inappropriate tests that were not conducted in a scientific manner. The experiments did not represent appropriate testing.

Thus politics, not scientific proof, became the basis for the decision on cyclamates. As a result, saccharin was the only artificial sweetener on the GRAS list until aspartame (manufactured by G. D. Searle and Co.) won FDA approval in 1974. Later this approval was temporarily withdrawn until 1981, when the FDA approved aspartame for specific uses. Aspartame is 180 times as sweet as sugar and has received FDA approval.

An added effect of this decision in its impact on the public, was to make the health food binge that followed the billion-dollar business it is today.

Diethyl Stilbesterol

In 1972 a ban was placed on the estrogen diethyl stilbesterol (DES), which had been used as a cattle-growth stimulant since 1954. During the 1960s DES usage in cattle was linked to the use of DES during pregnancy by women whose daughters developed vaginal cancer and sons developed genital abnormalities. Publicity of this finding led to a ban on DES. After an FDA rejection of the plea of the DES manufacturer for a hearing, the manufacturer appealed to the U.S. Court of Appeals, which ruled that marketing of DES could continue until the FDA held a hearing.

The DES ban was another action prompted by the Delaney clause. Its effect was to impress beef consumers that the cattlemen were intentionally poisoning them. Actually they were using materials which to the best knowledge of the scientific community were safe. In fact, a ban was placed on DES by the FDA on November 1, 1979.

Saccharin

The carcinogenic character of saccharin has been shown. The ban was delayed in 1978 by a public opinion backlash to the FDA decision. Congress extended the use of saccharin for an additional 18 months when the Saccharin Study and Labeling Act was signed into law by President Carter on November 23, 1978. Labeling is required to state that "Use of this product may be hazardous to your health. This product contains saccharin which has been determined to cause cancer in laboratory animals."

A Way Out of This Dilemma

Additives are on trial. Where this situation will end is not known. Sugar, vitamins A and D, monosodium glutamate, nitrates and nitrites, and hundreds of other GRAS substances are being reviewed.

Table salt or sugar or, in fact, any chemical in improperly designed or conducted experiments can induce cancer in animals. In the opinion of the author, the law should read, "if found to induce cancer when ingested by man or animal in amounts and under conditions of its intended use." Meanwhile the law, based on the Delaney clause, prevails at high cost and negative returns to all concerned.

The Congress, in cooperation with the NAS/NRC Food Protection Committee, should define the meaning of:

Tests appropriate for evaluation of safety

Reasonable levels of risk above which the chemical may prove hazardous to health

A risk to benefit ratio to be used as a basis for judging whether a ban or a warning be imposed

These definitions should be based on feeding levels of the chemical in test animals no higher than that equivalent to 100 times the concentration used in our foods, beverages, and water supplies. Otherwise we may ultimately destroy the food supply we are trying to make safer.

Safety of Food Additives Is Proved

Selenium salts once thought to be toxic have now been found to be safe and essential to health below specific levels. Cyclamates could someday return. Salt can often be fatal to infants when used in their milk formulas. The relative safety of food is a tribute to the zeal and dedication of food scientists in industry, government, and university laboratories. We can also thank the efficiency of our bodies natural detoxification system for this blessing.

Recent Regulatory Action

Federal regulatory agencies have long been concerned about both direct and incidental additives that increase cancer risks. Some recent examples of regulatory action and studies follow.

Diethyl stilbesterol (DES) a carcinogenic chemical used to promote livestock growth, was banned by the FDA on November 1, 1979.

The FDA has proposed that the artificial sweetener saccharin be banned from food.

Sodium nitrite used to improve the color and flavor as well as to preserve cured meats may be the precursor of carcinogens found in certain cured meats.

Butylated hydroxytoluene—an effective antioxidant when added to food—may cause lung tumors in mice and may cause behavioral changes. Testing continues.

Red dye No. 40 may be slightly carcinogenic and may also affect child behavior. Testing is in progress.

Caffeine is teratogenic (causes birth defects) and may affect the central nervous system. Testing continues.

Antibiotics used in animal feed to promote growth may increase resistance of human pathogens to antibiotic treatment. Testing continues.

Residues of PCB, PBB, Kepone, mercury, and other toxic industrial chemicals and pesticides have been found in numerous foods.

The exact number of deaths due to cancer-causing additives cannot be determined accurately. It is unfortunate that people have to be troubled about chemicals that pose only a slight risk to a given individual. In fact regulatory agencies were set up, in part, to save people the trouble of worrying about each and every little hazard (Jacobson 1980).

How Safe Is Safe?

Proving a negative is impossible, and safety is a negative, namely, the absence of harm. Numerous tests can be made without showing harm. Then a more sensitive testing method may identify the presence of some harmful chemical not previously identifiable. When this chemical is fed to test animals at high enough levels or injected into the animal it might do harm, especially in a weak or highly sensitive species. Such tests are not very reliable. The real criterion is how much of the chemical put into food by either man or nature is ingested.

Potatoes and watercress, in the raw state, contain poisons. Raw cabbage, spinach, onions, lettuce, tea, and cranberries contain carcinogens. Yet the human detoxification system handles these and many other poisons.

There are no safe or unsafe food additives. Instead we need to be concerned about safe and unsafe levels of use or kinds of uses. In order to assure safety, toxicologists, analytical chemists, nutritionists, and other scientists perform the never-ending task of studying feeding levels and the effects of cooking, processing, and storage practices on these chemicals.

QUESTIONS OF DOSAGE LEVELS

Gas chromatographs, mass spectrometers, and other incredibly sensitive instruments can detect the presence of chemicals in foods at levels as low as parts per billion and even parts per trillion in some instances. However, the sensitivity of testing methods is not the criterion by which chemical safety should be judged. Toxicity is dependent on dosage. For example, the toxic metals, arsenic and lead at certain levels may be therapeutic. Curare, a deadly poison used by South American Indians to coat their arrow tips, is now used in medicine. Digitalis in foxglove a deadly poison, has been used to save the lives of countless heart attack victims.

When does a toxic substance become a poison? Toxicologists call this the dose to response relationship. Toxicity occurs when the detoxifying capability is exceeded. Standards for safety testing are set by the government at the National Center for Toxicological Research. Industry has established its own Chemical Industry Institute of Toxicology. Each facility is dedicated to developing better, quicker, less costly, and more effective testing methods to assure the continued safety of our food supply.

Zero Tolerances

Under provisions of the 1954 Pesticide Amendment certain pesticides used on certain crops were required to leave absolutely no residues. Scientists have found that no analytical method can prove that zero amount of a material is present. This problem of zero tolerances became acute and was widely publicized in 1965 when the District of Columbia Department of Health prohibited sale of nearly a million dollars worth of milk from Maryland, Pennsylvania, and Virginia. The milk contained trace amounts of the pesticides heptachlor, heptachlor epoxide, and dieldrin, which are used to control weevils in the alfalfa fields on which the cows were fed. Detection was possible only because a newly purchased gas chromatograph was used, and it was sensitive enough to pick up trace amounts that were previously unmeasurable. Dumping of the milk led to a study of the problem by the National Academy of Sciences–National Research Council in 1965.

The study by a committee of scientists concluded that zero tolerances (established by the FDA) and no-residue (established by the USDA) "were scientifically and administratively untenable and should be abandoned." In the same year, the FDA announced that finite "negligible-residue" tolerances for pesticides—chemical by chemical, use by use—would replace zero tolerances whenever possible. Studies on no-residue replacement by safe tolerances led to cancellation of no-residue requirements on 31 December 1967.

GRAS SUBSTANCES

A survey conducted by the Flavoring Extract Manufacturers Association (FEMA) in 1971 of over 1400 flavoring ingredients showed that about 75% were used in foods at levels not exceeding 100 ppm (Oser and Ford 1977). Furthermore, the annual usage of 71% of GRAS flavorings totaled less than 1000 pounds or, on a per capita basis, the equivalent of 0.1 μg/kg of body weight per day. Considering the fact that nearly all of the so-called synthetic flavorings are analogous to their counterparts in foods or body tissues, are simple chemical structures, and are readily metabolized and detoxified in mammals, such low use levels of flavoring materials have been regarded as insignificant from the viewpoint of potential toxicity. The FEMA expert panel did not modify its GRAS determination of saccharin (Hall and Oser 1965), notwithstanding the FDA proposal in 1977 to ban its use (Oser and Ford 1978). Questions were raised concerning the study (especially the methodology employed) and then weighed against the total evidence concerning the tests and use of saccharin.

FOOD CHEMICALS CODEX

The Codex work by the Food Protection Committee of NAS/NRC began in 1961. On July 1, following the committee's publication of the first bound edition of the Committee report covering about 500 food additives, Dr. James L. Goddard, Commissioner of Food and Drug Administration at the time, wrote the director of the Codex, "I am pleased to endorse the specifications in this Food Chemicals Codex prescribing minimum requirements of purity for an appropriate grade of food chemicals for intentional and purposeful use in the food of man. The FDA will regard the specifications in the Food Chemicals Codex as defining an 'appropriate food grade' within the meaning . . . of the food additive regulation. . . ."

The published standards are sure to increase the purity of many commercial food-grade chemicals. These standards should also have other important effects. Dr. Tuthill of Mallinckrodt Chemical Co. stated, "A public relations program emphasizing the publication and function of the Codex should help materially to improve the public opinion on food chemicals." From its modest beginnings the Food Chemicals Codex has grown to include about 3000 food chemicals in the second edition (1972) and the first and second supplements to the second edition published in 1974 and 1975.

Industry scientists participated with university and government experts as members of the NAS/NRC committee that developed the Food Chemicals Codex.

ENVIRONMENTAL CANCER RISKS

Cancers may be caused by viruses or by environmental factors. Geography, heredity, employment, occupation, industrial pollutants, smoking, radiation and sunlight exposures, and even sex life have been statistically related to cancer.

Stomach cancer is the number-one killer in Japan and Iceland. In the United States there has been a dramatic drop in stomach cancer cases in recent years, perhaps due to the usage of BHA and BHT. Unfavorable effects have been observed in animals fed BHA and BHT at levels of 1000 to 5000 ppm in the diet. However, it is estimated that using BHA or BHT at the maximum level prescribed in foods would yield a maximum intake of about 4 ppm, an entirely safe level. Actual usage is substantially less. Cumulative effects in the test animals are offset by the human detoxification system.

We in the United States hold the world records for lung cancer and colon cancer. Africans die more from cancer of the esophagus than people of other locality do. Figure 1 shows male cancer death rates by sites for 1930–1970. We know that diets high in smoked food cause stomach cancer as do diets containing a large amount of charcoal-broiled foods. This occurs when fats that drop into the coals are converted into polynuclear hydrocarbons. These volatile chemicals remain on the meat following volatilization. Lijinsky and Shubik (1964) found more than 20 suspect compounds, including benzopyrene (a known carcinogen present in cigarette smoke) on charcoal-broiled steaks.

It is known that intestinal bacteria convert nitrates (used to cure meats) into nitrites, which in turn form nitrosamines that in large enough doses may produce cancer. Nitrosamines formed from nitrates in cured meats are probably at levels too low to pose any threat of cancer in humans. Furthermore, there is no evidence that nitrosamines could do so.

When eating vegetables we ingest far higher levels of nitrates than we get from cured meats and fish. Hence, a ban of nitrates and nitrites in cured meats because of the extremely remote possibility of cancer caused by nitrosamine formation in the body seems ridiculous, especially when their elimination from ham, sausage, bacon, corned beef, and other cured meats greatly increases the risk of botulism, the most deadly of all commonly encountered food poisons. "Until the all-purpose agent comes along, or until consumer preference changes, the best compromise probably will be continued use of nitrite in conventional amounts with vitamins C and E added to block formation of nitrosamines," according to the NAS Committee on Nitrite and Alternative Curing Agents in Food (1982).

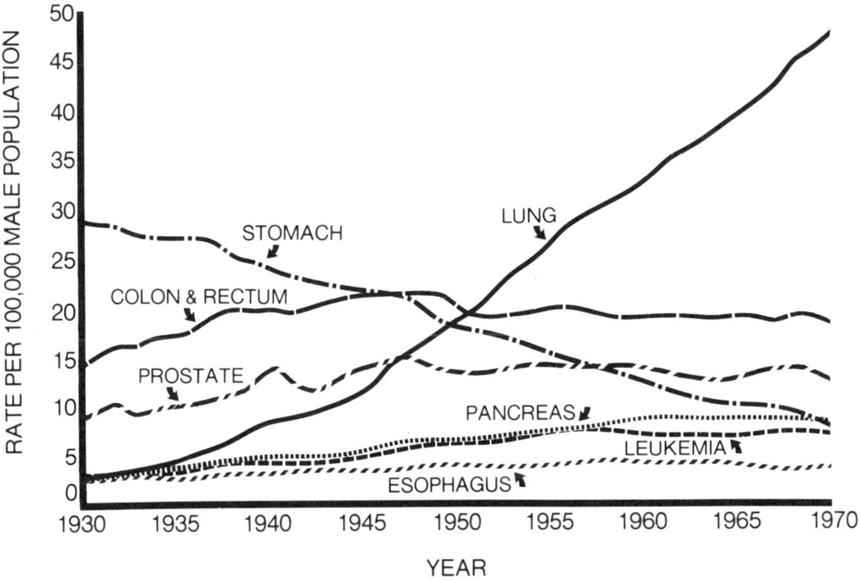

Fig. 1. Male cancer death rates by site, United States, 1930–1970. *From American Cancer Society.*

Toxicants from Tobacco Products

Cigarette, pipe, and cigar smoking are increasing despite the report of the U.S. Surgeon General of more than 10 years ago. These insidious toxicants unfortunately do not limit their carcinogenic and other health-destroying properties to the smoker. Instead, they may pose an even greater danger to the nonsmoker who is exposed to them.

Furthermore, residues of these toxicants are embedded in clothing, books, telephones, furnishings of all kinds, and exposed foods. There is a need to educate smokers concerning the harm that their noxious effluents cause. Certainly we must find more effective and intelligent ways to improve both human relations and health by properly controlling this habit that many possess and use to the detriment of all.

Screening Environmental Chemicals

Screening by the National Cancer Institute of 6000 chemicals in our environment resulted in the identification of 1000 that cause cancer in animals. Any environmental chemical suspected of having carcinogenic properties should be either controlled or removed from the environment.

ENVIRONMENTAL FOOD CONTAMINATION

Murphy's Law states that "if anything bad can happen, it will." While humorous, the phenomenon is constantly at work ruining some of our food supplies. The Office of Technology Assessment counted at least 243 cases of environmentally caused food contamination since 1968. The biggest loss in Michigan was caused by polybromobiphenyl (PBB), a fire-retardant chemical, shipped to the Farm Bureau at Lansing by mistake in 1973.

The feed-blending operators unfortunately failed to look carefully at the label and carelessly blended the fire retardant into numerous lots of feed. The retardant was mistaken for the feed supplement normally used, as it was packed in the same paper bags, with the same type of tag label sewn into the bag top when the bags were closed at the chemical plant.

The ultimate cost to the state of Michigan cannot be measured in dollars, as health and livelihoods of people have been lost. Many farmers had to destroy herds of cattle, droves of hogs, and flocks of chickens that, in some instances, took a lifetime to build. According to the Lansing State Journal, the cost in dollars may exceed a billion by the time the matter is finally settled, which will take years.

Kepone contamination of the James River in Virginia in 1973 by a subsidiary of the Hooker Chemical Co. destroyed the fishing industry and spread deadly poison along the east coast estuaries at untold cost. A similar environmental contamination of food supply occurred when a power transformer stored in a shed at the Pierce Packing Company in Billings, Montana, leaked polychloro biphenyl (PCB) coolant into the internal sewage system for animal wastes of the slaughterhouse. The wastes were collected, rendered, and added to animal feeds and sold throughout at least nine western states, resulting in high levels of PCB in the meat of animals fed the feed. Thousands of animals had to be destroyed as a result.

What causes regulatory failure in these environmental food poisoning episodes? A test sample taken from a poultry plant in Provo, Utah, while a federal inspector was on vacation revealed environmental pollution in the products of the plant. Five days passed before testing began, which took 10 days. The regional office of the USDA was not notified for an additional 5 days, a total of 20 days. Subsequently, weeks elapsed before state health officials and the FDA were notified. An alert to the public was not made until 2 months after the sampling. By then contamination of the food supply had begun.

Eggs, poultry, mayonnaise, cakes, and other foods were destroyed in this case, but, as in the similar cases already mentioned, authorities were unable to determine how much potentially dangerous food had been consumed. Under the current testing system for environmental contaminants in food, incidents of this type could go undetected.

An overhaul of its system by the FDA is now in progress. This will be designed to do the following: (1) test for the presence of suspect chemicals in food, (2) improve surveillance, (3) develop more rapid methods of analysis, and (4) tighten coordination and cooperation with other agencies.

Major obstacles in the path of this effort include both the cost of equipping and staffing laboratories to do this work and the costs of identifying each suspect chemical. Certainly, the old adage, an ounce of prevention is worth a pound of cure should convey the thought that strict quality control standards at the sources, namely, the packing plant and feed manufacturer quality control departments, would provide a better solution to this problem.

THE SAFETY COMMITTEE ON GRAS SUBSTANCES (SCOGS)

Under the rules pertaining to GRAS substances a chemical must not be added to the list or removed from the list without a public hearing. These hearings are announced by the FDA in the Federal Register. During a hearing industry and government scientists are on hand, together with any other interested parties. Frequently the FDA will ask neutral scientists from universities, institutes or foundations to challenge or refute industry findings. All of these invited participants attend and testify at government expense.

Following a hearing the FDA has the power to dispute industry reports supporting a given food additive. This is done by hiring a consulting laboratory to retest the substance in animal feeding tests. When all results are in, the FDA reviews all the data and concludes either that the additive is GRAS and should remain on the list or that it is not GRAS and should be removed from the food supply.

Industry has the right to appeal if the ruling is negative. However, the entire process is a costly one in time, talent, and dollars. As in the case of cyclamates, the manufacturer may decide to withdraw his product from the marketplace and apply later for reinstatement to the GRAS list.

FOOD SAFETY COUNCIL APPROACH

Dr. Sanford A. Miller, Director of the FDA Bureau of Foods, stated in a letter (Miller 1979), "the maintenance of a safe food supply in the United States will ultimately require the dedicated efforts of a broad-based spectrum of the American scientific community. I have always felt that the continuous controversy amongst consumer advocacy groups, industry, and the government has been counterproductive." He further stated that The

Food Safety Council represents the only forum, to his knowledge, in which the differences between the consumer advocacy community and industry are being discussed in an open atmosphere of cooperation, not controversy. The Food Safety Council board is comprised of an equal number of members from the food industry and allied fields of those representing the public interest from academia government and professional organizations. Its aims are, "to foster criteria for the safety and wholesomeness of foods and food ingredients, to provide the public, consumers and food scientists with scientifically sound information . . . to assist national and international . . . governmental bodies in formulating sound policies, laws and regulations to insure the safety, wholesomeness, and abundance of food."

Risk to Benefit Approach Needed

The NAS/NRC reported that a broad and total revision of the food safety provisions of the Federal Food Drug and Cosmetic Act is needed and recommends that consistent and uniform food safety standards should be adopted as follows:

The safety of food must be determined on the basis of an acceptable level of risk.

Each source of risk must be reviewed, evaluated, and controlled in a fair and consistent manner.

We must establish different regulatory controls based on differing levels of risk in our food supply.

Label warnings should be given when risks are high, and use levels should then be minimal.

Judgment of acceptable risk levels for a food or food substance should be based on expert scientific knowledge and experience by taking into account the conditions of use, levels to be used, and cumulative effect in the diet.

SYNTHETIC FLAVORS AND FOOD COLORS

There are hundreds of synthetic flavors on the GRAS list. Commercially produced food and beverage flavors that closely match or are even better than true flavors are now available and FDA-approved for use at parts per million levels. Food scientists have been solving many flavor problems by using gas, liquid, and thin-layer chromatography and spectrometry first to analyze natural flavor volatiles and then to match them synthetically. These imitations are more convenient to use and are more shelf stable and economical than their natural counterparts.

Imitation bacon, ham, beef, and chicken aromatics have been blended so that they can be combined with soy to somewhat simulate the corresponding meats (Ziemba 1969).

Synthetic Vegetable Flavors

Food processing causes natural vegetable flavors to decompose. A new era in flavor synthesis began with the recently successful development of delicate vegetable flavors. Using gas chromatographic analysis flavor chemists have successfully synthesized celery, onion, garlic, potato, parsley, pepper, mushroom, and tomato flavors. Required levels range from 0.002 to 0.02% of finished product by weight. Improvement in instant mashed potatoes and other processed vegetables is now possible (Lawler 1973).

Imitation Dairy Products

Milklike products including imitation milks, margarine, whipped toppings, coffee whiteners, and Mellorine, an imitation ice cream, are being marketed. Vegetable fat replaces butterfat in these products (Gemmill 1969). Synthetic flavor blends are used in all of these food substitutes.

Synthetic Food Colors

Dairy products, beverages, baked goods, spices, jellies, candy, maraschino cherries, meat product casings, and Easter egg dyes are a few uses of synthetic colors. According to the NAS/NRC, total use of food colors in the United States is about 0.012 lb (5.4 grams) per person per year. Manufacturers have made thorough teratological (mutagenic) studies on all of the certified food colors. To date, tests have shown no adverse effects.

Eleven FD&C dyes are approved by the FDA: Blue No. 1, Blue No. 2, Green No.3, Yellow No. 5, Yellow No. 6, Red No. 2, Red No. 3, Red. No. 4, Red No. 40, Orange B, and Citrus Red No. 2. Eight may be used for foods generally, while three are restricted to specific uses: FD&C No. 4 only for coloring maraschino cherries in amounts not exceeding 150 ppm; Orange B only for coloring the casings or surfaces of frankfurters and sausages in amounts not to exceed 150 ppm; Red No. 2 only for coloring the skins of oranges not intended for processing in amounts not to exceed 2.0 ppm based on the whole fruit weight (Weissler 1975).

In 1972 the FDA banned Red No. 2 from other uses, though it had been the most widely used red coloring agent, because tests in animals could not resolve whether it caused cancer.

Natural Food Colors

Natural food colors have a long history of safe use for human consumption, although this fact is difficult to verify by modern toxicological procedures (Dinesen 1975). The toxicological evaluation of vegetable extracts is made complex by the many compounds present other than the one being investigated.

Recent studies indicate that betalaines, the pigment in red beets, may find commercial application in selected foods when large-scale purification methods have been developed (von Elbe 1975). The properties, food uses, and advantages of carotenoids as food colors was reported by (Bauernfeind 1975). The arithocyamins from wine or Concord grape juice lees (sediment) are abundant, hard to recover, and not chemically stable. This accounts for their limited use as food colorants (Francis 1975).

Color Lake Pigments

FD&C color lake pigments have helped to create new convenience foods by solving many color problems when soluble color dyes were not satisfactory. In instant dessert and gravy mixes, breakfast drinks, and cake and cookie mixes combinations of lakes and dyes are used; each performs a special function. Color lakes are also used in tableted candy produced by first dry-blending sugar, flavor, and color lake pigments and then compressing the mixture.

Imitation chocolate confections, fruit and mint-flavored hard fat confections, and soy protein products simulating meats and nuts are given color stability by the use of lake pigments (Signorino and Furmanski 1975).

Nonabsorbable Polymeric Food Colors

February 28, 1977, four years after initiating an intensive research effort and currently involving a staff of 80—the first member of a family of nonabsorbable, polymeric food dyes began long-term chromic feeding studies slated for inclusion in the battery of supporting documentation required to petition FDA for approval. Dynapol Corporation of Palo Alto, California, has successfully demonstrated that colors, primary dyes, and leashed polymers will pass through the body without being absorbed. They will not offer the potential toxic effects of absorbed ingredients in man after a long history of daily consumption. With this technique the additive-polymer would perform its function in the food and pass through the gastrointestinal tract with elimination via the feces (Furia 1977).

The poly dyes and lakes have a wide applicability in foods including beverages, fountain syrups, extracts, concentrates, gelatin desserts, puddings, toppings, icings, ice cream, sherbet, and yogurt.

Although oil insoluble, they are emulsifiable and can be used in sauces, dressings, and spreads. Their high thermal stability makes them ideal for high temperature processed foods. Color fidelity in hard candies and baked goods is also outstanding.

Success of poly dyes could lead to further applications of polymer additives, especially poly flavors.

THE 5′ NUCLEOTIDES: FLAVOR POTENTIATORS

Nucleotides originated in Japan and are derived from yeast. This process yields a natural 50:50 blend of disodium inosinate and disodium guanylate.

Inosinic acid was established in 1913 as a major taste component of dried bonito, a fish species. Japan used it as an important seasoning material. It exists naturally in many meat tissues. Guanylic acid was found later to be a major taste component in many strains of mushrooms. The taste-enhancing effect of disodium inosinate is about one-fourth that of disodium guanylate.

Use Level Standards

These flavor potentiators improve and mellow the taste of food to a degree unattainable with monosodium glutamate (MSG) alone (see Chapter 4). As they impart a strong meaty flavor, a cost saving may be realized in obtaining stronger meat flavor. Time is saved in preparing meaty-tasting foods without reducing taste. The quantity of nucleotide used in a food varies between 0.0005 and 0.03% on an as-served basis in soups, bouillons, sauces, gravies, dressings, certain vegetables, and most meat, poultry, and fish-based products. It may be used as a replacement for beef extract and to upgrade the quality of hydrolyzed proteins.

Disodium inosinate and disodium guanylate are approved by the FDA and the Meat and Poultry Inspection Divisions of the USDA in certain products under their inspection control.

Nucleotides used with MSG improve its effectiveness and may allow a reduction in MSG level. Usually a nucleotide mixture of 50:50 inosinate–guanylate is added to MSG in a proportion of 5 parts nucleotide to 95 parts MSG. As the nucleotide mixture costs 20 times as much as MSG, it must be used judicially and only where it proves effective. Its use in the kitchen, as with MSG, is most efficacious when incorporated into a food base.

Stability

Nucleotides are stable under nearly all food processing conditions and do not decompose under normal storage conditions, but they can be decomposed by phosphatase enzymes.

Recovery of nucleotide after heating at pH 6 for 40 min at 115°C is 81%; after heating at pH 4.5 for 40 min at 115°C, 75%; and after heating at pH 3.0 for 40 min at 115°C, 71%.

Mixed with dry flour the nucleotide recovery in a tight container at 40°C and 60% relative humidity (RH) for 11 weeks, 81%; at 40°C and 80% RH for 11 weeks, 29%.

In wet dough nucleotide decomposes completely at 30–60°C within 40 min.

Beef Extract Replacement

Formula for replacement of 1 lb beef extract:

Nucleotide	0.3 oz
Yeast extract	0.5 lb
Glucose	0.48 lb
Caramel	0.3 oz
	1.58 lb

This replaces half of the beef extract used in a formula.

Specifications

Nucleotides are odorless, white or nearly white powders that have a characteristic taste. Solubility is 20 g/100 ml in water and acetic acid and 0.2 g/100 ml in 50% ethanol at 20°C. The pH is 7.0–8.5. Arsenic and heavy metal contents are less than 2 ppm and 20 ppm respectively. The powder form contains 26% water. Purity is not less than 98% on a dry basis. The bulk density of the mixture is not less than 1.1 and not more than 1.5 ml/g.

Microorganisms should be as follows:

Total—not more than 20 colonies/g/2 plates
Thermophiles—not more than 2 colonies/g/2 plates
Coliform—none
Molds—not more than 2 colonies/g/2 plates

Presence and Use of Inosinic Acid in Food

Inosinic acid is naturally present in meats. In chicken meat the concentration reaches a maximum 8 hr after slaughter and then decreases by the following changes: ATP → ADP → AMP → Inosinic Acid → Inosine → Hypoxanthine.

In tests the meat taste was preferred at the peak concentration of inosinic acid 8 hr after slaughter versus 4 days and 6 days after slaughter, when the concentrations diminished by 50% after 4 days and to 0% after 6 days.

Experiments carried out on eight varieties of hot-pack (water-boiled) canned vegetables such as asparagus, green peas, mushrooms, sweet corn, green beans, tomato juice, and carrots indicated an improvement in taste when levels of 0.02 to 0.04% were used.

Table 8 shows the nucleotide level in various natural soup stocks having no added nucleotide.

TABLE 8. Nucleotide Level in Soup Stocks

Soup Stock	Concentration (g/100 ml)	Nucleotides (mg/100 ml) 5′ AMP	5′ IMP	5′ GMP
Beef	30	1.64	6.0	0
Chicken	40	2.26	5.84	0
Fish	50	2.72	8.84	0
Dried bonito	2.4	2.5	13.25	0
Shrimp	1.0	1.0	1.13	0
Prawn	8.0	8.0	1.0	0
Shell ligament	3.0	3.0	0	0
Cuttlefish	13.0	13.0	0	0
Cortinellus shutake	2.0	2.0	0	1.23
Indian bean	10.0	10.0	0	0

At the 0.05% level of nucleotide, fish paste taste is definitely improved.

Do not use in cream soups because of possible phosphatase in flour that would destroy the nucleotide.

Annual production of nucleotides now exceeds 3 million lb/yr. RNA (ribonucleic acid) from yeast is the raw material from which nucleotides are obtained by enzyme action on the yeast cells. The phosphoric acid group is located at the 5′ position (hence the name, 5′ nucleotides). The chief point of weakness is the phosphate linkage. This is easily split off by phosphatase enzymes, which are widely distributed in both plant and animal products. The addition of nucleotides improves flavor for the same proteinaceous foods that show improvement with MSG addition.

SPECIAL USES OF FOOD ADDITIVES

Irradiation: A Food Additive

Heading the list of unexpected food additives is the use of radiation for food preservation. For many years the U.S. Army Laboratories in Natick, Massachusetts, have been experimenting with radiation as a means of preserving army rations. As a result, the FDA has thus far approved three uses for ionizing radiation in foods: (1) preserving canned bacon, (2) destroying insects in wheat and wheat products, and (3) inhibiting the sprouting of white potatoes.

Under the 1958 Food Additives Amendment to the Federal Food Drug and Cosmetic Act of 1938, ionizing radiation used to preserve foods is regarded as a food additive. The rationale for this is that radiation can bring about harmful changes in food and may cause the food to be radioactive as a result of heavy doses of radiation. Damage is self-limiting, though, as an overdosed food becomes so unpalatable that it is inedible. Antioxidants have been added prior to irradiating foods to help preserve color and flavor.

Irradiated foods are expensive, and their flavor acceptance ratings are low.

Freeze Drying

Freeze drying is another expensive processing method that has had limited success; popular items include freeze-dried instant coffee, chives, and shrimp. However, this process has not fulfilled the great expectations predicted for it. In fact, without the use of additives to improve solubility or wetting, taste, flavor, aroma, texture, or other properties the process could not be used because quality levels would be unacceptable.

Fabricated Foods

Fabricated foods include bacon, coffee whitener, and imitation orange juices; these items use large numbers of food additives. Space foods have used some food additives to make them nutritious, flavorful, palatable, and attractive. Tang, an orange juice replacement, is a typical example of a space food. Others include dehydrated meats, vegetables, fruits, cereals, and desserts packaged in cans, flexible pouches, and plastic dispensing tubes; thermally processed canned, semi-solid foods in aluminum dispensing tubes; bite-sized foods enrobed with edible coatings, and tablets in dispensing containers. (Werntz 1962).

WHAT NEW ADDITIVES ARE NEEDED?

New additives may be developed and used by the food industry. However, we have enjoyed a remarkably safe, nutritious and economical food supply at economical prices in the United States for many years. With increased cooperation between producers, processors, shippers, distributors, consumers, government agencies, and universities our food chain can be strengthened and improved as needed to provide an adequate supply of high quality standard foods in the future.

Besides the further development of the nonabsorbable polymeric food colors already discussed, new additives that are needed include:

Nonnutritive sweeteners that taste more like sugar.

Flavor enhancers that improve flavor in high-carbohydrate foods as MSG in does in high-protein foods.

More effective antioxidants soluble in both water and oil.

Better freeze-dried food improvers.

Better antistaling compounds for bread.

Flavorings that give bread a homemade flavor.

Flavorings that match rich roast beef flavor.

Flavorings that give low fat foods the taste of fresh butter.

Additives that extend the shelf-life of draft beers.

Wine aging accelerators for red wines.

Wine deterioration retardants for white and rose wines.

BIBLIOGRAPHY

ANON. 1959. Charcoal flavored steaks without charcoal—a menace to consumer's health. Consumers Bull. *42*, 33 (5/6/59).

ANON. 1963. Defective trees and sawdust used to make charcoal briquettes. Science News Letter *84*, 72.

ANON. 1977. Food Safety Council. Food Technol. *31*(1), 24.

BAUERNFEIND, J.C. 1975. Carotenoids as food colors. Food Technol. *29*(5), 48.

CLAUSI, A.S. 1979. Revising the U.S. food safety policy: An industry viewpoint. Food Technol. *33*(11), 65.

COON, J.M. 1973. Toxicology of Natural Chemicals, Second Edition. Food Protection Comm., NAS–NRC, Washington, D.C.

DAVIS, A. 1972. Let's Have Healthy Children. Harcourt, Brace, Jovanovich, New York.

DINESEN, N. 1975. Toxicology and regulation of natural colors. Food Technol. *29*(5), 40; *31*(5), 34.

FEINGOLD, B.F. 1975. Why Your Child Is Hyperactive. Random House, New York.

FENAROLI, G. 1975. Fenaroli's Handbook of Flavor Ingredients, Second Edition. CRC Press, Cleveland, Ohio.

Food Protection Committee. 1965. Chemicals Used in Food Processing. Publ. 1195. NAS–NRC, Washington, D.C.

FRANCIS, F.J. 1975. Anthocyamins as food colors. Food Technol. *29*(5), 52.

FURIA, T.E. 1977. Nonabsorbable polymeric food colors. Food Technol. *31*(5), 34.

GEMMILL, A.V. 1969. Imitation dairy products. McGraw-Hill Yearbook of Science and Technology. McGraw-Hill Book Co., New York.

GENERAL FOODS. 1976. Today's Food and Additives. General Foods Corp., White Plains, New York.

GONZALES, N. 1977. What's eating you? Family Health/Today's Health, 22 November, p. 22.

GRAHAM, D.M. 1976. Food additives and hyperactivity. Cereal Foods World. *2*(6), 248.

HALL, R.L. and OSER, B.L. 1965. III. GRAS substances. Food Technol. *19*, 2,151.

JACOBS, M.B. (Editor). 1951. The Chemistry and Technology of Food and Food Products (3 vols., Second Edition) Interscience Publishers, Inc., New York.

JACOBSON, M.F. 1979, Diet and cancer. Science *207*(4428), 258.

LAWLER, F.K. 1973. Synthetic vegetable flavors. McGraw-Hill Yearbook of Science and Technology. McGraw-Hill Book Co., New York.

LEHMAN, P. 1979. More than you ever thought you would know about food additives. FDA Consumer, HEW Pub. No. (FDA) 79–2115, Washington, D.C.

LIJINSKY, W. and SHUBIK, P. 1964. Benzo[a]pyrene in charcoal-broiled steak. Science *145*, 53, 5J.

McGraw-Hill Encyclopedia of Science and Technology. 1960. Functional characteristics of food additives, Vol. 5, pp. 316–319. McGraw-Hill Book Co., Inc., New York.

MILLER, S.A. 1979. Letter to M. Jacobson. Center for Science in the Public Interest. May 23.

NAS. 1973. Toxicants Occurring Naturally in Foods, Second Edition. NAS, Washington, D.C.

NAS. 1982. Committee on Nitrite and Alternative Curing Agents in Food. News Report *32*(7).

OSER, B.L. and Ford, R.A. 1977. Recent progress in the consideration of flavoring ingredients under the food additives amendment. Food Technol. *31*(1), 65.

OSER, B.L. and FORD, R.A. 1978. 'Idem.' Food Technol. *32*(2), 60.

POMERANTZ, F. 1980. Food additives: An expanding market in the 80's. Food Prod. Dev. *14*, 12, 36–40.

ROSE, A. and ROSE, E. 1961. The Condensed Chemical Dictionary. Reinhold Publishing Company, New York.

SANDERS, H.J. 1966. Food additives. Chem. Eng. News *44*(42), 100.

SCHRAYER, D.W. 1978. Consumer response to nutrition labeling. Food Technol. *32*, 12, 47.

SIGNORINO, C.A. and FURMANSKI, E.R. 1975. Dyes cause color problems? Try certified lakes. Food Eng. *47*, 76.

STEPHENSON, M. 1978. The confusing world of health foods. Consumer HEW Pub. No. (FDA) 79–2108.

TRAGER, J. 1970. Foodbook. Grossman Publishers, New York.

TRAGER, J. 1972. Bellybook. Grossman Publishers, New York.

VON ELBE, J.H. 1975. Stability of betalaines as food colors. Food Technol. *29*(5), 42.

WALTON, P. 1976. Food Additives—Who Needs them? Manufacturing Chemists Ass'n. Washington, D.C.

WEISSLER, A. 1975. FDA regulation of food colors. Food Technol. *29*, 5, 38.

WERNTZ, O.G. 1962. Feeding man on the moon. Activities Report of the Research and Development Associates, Vol. 14, p. 221. Food and Container Institute, Inc. (U.S. Army QMC). Champaign, Illinois.

ZIEMBA, J.V. 1969. Synthetic Flavors. McGraw-Hill Yearbook of Science and Technology. McGraw-Hill Book Co., New York.

4 A Primer on Monosodium Glutamate

Monosodium glutamate and the 5′ nucleotides (see Chapter 3) are flavor potentiators for foods that contain proteins, mainly meat, fish, poultry, and vegetables. Their efficacy does not extend to acidic or sweet foods. They have no effect on carbohydrates. However, maltol is a flavor potentiator that accentuates flavors in fruits, jams, gelatin desserts, soft drinks, fruit flavors, and foods that have a high sugar content.

Monosodium glutamate is the sodium salt of glutamic acid. It is a fine white crystal—pure, stable, easy to dissolve in water, similar to salt or sugar in appearance.

Glutamate is classified as a nonessential amino acid in the human diet because the human body produces it. It is beneficial because these non-essential amino acids provide important sources of nitrogen and conserve essential amino acids that the body cannot produce but must obtain from ingested food. That is one reason it is meaningful that glutamic acid be in foods.

HISTORY AND SOURCES

Glutamate has been used to enhance the flavor of foods ever since Oriental cooks discovered over 2000 years ago that some foods prepared with a soup stock made from a certain seaweed tasted better. They were not aware that the seaweed, *Laminaria japonica*, contained generous amounts of naturally occurring glutamic acid and that it was this substance that enhanced the flavor of their basic diet.

The link between seaweed, monosodium glutamate, and flavor was discovered in 1908. In that year Professor Kikunae Ikeda of the University of Tokyo isolated monosodium glutamate while experimenting with the dried seaweed in an attempt to unlock the flavor-enhancing secret. He believed that what the Japanese called *umami*, or tastiness, existed in addition to the basic tastes—sweet, sour, salty, and bitter—and could be crystallized from foods.

Dr. Ikeda became so impressed with the effect of MSG on food flavor that the production of monosodium glutamate was immediately undertaken on a commercial basis in Japan. Production in the United States began in the 1940s. Today in the United States, MSG is produced from natural sources by fermentation of sugar beet molasses.

PROTEIN FLAVOR ACCENTUATION

Monosodium glutamate (MSG) accentuates flavor in proteinaceous foods. Toby Bishop of International Minerals and Chemicals Co. named it Accent. Evidently it acts by sensitizing the taste buds to protein-type flavors. When the Campbell Soup Company tested MSG in the late 1920s, they found that chicken soup flavor could be amplified by it several-fold using less meat. MSG brings out the flavor that is present. When the flavor is good it becomes very good, but when it is below average it tastes bad. For example, boar meat flavor in sausage is magnified perhaps a hundredfold. This means that MSG is an indicator of flavor in foods.

MSG is an agent that makes a vegetable dish tolerable to a meat eater. Chinese chefs call it chicken powder. Other tasters say it tastes beefy. Orientals discovered it first; they use MSG to enliven their predominantly vegetable diet, and table-settings will sometimes have an MSG container to accompany the salt and pepper.

In the United States, food manufacturers use MSG to restore flavor lost in harvesting, processing, storage, and transportation. Its use improves the flavor of consumer items.

Foodservice kitchens use MSG in a different form. Instead of working with the pure product, which is expensive and difficult to control with regard to over-use, cooks rely on high quality food bases from which their stocks and seasonings are derived to get the MSG they need. In this way the MSG is provided in an accurate and standardized form to insure uniformity, to reduce potential waste, and to avoid meticulous measuring or weighing procedures that take time. With a high quality food base used according to directions, the MSG concentration will be in proper ratio to other ingredients.

No one knows accurately how many people are allergic to MSG. Probably not more than one in ten thousand, although estimates as high as one or two per thousand have appeared in the literature. Recent experiments with MSG-sensitive subjects demonstrated that when a piece of bread, a glass of milk, or other carbohydrate-rich food is eaten several minutes prior to the customary won ton soup, the syndrome disappears (Glutamate Association 1978).

Cristol (1981) states that "since Chinese Restaurant Syndrome is not a phenomenon associated generally with processed food the FDA should, on the basis of extensive scientific evidence, classify MSG as a category 1 GRAS substance."

PRODUCTION OF MSG[1]

Glutamate is a naturally occurring substance, a component of virtually all protein in our food (Table 1). Glutamate is also produced in the organs and tissues of our bodies.

TABLE 1. Percentage of Protein in Selected Products That Is Glutamate

Product	Glutamate as percentage of protein
Wheat	50
Mother's milk	16
Casein	23
Camembert cheese	27
Eggs	13
Chicken	21
Beef	19
Salmon	17
Peas	24
Corn	10
Tomatoes	1

Glutamate as the sodium salt, monosodium glutamate, is commonly referred to as MSG. Monosodium glutamate is one of the substances categorized as GRAS by the FDA. Conditions for its safe use have been established by the FDA, USDA, and other countries as well as the Food and Agriculture Organization/World Health Organization (FAO/WHO).

[1]The information that follows in this chapter is courtesy of the Glutamate Association, United States, 1978.

Consumption of MSG added to food for flavor enhancement purposes results in only a slight increase over the amount of glutamate normally ingested in a typical day. Examination of blood levels for glutamate, a commonly used research technique, clearly demonstrates that the use of MSG as a flavor enhancer is no different from eating a protein meal.

By using MSG to enhance flavor, the consumer or food manufacturer is making use of a component that occurs naturally in food and the human body. Frequently the manufacturer is returning a substance to the food that nature placed there originally. This helps to restore the natural flavor. But more importantly, by improving palatability and increasing the pleasure of eating good food, MSG indirectly aids nutrition.

GLUTAMIC—THE MOST ABUNDANT AMINO ACID

Food is usually considered to be composed of three major parts: fat, carbohydrate, and protein. Glutamate is naturally present in virtually all foods including meat, fish, poultry, milk, milk products, and many vegetables, in the form of protein and free amino acid. Each time these foods are eaten some glutamate is consumed. Additionally the human body as part of its normal function produces glutamate continually in many of its tissues and organs. Of all the naturally occurring amino acids glutamate, by a wide margin, is the most abundant.

MSG added to food as a flavor enhancer accounts for only a small fraction of the total amount of glutamate ingested as a natural part of food or made in the body. For example, the average human body contains about 2000 grams (4.4 lb) of naturally occurring glutamate. About 20 additional grams (⅔ oz) of naturally occurring glutamate are ingested per day by the average person as part of normal food intake. Most of this occurs as a component of protein. Depending on the food, 1–2 g (1/15 oz) may be present as the free amino acid, glutamate. Another gram (1/30 oz) per day might be consumed by eating commercially prepared food to which glutamate has been added. If the person adds glutamate to food in the kitchen or at the table an additional 1–2 g (1/15 oz) a day might be consumed. Glutamate ingested in the form of added MSG represents a very small fraction (in the order of 1/1000th) of the total glutamate naturally present in the body, even though actual amounts may vary depending on food choices, use levels of MSG, and eating habits.

HOW IT WORKS

MSG enhances numerous natural flavor components of foods. The use of MSG will make good foods taste better. As the primary purpose of the addition of MSG is to enhance flavor of food, it has real value because even the most nutritious food will not be eaten unless it tastes good. Thus flavor enhancement is important to good nutrition.

MSG works well with foods already containing high levels of naturally occurring glutamate such as meats, poultry, seafood, and some vegetables. Some vegetables, for example, lose part of their naturally occurring glutamate within 24 hours after harvesting. Even when refrigerated, they may continue to lose glutamate, especially after initial cooking. MSG gives food a glutamate boost and restores its natural flavor level. Mushrooms and tomatoes, often used to flavor other foods, contain much free glutamate, again suggesting a link between glutamate and tastiness.

USE LEVELS

In the United States, MSG is usually added by the food processor at levels well within the normal range of free glutamate naturally found in foods; the percentages added generally range from 0.1 to 0.8, based on the weight of the food as it would be consumed. This compares to levels of 0.001–2.0% of naturally occurring free glutamate in foods.

In the home MSG may be used to meet personal tastes by using the general guideline of ½ teaspoon per pound of food (for four to six servings).

SAFETY

In determining the safety of a food or a food ingredient, the following three factors must be considered:

The reasonably anticipated patterns of consumption of the food or food ingredient and of any substance formed in or on food because of its use

The cumulative effect of the food or food ingredient in question and any chemically or pharmacologically related substances in the diet of man or animals

Safety factors appropriate for the utilization of animal experimentation data

Under these criteria, the extensive research by a large number of scientists throughout the world clearly supports the statement that "monosodium glutamate is safe for humans in terms of its conventional levels of use in foods." Scientific evaluations of more than 1000 studies occurring over 50 years confirm this conclusion.

During the past decade extensive worldwide laboratory research has been completed on the effects of MSG on the central nervous system. A wide variety of animals as well as human subjects have been studied at the University of Iowa; the University of Illinois; the Huntingdon Research Centre in Huntingdon, England; the Mario Negri Research Institute in Milan, and other institutions.

Animal Feeding Experiments with MSG

Studies in sensitive animal species, usually following the injection or forced feeding of high doses and high concentrations of a test MSG solution, indicate that glutamate, among other food components, can induce a variety of possible health problems. However, the levels required to induce toxicity represent amounts and dietary patterns not experienced by humans. When glutamate is administered to a test animal species by the same rates, routes, and concentrations as used by humans, no toxic effects are seen even in the most sensitive animal species.

In studies done on mice, high doses of MSG were shown to produce brain damage but only if the compound was force-fed or injected. After analysis of blood levels and the metabolism of MSG in the mouse, it was reconfirmed that mice react to MSG in a manner that is markedly different from humans. Treatment of mice with MSG by force-feeding or injection creates sufficiently high blood levels apparently to force enough MSG into the brain to induce toxicity. Humans never show these high blood levels after ingestion of MSG, and they also metabolize MSG differently from mice. Therefore toxicity in the mouse must be distinguished from effects in the human.

There are no reports in the literature of mice developing brain lesions as a result of the dietary feeding of MSG. This is true even though it is well recognized that the mouse is one of the most susceptible animals to the induction of brain lesions from a variety of substances. Even in this sensitive species, dietary feeding of MSG in amounts and concentrations greatly in excess of its use by man (over 12,000 times its maximum anticipated level of use) was without toxic manifestations in the brain.

In experiments involving other toxic manifestations such as retinal and hypothalamic damage in fetal, newborn, and young rodents, subcutaneous injections or gavage (oral force-feeding) was required.

Studies in monkeys, a species closer to humans, were conducted at the University of Illinois and the Huntingdon Research Centre to determine whether brain damage occurs in this species. Scientists at both laboratories found that the monkey was similar to humans in terms of both blood levels and metabolism of MSG. In studies involving about 200 monkeys there was evidence that brain damage had not occurred. Also extensive clinical studies in primates, including humans, revealed no evidence of the abnormalities that had been observed in rodents and that would have been anticipated in primates had brain damage occurred.

The technical capabilities of the investigators were demonstrated by their ability to induce and detect central nervous system damage in the mouse following high-level dosing with MSG. Therefore, when brain lesions did not occur in nonhuman primates orally fed high doses of MSG, the evidence strongly supports the finding that no brain lesions occurred rather than the contention that the investigators missed finding them or did not have the ability to induce them.

Effect of MSG Addition to Food

It is important to note that glutamic acid added to food in the form of MSG causes a blood level response in humans essentially the same as the response when glutamic acid is ingested by eating food containing protein. This means that, based on blood level studies—a commonly used technique in research—use of MSG for flavor enhancement purposes has no different effect on the level of glutamic acid in the blood than eating protein.

There is ample evidence that MSG does not pass the placental barrier from mother to unborn child. Thus MSG ingested by the mother as a flavor enhancer does not enter the fetus.

Studies have also determined that while a nursing human baby will ingest 150 to 200 mg (0.005 to 0.007 oz) of free glutamate daily, which is present naturally in mother's milk, there will be no significant increase in the glutamate level of the milk after the ingestion of glutamate whether it is naturally occurring in the food of the mother or added to the food as a flavor enhancer. This has been found to be true even after nursing mothers have been fed large quantities of MSG.

Food Sensitivities

Glutamate in heavy dosage taken on an empty stomach may cause the so-called Chinese Restaurant Syndrome (CRS)—headache, dizziness, facial pressure, burning sensations on the back and neck, and so on. As glutamate is a protein substance, an allergenic response might be expected, because there is no known protein substance to which someone is not allergic.

One report claimed that 25% of those consuming Chinese foods believed they had experienced Chinese Restaurant Syndrome, presumably attributed to its MSG content. A later study by a research group found that more than 30% of those asked whether they were susceptible to CRS answered yes when the syndrome was mentioned in the questionnaire. However this figure dropped markedly to only a few percentage points when the questionnaire was designed to minimize the use of such subjective key terms as "MSG" or "CRS." Various investigators used human volunteers from a general, unselected population and double-blind techniques (wherein neither the investigator nor the volunteers knew whether the test or the control had been administered). There were no significant differences in the incidence of symptoms between groups ingesting large doses of MSG and control groups.

Special Diets

Many people today are on special diets for various reasons. Some need to be on low sodium diets to cut down on water retention; others opt to limit salt intake because of temporary water retention. Table salt (sodium chloride), is 39% sodium. Can people who want to limit their use of sodium use MSG in their food? Often the answer is yes.

Although all dietary sources of sodium—table salt, the natural sodium content of food, and MSG—must be considered by those on very special low- or no-sodium diets, by way of comparison it should be noted the MSG contains 12% sodium, which is about ⅓ the concentration in table salt. When MSG is used at the table or in cooking according to package directions, approximately 0.5 g of sodium a day would be ingested in a usual menu of meat, vegetables, and salads. This amount is exactly what typical sodium-restricted diets allow. Table 2 presents the contribution of sodium to the diet by the use of MSG.

Persons on totally restricted sodium diets that required that no sodium be added in cooking or at the table can improve the flavor of their food by using potassium and ammonium glutamates, which are available in a variety of salt substitutes.

IDENTIFYING MSG

A question frequently asked about MSG is how the consumer will know when it is added to food. There are now existing or proposed regulations that

TABLE 2. Contribution of Sodium to the Diet by Use of MSG

Meal	Food	Typical portion	MSG use level	g of MSG	Sodium from MSG (g)
Breakfast	Sausage	1 oz	0.4%	0.113	0.014
Lunch	Ground steak	4 oz	½ tsp/lb	0.625	0.077
	Green beans	1 cup	½ tsp/4 servings	0.625	0.077
Dinner	Soup	8 oz	0.5%	1.134	0.139
	Chicken	6 oz	½ tsp/lb	0.938	0.115
	Corn	1 cup	½ tsp/4 servings	0.625	0.077
Total				4.060	0.499

Source: Glutamate Association 1978.

would require that all food sold in the United States to which MSG has been added must state this fact on the label. It should be kept in mind, however, that glutamate is a natural component of many foods that, as such, cannot be eliminated from the diet.

Regulation

Monosodium glutamate and its use in food is subject to a variety of standards and regulations on a worldwide bases. The Joint Expert Committee on Food Additives of the FAO/WHO of the United Nations has periodically reviewed and endorsed the conditions of the safe use of MSG. This committee has established an acceptable daily intake (ADI) and has set standards of purity for MSG entering into international commerce. The ADI for a human being, expressed on a body weight basis, is the amount of food additive that can be taken daily in the diet, over a lifetime, without hazard to health.

The acceptable daily intake of MSG for a human is 153 mg/kg of body weight, including the intake of free glutamate from all dietary sources. This translates to almost 10 g (⅓ oz or approximately 2 teaspoons) of MSG per day for a 65 kg (140 lb) person.

Various national scientific organizations have also established standards of purity for glutamates. For example, monographs of identify and purity are listed in the U.S. Food Chemicals Codex and the Japanese Standard of Food Additives.

MSG Is GRAS Listed

In the United States, MSG has been listed on the GRAS list of food substances. In addition, its use has been provided for in a number of regulations for standardized foods promulgated by the FDA and the USDA.

> MSG is specifically authorized in the Standards of Identity of many foods under Title 21 of the United States Code of Federal Regulations (CFR), but its presence must still be disclosed on the label among such foods as mayonnaise, french dressing, canned tuna and breaded shrimp.
>
> Recently, the Select Committee on GRAS Substances (generally regarded as safe), commissioned by the U.S. Food and Drug Administration, issued a supplement to their report on glutamates. Monosodium glutamate was reclassified to a more liberal status (from category 30 to 2). The opinion of the Sales Committee reads, there is no evidence in the available information on . . . [all common forms of glutamate] . . . that demonstrates or suggests reasonable grounds to suspect a hazard to the public when they are used at levels that are now current and in the manner now practiced (IFT Expert Panel on Food Safety and Nutrition 1980).

The report goes on to state that some persons may react to relatively small doses of MSG because of metabolic idiosyncracies and that research is underway on this phase of glutamate evaluation.

SUMMARY

It is clear from reviewing the literature available that MSG is one of the most thoroughly studied materials in the food supply. The following is fact:

Consuming MSG as a food flavor enhancer is no different from eating food that naturally contains free glutamate.

Based on blood level studies, use of MSG for flavor enhancement purposes has no different effect on the body from that of eating protein.

Extensive research by a large number of scientists throughout the world clearly supports the statement that monosodium glutamate is safe for humans in terms of its conventional levels of use in foods.

Regulatory bodies throughout the world have reviewed the safety and efficacy of MSG to assure that it is used under conditions that are both safe and effective.

Glutamate, in one form or another, has been used in the diet of human beings for at least 2000 years.

Glutamic acid is the most common of all amino acids. Almost all protein foods contain this amino acid as a component.

Glutamate is produced in many organs and tissues of the body and plays an important role in many metabolic reactions.

MSG is effective in enhancing the flavor of a wide variety of foods.

Addition of MSG to food for flavor enhancement purposes results in only a slight increase in the amount of glutamate normally ingested in a typical diet.

Studies have also determined that, while a nursing human baby will ingest 150 to 200 mg of glutamic acid daily in its mother's milk, there will be no increase in the glutamate level of the milk after the ingestion of reasonable amounts of MSG by the mother.

Contemporary research indicates that food science will continue to seek nutritious, economical foods. It is also clear that palatability will continue to be the critical factor in their acceptance by the public.

Flavor enhancement is important to good nutrition. The most nutritious food in the world is of no value unless it is eaten. If food does not taste good, the chance that it will be consumed is reduced. Thus, the role of MSG is to make good food taste better and therefore more acceptable.

REFERENCES

ANON. 1978. MSG-update—A fact-finding guide to monosodium glutamate. The Glutamate Association, United States, Atlanta, Georgia.

COMMITTEE ON SPECIFICATIONS. 1972. Food Chemicals Codex. 2nd Edition. Committee on Food Protection, NRC–NAS, Washington, D.C.

CRISTOL, RICHARD E. 1981. The Glutamate Association—Member Update—September 18, 1981. The Glutamate Association, United States, Atlanta, Georgia.

IFT EXPERT PANEL ON FOOD SAFETY AND NUTRITION. 1980. Monosodium glutamate. Food Technol. *34* (10), 49–53.

5 Food Flavor Standards

THE IMPORTANCE OF FLAVOR

Food may be nutritious and possess maximum eye appeal, but when flavor is lacking the food is neither acceptable nor marketable. Nature provides many interesting examples. Apples having a beautiful, lustrous red color may be discarded after one bite if they are dry and pithy. It is a rare treat to taste a really good melon. Some meat can look tempting when it is purchased but, no matter how it is cooked it remains tough. Chicken breast meat or lobster meat with eye appeal may be tasteless, dry, and tough after preparation for the table.

Research and quality control have been helpful in combating either quirks of nature or a combination of handling, storage, and cooking variables. Yet, within limits, products still vary. Generally we must admit that the most nutritious products occur when the fruit, vegetable, meat, poultry, or fish has attained its ripest, tenderest, and most succulent stage. Accordingly, tenderometers are applied to representative samples of fruits and vegetables prior to harvest in order to check their maturity. Meats and poultry are tested with shear presses. Many other physical and chemical methods are employed in upgrading and safeguarding the yield, nutrition, and flavor of our food.

Ecologically speaking, the simple relationship between food and humans is better appreciated than the interrelationship of food nutrition, food flavor, and humans. Perhaps one of the most memorable instances of this neglect of flavor occurred during World War II with respect to the Army canned C-rations (meat and vegetable stew, meat and vegetable hash, meat and beans, and so on). These rations were models of nutritional balance. But they were found unpalatable by the soldiers because of a combination of factors, including effects of canning and storage as well as the lack of added flavoring or flavor enhancers.

Proof of this flavor inadequacy was obtained by a fortuitous circumstance. Hungry soldiers would not eat their rations, indeed, Caul reported that soldiers stationed in the Arctic region preferred hunger to unpleasant-tasting though nutritive foods. Then, the soldiers by experimentation learned that the bouillon powder contained in their K-rations could be used to flavor the C-rations and thus improve palatability (Caul 1958).

Another valuable lesson was learned at a later date in connection with the Marshall Plan program of feeding Europe after the war. Grain, vegetable oil, and milk powder combinations were formulated with and without added monosodium glutamate, hydrolyzed plant proteins, and spices for flavoring. Since the flavor additives increased cost about 5%, the procurement officers decided that flavoring was unnecessary. They maintained that the primary object was to provide calories and protein, not flavor. When General Lucius D. Clay attempted to feed these unseasoned products to the hungry masses of Europe, they were rejected. Eventually General Clay ordered millions of pounds of this unpalatable food dumped into the ocean.

Daily thousands of kitchens in the United States prepare food items that are either partly or entirely rejected at the table. Garbage cans and disposals are frequently filled with discarded or uneaten protein foods. This wanton waste could be eliminated by intelligent leadership in the foodservice industries, for example, by giving proper recognition to the importance of flavor in food preparation. Chef-less food preparation in a quantity kitchen for a captive pensioner audience should be as acceptable as a chef prepared-to-order food for a millionaire.

The American food scientist, I. J. Hutchings, stated that "Food must be made not only nutritious but more appealing to the consumer. Food scientists have been negligent in the area of developing or creating food flavors." In a similar vein, the nutritionist and late president of Wisconsin University, C. A. Elvehjem, predicted:

> Just as individual nutrients such as vitamins were identified, isolated, synthesized, and then used for enriching foods, so a similar attack will be made on flavors and aromas present in foods and food products. By 1980 foods combined to meet specific nutritional requirements may be enriched with these factors just as we now enrich with vitamins (Smith and Minor 1974).

WHAT IS FLAVOR?

Flavor may be described as consisting of three fundamental parts: (1) taste or the nonvolatile constituents including sweetness, saltiness, sourness, bitterness, and monosodium or nucleotide enhancing effects (which emphasize taste bud sensitizing and mouth feel in protein foods); (2) odor consisting of the volatile constituents of fruits and spices and of cooked meat, poultry, fish, vegetables, and eggs; and (3) kinesthetic factors such as texture and other physical qualities that may affect the senses of sight, touch, or hearing.

Numerous definitions of flavor could be given, but the one chosen here is that of Kazeniac (1961), who used four designations as proposed by Sjöstrom and Cairncross (1950). The first was taste, consisting of saltiness, sweetness, sourness and bitterness, to which Moncrieff (1965) has added metallic. The second was aroma, which described odor sensations. The third was body, which referred to the texture or sensation caused by chewing but has nothing to do with taste or aroma. The fourth was mouth satisfaction, which implied salivary stimulation, blending, and pleasantness. Thus defined, flavor is an interaction of these four basic sensations.

Taste and smell are our chemical senses. By realizing that all matter is electrical in nature and that temperature affects reaction rates, we may conclude that our chemical senses are affected by both electrochemical and thermochemical phenomena. Salivary enzymes (protein catalysts) often cause chemical changes to occur within the food even while it is being chewed. Texture must also be considered in any overall concept of taste. Tactile sensations (which affect the sense of touch) and responses resulting from seeing or hearing the food (as in chewing water chestnuts or popcorn) are useful in evaluating its physical characteristics. Hence, both kinds of taste effects, the chemical and the kinesthetic or physical, are important.

Since the two chief parts of flavor are taste and odor, separate discussions on each follow.

TASTE

Taste is a relatively simple physical sensation that originates in the taste buds. The taste buds are stimulated by the chemical make-up of food, its temperature, its pH (relative acidity), and the interplay of other senses: smell, touch (biting, chewing, tongue feel, swallowing), visual appearence, and so on. Taste and odor work together, reaching the taste buds with or without other sensory side effects such as sight and hearing. The brain combines these sensory reactions into the complex response called flavor.

Taste Physiology

Taste is one of our simpler senses. There are only five principal dimensions in taste as compared to countless varieties of odors. Yet the innervation of taste is more complex than that of smell (Moncrieff 1944).

Taste receptors, called taste buds, are located in the mouth cavities of human beings. Our taste buds are embedded in the covering of papillae, which are minute projections located mostly on the tongue but also found on the inside surface of the cheek and on the epiglottis. There are about 245 taste buds in each papilla and approximately 9000 taste buds in all (Beidler 1958).

Taste buds consist of sensory cells in the mouth surface tissue or epithelium (see Fig. 1). Taste occurs when a chemical compound in solution or dissolved in the saliva seeps into the taste bud and stimulates the nerve ending that transmits an electrical impulse to the brain. Tasting does not always require ingestion of the compound directly into the mouth. For instance, when an antibiotic is injected into an arm or thigh, the patient may experience a bitter taste almost instantly as the taste buds absorb it from the blood (Beidler 1958).

The tongue, the principal instrument of taste, can differentiate between two separate stimuli occurring simultaneously only 0.05 in. apart (Langley and Cheraskin 1951). Tasting is a rapid reaction. Experimental results show that the papillae of the rat will respond to the taste of a sodium chloride solution within five one-hundredths of a second (Nejad 1961).

According to Kazeniac, sweetness is detected mainly at the tip of the tongue, saltiness at the frontal edges, sourness at the sides, and bitterness at the back of the tongue (Kazeniac 1961). Taste perception zones shown by Crocker (see Fig. 2) deviate appreciably from those ascribed to the tongue by Kazeniac. However, as will be clarified later under the heading "Taste Theories," this appraisal of taste bud functions with respect to location may be out-of-date. Taste buds have been known to migrate with age. Sweet-sensitive buds located in the cheeks of infants and small children disappear as the children mature.

Dysautonomic patients (persons with malfunctioning autonomic nervous systems) are unable to perceive taste or discriminate between tastes (Smith *et al.* 1965). But in most people tasting ability is taken for granted, although it can be dulled or sharpened. Smokers and heavy coffee or liquor drinkers sustain a fatiguing effect on their taste buds. One distinguished epicurean club called Quando Manducamus (When Do We Eat?) has placed a taboo on smoking until after dining is completed and coffee has been served (Barthel 1966). A glass of sherry and a cup of consommé preceding the meal serve to attune the taste mechanism by stimulating the flow of gastric juices.

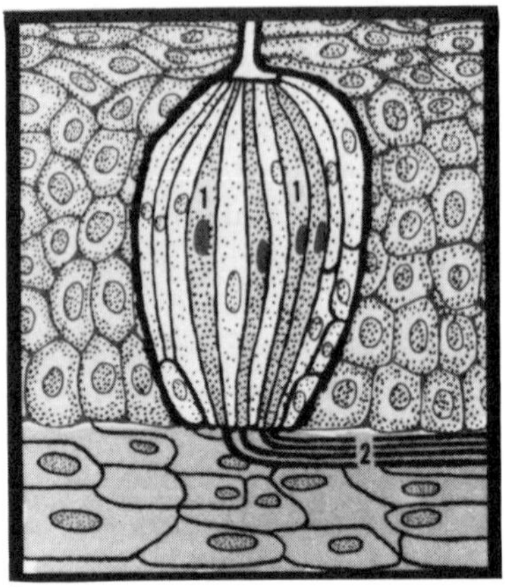

Fig. 1. Taste buds
From Better Homes and Gardens 1966.

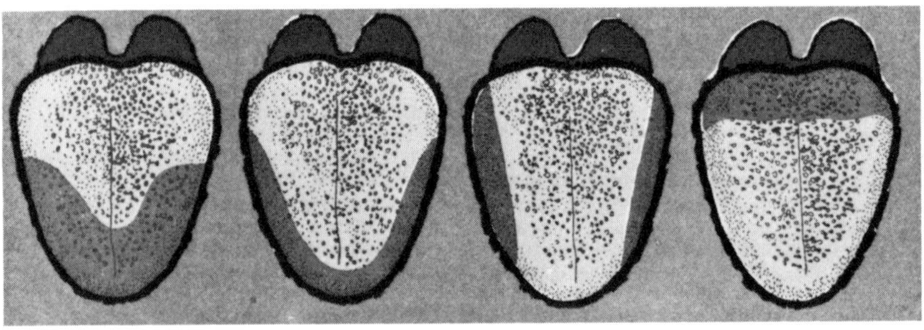

Tobacco chewers as distinguished from smokers are often proficient tasters. One might assume that constant mastication stimulates the salivary gland and cleanses the taste buds.

A series of classical experiments concerned with the salt, sour, sweet and bitter tastes were reported by Moncrieff (1950–1952). Later, this same worker showed that bitterness in chemical compounds increases in direct proportion to the molecular weight (Moncrieff 1955).

Taste Theories

Von Békésy (1964) proposed a duplexity theory of taste. First he studied the relationships between warm and cold stimuli and the four basic taste stimuli—sweet, salty, sour, and bitter. Then he separated the tongue sensations into two general groupings: (1) bitter, warm, and sweet and (2) sour, cold, and salty. He also concluded that sour and salty tastes merge together at the center of the tongue, whereas sweet and sour tastes do not.

The newest concept of taste bud action is based on studies of electron micrographs of taste buds. Two cell types exist, one light and the other dark.

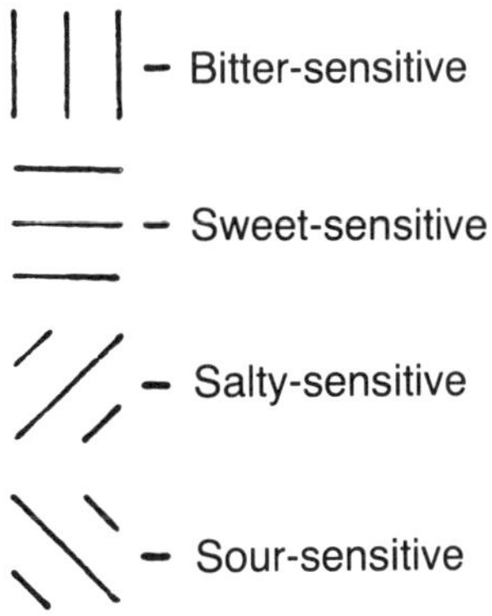

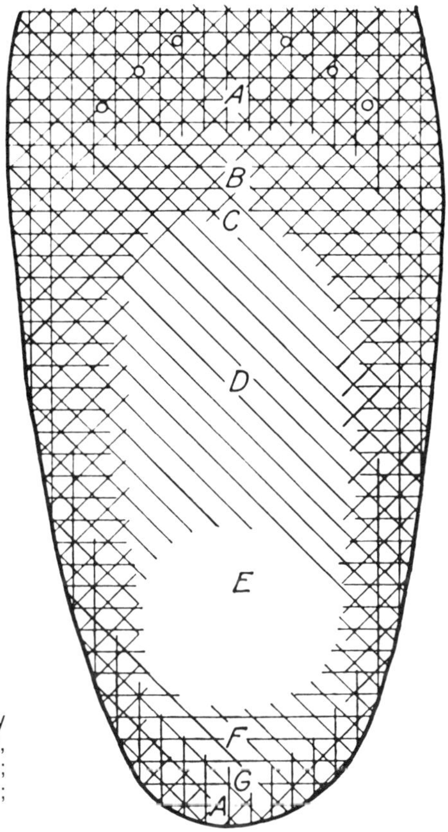

Fig. 2. Taste perception zones ascribed by Crocker (1945). A, all sensations; B, sweet, salty and sour; C, salty and sour; D, sour only; E, insensitive to all tastes; F, sweet and sour; G, bitter, sweet and sour.

The light-colored cells are compared to bricks in a building, and the darker cells are likened to the mortar as they serve to bind the lighter cells together. Dark cells absorb the chemical, osmium, but light cells do not. Both kinds of cells, together with a hairlike nerve cell that transmits taste responses to the brain, are present in taste buds. Taste buds vary in shape, and their position in the epithelium (surface tissue) may undergo change. Accordingly, experimental evidence indicates that the nature of the taste bud may be that of a migratory lymph cell (Farbman 1965).

Taste Psychology

Historically, taste classification is based on phenomenological evidence. The Swedish botanist Carolus Linnaeus (1707–1778) enumerated eleven tastes: sweet, sour, salty, fatty, bitter, aqueous, viscous, astringent, nauseous, sharp, and insipid. Wilhelm Wundt (1832–1920), founder of the first experimental psychology laboratory, reduced the number of tastes to six: sweet, sour, salty, bitter, alkaline, and metallic. Later, Wundt held to the basic four consisting of sweet, sour, salty, and bitter as proposed by Crocker (1945). General acceptance of this four-dimensional characterization of the taste phenomenon led Henning to develop the taste tetrahedron concept. Moncrieff (1965) holds that it is necessary to add metallic to the four primaries of Crocker.

A psychophysical scale that measures gustatory values of different foods has been devised by Beebe-Center and Waddell (1948). Since taste is synonymous with the term gustation, a unit of taste called the gust was devised. The gust is based on the taste of a 1% sugar solution. On the scale, undiluted lime, lemon, or pickle juice has a rating of over 100 gusts. Acceptable foods rarely exceed 50 gusts, and the average limit of tolerance is about 100 gusts. Therefore, we usually serve foodstuffs that occupy positions near the middle of the scale.

Off-tastes can profoundly influence likes or dislikes for food. Tomato juice or other fruit or vegetable juices from a can may have a fishy or metallic taste caused by the reaction between the acid in the juice and the metals in the container. Packing in glass or in drawn metal cans having acid-resistant enamelled surfaces corrects this problem. Orange juice served warm and coffee served cold have objectionable tastes. Foods that should be sweet but taste salty or vice versa are highly unacceptable. Too much monosodium glutamate (MSG) is not good either.

In foodservice firms a common fault is leaving onion soup or consommé on the steam table too long before tasting it to see if evaporation has caused too high a salt concentration. Adding the correct amount of water is a simple antidote, but often overlooked. Food should always be tasted prior to serving and checked at frequent intervals whenever it is held hot. A good cook, according to Escoffier (1941) uses the freshest and finest ingredients, exercises utmost care in meal preparation, and uses both his nose and his tongue to test the food.

Sometimes our sense of taste can warn us that the food we are eating may be harmful to health. For example, medical researchers find that burned fat volatiles deposited on charcoal-broiled steaks contain benzopyrene, a cancer-causing chemical found in cigarette smoke (Lijinsky and Shubik 1964). Charred meat may cause cancer to start in the intestinal tract; and spent fat from the potato chip industry, when added to chicken rations, causes cancer in the chickens. For meats other than pork, cooking time and temperature should be held to a minimum. A diner is warned of the presence of this harmful chemical by the charred or burned taste of fat in the food (Anon. 1959).

Taste blending is important. Salt enhances sweetness and masks sourness. Monsodium glutamate (MSG) reduces earthiness and/or bitterness in potatoes, onions, and bean sprouts. Nucleotides and monosodium glutamate act synergistically to reduce bitterness and disguise other bizarre notes in vegetable products such as onions. These flavor potentiators (Meyer 1960) can make a vegetable dish tolerable to a meat eater by improving the flavor profile (Caul 1957).

Often two similar products can be combined to form a single superior product. Tomato juice from the West Coast is added to tomato juice from the Midwest to reduce the acidity and improve the color of the Midwestern product. Likewise Niagara and Concord grape wines of the East and Midwest are blended with California wines because the fruits from California are sweeter and less acid than those from the eastern United States and yield wines of higher alcohol content.

Our food patterns and tastes are in a constant state of flux. For examples, at present, pickles are milder, ham is less salty, and wieners are seasoned with MSG, as are soups and meat foods. Within the past 25 years food scientists have learned to make these and many other changes in order to increase consumer acceptance.

Taste Control

Taste may be controlled, within the limits of natural variance, by taste-testing together with careful grading, weighing, processing, and handling of foods. Taste-testing may be done directly by the organoleptic methods of feeling, smelling, and tasting or indirectly by chemical and instrumental testing. Taste-testing in the manufacturing of foods requires stringent control of the seasoning profile and careful consideration of the kinesthetic and chemical factors in taste (Rietz and Wanderstock 1965). The influence of processing (chlorination, washing, heating-cooling, freezing-thawing) on sensory properties of food must likewise be controlled to insure taste acceptance.

Quality

Consumer preference, detection of difference, difference–preference, selection of the best sample or process, and determination of grade or quality level may be studied by taste panels (Kramer and Twigg 1962). The attributes of quality included under taste are texture, temperature, appearance, sweetness, bitterness, and metallic. Glutamate and nucleotide effects should also be considered whenever these seasonings are added to protein foods. Fiber, moisture, fat, protein, carbohydrate, and ash are determined by chemical procedures (AOAC 1960). Minerals such as sodium, potassium, arsenic, and lead are assayed by spectrographic, polarographic, and X-ray diffraction or chemical techniques.

Texture

Characteristics of texture as related to touch and taste are measured directly by sight and by mouth or finger feel. Texture can further be determined by instrument testing: firmness and juiciness are tested by compression, chewiness by shear-pressure, fibrousness by comminution (cutting fine), and chewiness by tensile strength. Grittiness is measured by comminution, sedimentation, and elution (separation of material by washing). Mealiness is measured by starch or gum analysis. Color measurements have also proved useful in the realm of kinesthetic factors. Temperature is tested directly by feel and indirectly by either a thermometer or a potentiometer.

Taste Chemicals

The chemical tastes may be easy or difficult to measure. Sugar, salt, pH (relative acidity or alkalinity of the food), monosodium glutamate, and the 5′ nucleotides usually occur in natural or prepared foods at concentrations that permit either chemical or biochemical and physiochemical measurements. The Glutamate Manufacturers Technical Committee has published methods for determining the monosodium glutamate content of foods, and Pabst Laboratories has perfected techniques for the 5′ nucleotides. Constituents of food that impart bitter notes are difficult to assay because of their complex chemical nature.

Taste Stimuli

According to Sharon (1965) taste stimuli may cause both direct and indirect reactions. When food is put into the mouth, we have a direct response to it. Salivary and gastric stimulation may also result from seeing food that we have learned to like. This indirect response to taste stimuli can measurably increase pancreatic secretion when the food is being digested in the intestine later on.

There are other responses to eating besides the stimulation of the taste buds and the stomach. When lumps of meat are chewed, the soft palate tissue, tooth membranes, muscles, and joints are stimulated. Thus more gastric juice is elicited by eating stew than by eating hash.

Continuing research is essential in the taste area of food science. Currently, however, the emphasis is being placed on food odor analysis. The problems involved in first analyzing and then synthesizing or biochemically producing food odors is a timely challenge that food scientists have accepted.

NEW TASTE KNOWLEDGE

Recent studies on taste reveal that many odor compounds are taste-active. Peripheral taste systems, as labeled in Fig. 2, are responsive to various chemicals. These include inorganic ions, amino acids, peptides, amines, thiamine, monosodium glutamate and nucleotides (Boudreau 1980). Inosinic acid, glutathione, arginine, and other free amino acids including glycine, adenosine and cytosine monophosphates, sodium, chloride, and ammonium ions can be combined in model systems to obtain seafood, fish, and meat tastes.

Umami: A Brothy Taste

Flavor chemists at Ajinomoto and Company refer to a delicious brothy taste that is perceived at the back of the tongue and mouth as *umami*. This effect can be produced by combining amino acids, monophosphate nucleosides, and MSG. This taste, which occurs at distinct loci on the tongue, is found in fish, chicken, tomatoes, soy sauce, cheese, and mushrooms.

Taste Studies Lag Behind Odor Research

Taste-active compound studies lag behind the study of odorous compounds. Functions of taste are far more complex than formerly assumed, and psychophysical studies show that many more than the four basic tastes (salty, sweet, sour, and bitter) are produced.

The taste of our foods does not equal that of primeval days or our natural ecosystem. The impact of industry on our foods and their tastes is staggering in our closed ecosystem. We all have to eat food, good or bad. But better taste obtained by the use of taste compounds that occur naturally in our foods to fortify flavor may be beneficial just as vitamin and mineral fortification are. Of course, the use of any additives should be controlled and safe.

ODOR

Odor has been termed the most important sensory component of flavor by Moncrieff (1944). Evidence of the importance of olfaction can be obtained readily by holding the nose and tasting first an apple and then a potato. If you hold your nose when you are blindfolded, you cannot tell the difference between the apple and the potato. Moncrieff says, "gustation is to taste as olfaction is to smell."

Odor is a complex physiological response occurring at specific chemical receptor loci known as the hairs of the olfactory cell and due to electrochemical, thermochemical, and kinesthetic reactions at those specific sites. Whenever smell with or without superimposed feeling contacts the receptor site, the brain computes the overall effect of the complex response known as odor.

Odor Physiology

By comparing the chemical senses of taste and smell, Moncrieff (1965) found that the brain is capable of recognizing more than 200,000 different odors and that, the palate and tongue have thousands of taste receptors, the nasal cleft has millions of olfactory receptors. These olfactory receptors are embedded in the small patch of mucous membrane situated on each wall of the nasal cleft, which is a narrow space in the uppermost compartment of the nose.

According to Von Frisch (1964), rabbits, dogs, and eels possess many more olfactory receptors than man. The olfactory bulb of the rabbit contains 100 million receptor cells with 6 to 12 hairs per cell. The total in man is 50 million glomeruli receptors served by 45,000 secondary neurons connected to the olfactory section of the brain (Döving 1965). The rabbit has only 25,000 of the secondary neurons leading to the cortex of the brain.

In a series of classical experiments, Gesteland and Lettvin (1964) measured the electrical responses of individual olfactory nerve cells in the olfactory brain of the frog. Frog species are most frequently chosen for olfaction experiments because their neural anatomy resembles that of man. These workers connected microelectodes to the individual cells, and their experiments demonstrated that specific cells react selectively with specific odors. Eight kinds of odor receptors were identified in the frog, and five of these receptor types reacted with the seven primary odors that Amoore (1952) described. Thus, the experiments of Gesteland and Lettvin give support to the stereochemical theory of odor (see Odor theories, which follows), proposed by Amoore, Johnston, and Rubin (1964). These workers have been successful in establishing the fact that the sense of smell is governed by an electrical process that originates in the olfactory nerve whenever a whiff of odor hits the lining of the nose.

The human nose is an instrument of remarkable sensitivity and precision. Even though the sensitivity to odors varies between individuals, most people can detect vanillin at a concentration of one part in ten million. Odor thresholds also vary according to the chemical compound that is being smelled. For example, ethyl mercaptan—the active ingredient in skunk odor—may be smelled at a concentration as low as 0.00000066 mg/l

International Critical Tables value (Wenger *et al.* 1956). Yet this is equivalent to more than 19 billion (19×10^9) molecules of ethyl mercaptan (Hicks 1965). Odor sensitivity is about 10 thousand times that of taste sensitivity; as will be discussed later, ordinary chemical methods are often impractical in the study of food odors (Crocker 1945).

Odor Theories

More than 2,000 years ago the Roman poet Lucretius postulated that the palate contains small pores of various sizes and shapes (Amoore *et al.* 1964). Odor perception was attributed by Lucretius to the specific shapes of the odor molecules together with their capacity to fit particular pores in the palate.

Moncrieff (1949) proposed a so-called new theory of odor remarkably similar to the ancient one of Lucretius, but based on modern scientific evidence. According to the deductions of Moncrieff, the odorant must be volatile and has to possess a molecular configuration complementary to that of a specific site on the olfactory receptor. He stated that olfaction occurs in six stages: (1) odorant molecules pervade the air; (2) odor-containing air is inspired by the subject and sniffed into the nasal cleft; (3) molecules lodge themselves on site of suitable receptors; (4) lodgement may cause an energy change, such as a reduction in surface tension; (5) the energy shift in the receptors sends discrete electrical messages up the olfactory nerve to the brain; and (6) the brain processes and computes the smell.

About fifteen years later, after more than a decade of classical experimentation with hundreds of organic odor compounds, Amoore (1952) and Amoore and co workers (1964) proposed the stereochemical theory of odor. In analogy to the three primary colors, these workers chose seven primary odors: camphoraceous, musky, floral, pepperminty, ethereal, pungent, and putrid. The first five of these seven primary odors are complementary to the seven primary receptor sites, which resemble cavities and slots. According to Amoore, each of these first five primary odors can be identified by the size and shape of its molecules, and particular odors fit into specific openings. The other two primary odors, the pungent and putrid, are distinguished by electrical charge rather than by shape. Thus, these workers propose a complex odor spectrum for smell that resembles the simpler color spectrum for sight.

Experimental evidence substantiates the stereochemical theory of odor. The first direct support of the Amoore theory is the experimental discovery by Gesteland and Lettvin of differentiated receptor sites in the olfactory organ of the frog (1964). Obviously, the theory of Amoore is of great value, although it may prove to be an oversimplified explanation of the complex phenomenon of odor. Further studies will place the stereochemical theory of odor in proper perspective.

Instruments

Work is being done to develop better instruments for detecting odors. So far man has devised no instrument to equal the performance of the human nose and brain. In making such efforts, scientists are learning more about the way the human nose functions.

According to Moncrieff (1957, 1961), the smell stimulus is a physico-chemical adsorptive process, and the chemical molecules responsible for a particular flavor lend themselves to instrumentation. The mechanical nose he has developed is made up of a thermostat coated with a peanut protein film and a glass-enclosed thermistor having a resistance capacity of 2000 ohms, with a drop in resistance of 60 ohms per degree celsius rise in temperature. When an odorant vapor in air is passed over the coated thermostat at a controlled rate of one liter of air per minute, a temperature rise occurs that unbalances the Wheatstone bridge resistance circuit. This device, while more sensitive to acetone than the human nose, is inferior to the nose in detecting vanilla or must odors.

Investigations on the sense of smell were begun at Honeywell Research Center, Hopkins, Minnesota (1964). The ultimate goal of this research effort is to develop electronic sensors capable of detecting and identifying odors. The research team consists of director H. E. Heist, D. J. Landis, and B. D. Mulvaney. They have already been successful in separating individual olfactory cells and in making electron micrographs of the cell parts that are suspected of being odor receptors and/or transmitters (see Figs. 3, 4, and 5).

Rabbit cells have been separated and maintained as single cells for weeks at a time and have been subjected to various odor and visual tests. Prior to electron microscopy, the cells are embedded individually in an epoxy resin block for sectioning. An ultramicrotome is used to prepare sections of 50 nanometers (nm) thickness (about 0.000002 inches) for subsequent tests. Correlated studies using light microscopy are made with thicker sections averaging 1 ¼m in thickness (about 5/10,000 of an inch).

Results indicate that the hairs and olfactory vesicles hold the greatest promise for future studies. Heist, Landis, and Mulvaney have noted that each rabbit olfactory cell averages six to twelve olfactory hairs. These cells resemble those of other animals by displaying the conventional 9-plus-2 pattern of fibers at their proximal ends. Figures 6 and 7 illustrate the olfactory bulb location and the structure of the olfactory section of the brain.

Odor Psychology

Both good and bad odors exert remarkable psychological influence on our lives. Food appetites and personal performance can be whetted or dulled by the odors in the air we breathe. Emotional effects of odors can also profoundly affect food sales (Hicks 1965).

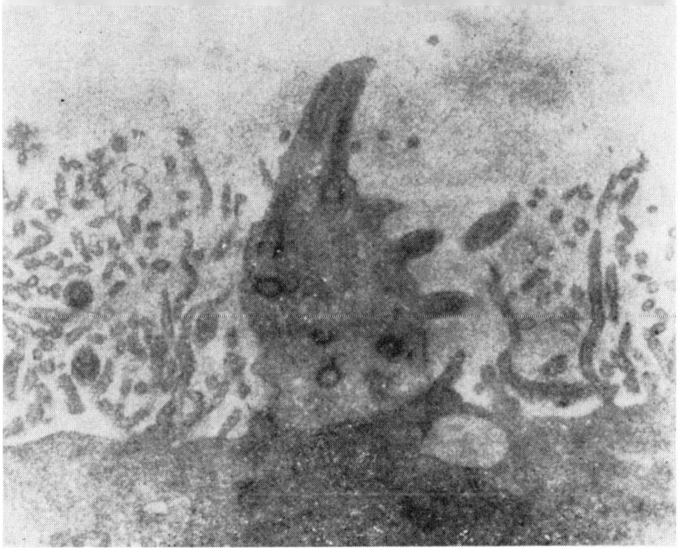

Fig. 3. Olfactory cell, longitudinal section, × 28,000. Electron photomicrograph of an individual bipolar olfactory cell, taken from a rabbit, shows olfactory hairs and vesicle.

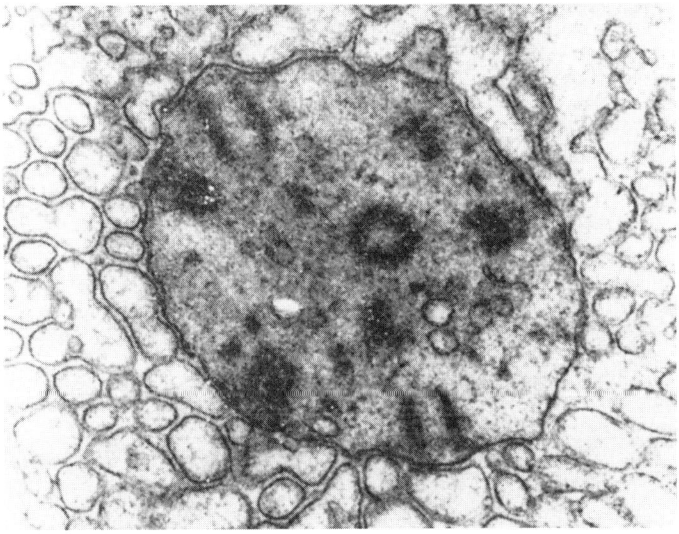

Fig. 4. Olfactory cell, cross-section, × 66,000. Electron photomicrograph of a rabbit's individual olfactory cell with double sets of lines at the periphery which are basal bodies of olfactory hairs.

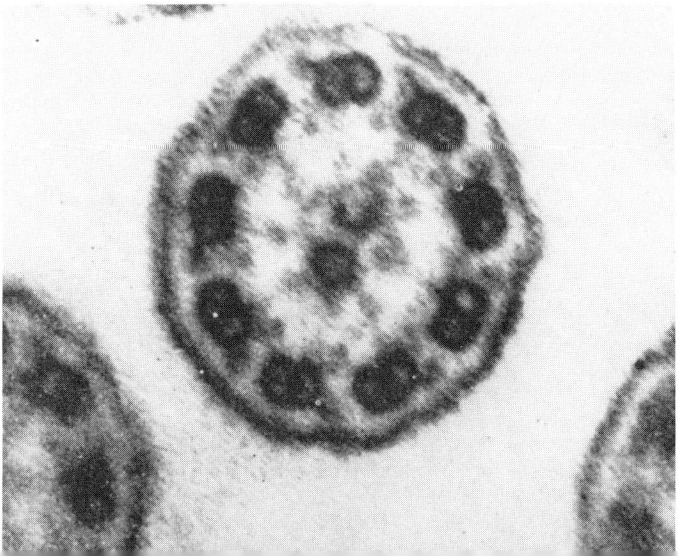

Fig. 5. Olfactory hair, cross-section, × 500,000. Electron photomicrograph of rabbit's olfactory hair with 9-plus-2 pattern of fibers, resembling the structure of other cell types found throughout the animal kingdom.

Figs. 3–5 from Honeywell Research Center 1964.

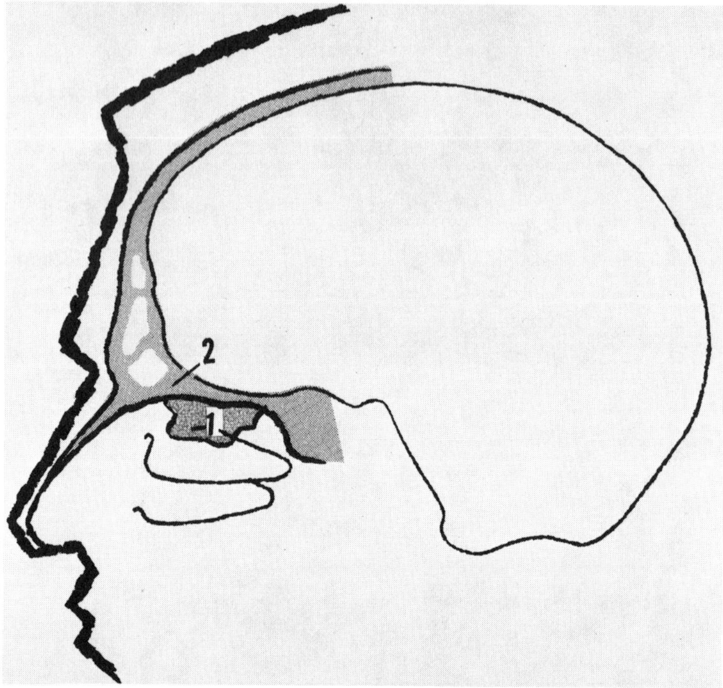

Fig. 6. Receptors for the sense of smell are located in a small patch of tissues (1) at the tip of the nasal cavity; nerves pass through apertures in the ethnoid bone (2) to the brain.
Courtesy of Better Homes and Gardens. From Family Medical Guide. 1966. Meredith Corporation.

Fig. 7. Smell structures in relation to nasal cavity and brain with magnified details. (A) The left olfactory bulb (1) receives nerve fibers that pass through the ethnoid bone (2) from the smell patch (3) in the roof of the nasal cavity. (B) Microscopic view of olfactory bulb shows fibers merging into oflactory nerve that leads to the brain. (C) Olfactory glands (4) produce mucus in which molecules of odorous substances are dillolved for detection by sensitive olfactory cells (5).
Courtesy of Better Homes and Gardens. From Family Medical Guide. 1966. Meredith Corporation.

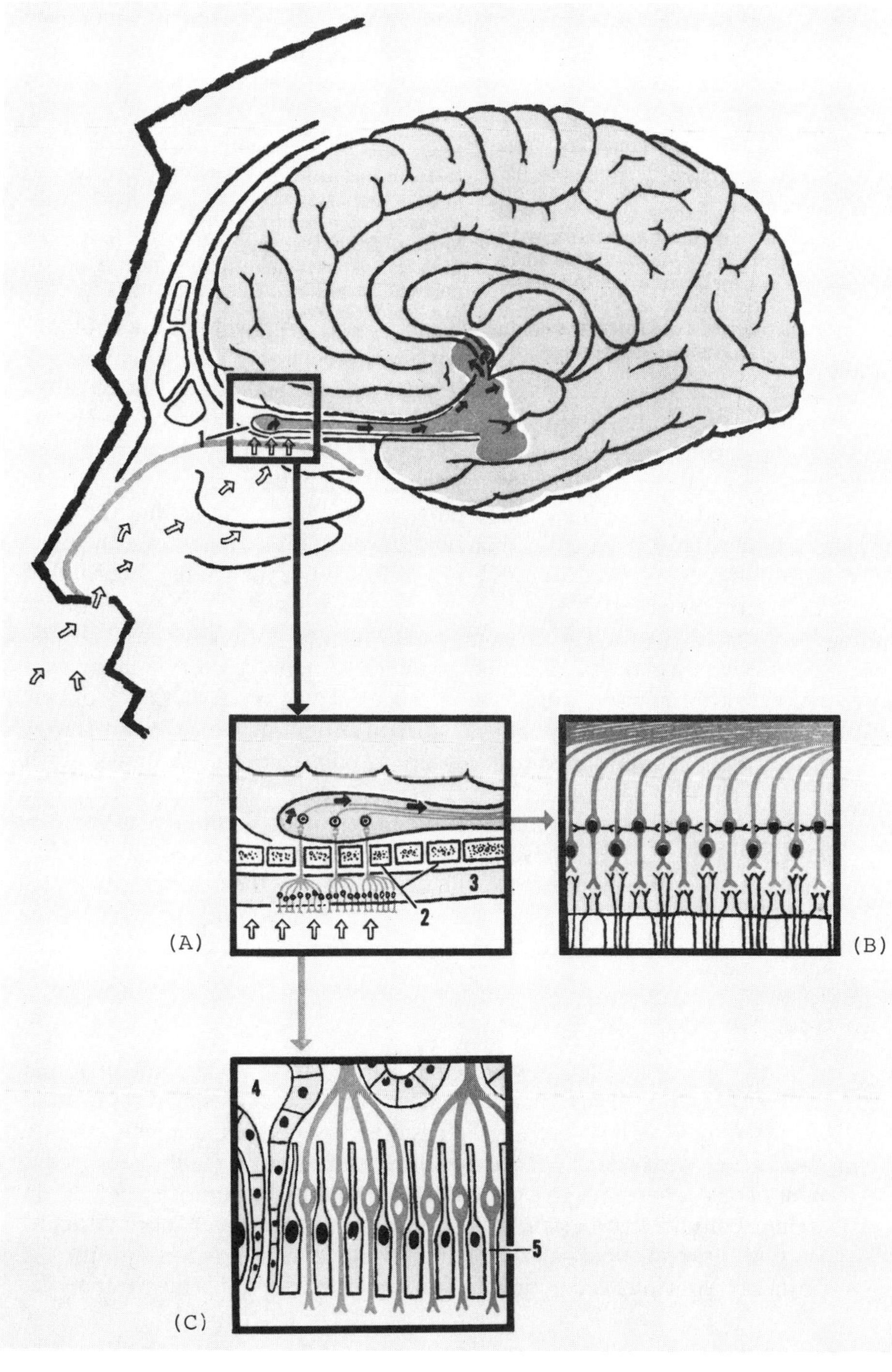
1
2
3
(A)
(B)
4
5
(C)

A pleasant feeling and salivary stimulation can result from inhaling food aromas. Consider for example: the fragrant essence of freshly picked tree-ripened oranges, apples, peaches, pears, or bananas; the yeasty aroma of homemade bread baking; the smell of beef roasting, corn popping, coffee percolating, cheese curing, hops brewing, or fudge cooling on a marble slab. These fragrances can cause us to recollect childhood smelling experiences and to reminisce. In contrast, the lachrymal effects of peeled onions cause tears to flow; the sickening gassy smell of sour milk, spoiled meat, or fermented fruits and vegetables turns the stomach and upsets the entire central nervous system.

Hazardous odors serve as a warning mechanism with the aid of our chemical senses. Gas leaks are identified by means of the mercaptan stench that is added to natural-gas supplies. Burned fat and heavy smoke odors warn us of the formation of carcinogens (cancer-producing chemicals) during improper char-broiling or smoking of meats, poultry, or fish. The application of excessive heat to fat when frying potato chips or other foods causes the release of these same polynuclear hydrocarbons that the nose may detect. (Lijinsky and Shubik 1964; Anon. 1959). Hence, our chemical warning system protects us today as it did primitive man many thousand of years ago (Moncrieff 1944).

Odor transfer problems have plagued engineers for many years. Design engineering is needed to minimize problems of odor transfers in apartment buildings, refrigerators, and food packages. Tests prove that fatty or oily materials are especially receptive to certain odors (McKinley 1958). Butter or chocolate can be ruined by exposure to paint and varnish fumes. Or if butter is cut with a knife that has not been cleaned after being used on fish, onions, or garlic, the butter flavor may be spoiled. Within a refrigerator, butter should not be exposed to raw fish, smoked ham, onion, garlic, sauerkraut, or limburger cheese volatiles.Chefs, on the other hand, sometimes use odor transfer advantageously. For example, they produce a lobster butter by incorporating cooked lobster essence into creamery butter.

Odor Analysis

Odor has been called the principal part of flavor. Consequently, the problem of odor analysis is being attacked with ever-increasing vigor by food scientists in all parts of the world. Taste analysis is comparatively simple. The taste or nonvolatile portions of flavor are fewer in number and occur naturally in foods at high enough concentrations to permit either direct chemical or microbiological analysis. Odor analysis is much more difficult. The odor or volatile parts of flavor are low in concentration to start with. As the many individual components are separated for subsequent analysis, further reduction in sample size occurs. Accordingly sophisticated chemical and instrumental methods of analysis are being developed to cope with the situation. Some of these will be described later.

There is a growing awareness that determining what chemicals constitute an odor may be the simplest part of solving an odor problem. For, beyond this, it is essential to determine the relative concentrations of all the chemicals constituting the odor. Since it is not uncommon for a food odor to contain more than one hundred different chemicals at varying concentrations, the tasks of analyzing a particular food odor and then matching it by synthesis are apparently extremely difficult both chemically and mathematically speaking.

Even this concept of food odor analysis is oversimplified, however, for food is living matter that is in a constant state of flux. Fruit enzymes, for instance, are constantly forming esters from acids and alcohols present in the fruit. Meanwhile other enzymes are hydrolyzing esters to form alcohols and acids. Many other chemical changes are occurring at the same time. These changes happen even while an apple, orange, or banana is being eaten. Analysis showed that crushed fresh strawberries contain 0.5 ppm of the alcohol hexene-2-ol, whereas none of this particular alcohol was present in the whole fresh fruit. Mere crushing, a physical effect, changes the chemical nature of the strawberries and alters their flavor.

In applying modern research instruments to the study of flavor (Figs. 8, 9, 10, and 11), scientists are continually discovering more complexity in the natural flavors of all foods, although there are a few common-denominator factors. Many of the same chemical compounds have been found in different foods at varying levels of concentration. Thus it has been established that there may be some qualitative chemical similarities, accompanied by both qualitative and quantitative chemical differences between foods.

Gas chromatographic methods for separating flavor volatiles are complex and expensive (Fig. 11). It is safe to estimate that the rate of improvement in gas chromatographs during the past five years has been at least five times as great as the rate of change in automobile models during the same period. Constant development and refinement of gas chromatographs is still going on.

For example, consider the results of a gas chromatographic study of cooked chicken volatiles by Minor *et al.* (1965). A total of less than 30 peaks representing at least that many chemical entities was obtained on each of the chromatograms for breast and leg muscle using a packed column and temperature programming. During the 2-year interim from the start of the study to the publication of the results, gas chromatographs equipped with electron capture detectors and capillary column fractionators resulted in the separation of about two hundred peaks indicative of that number of individual

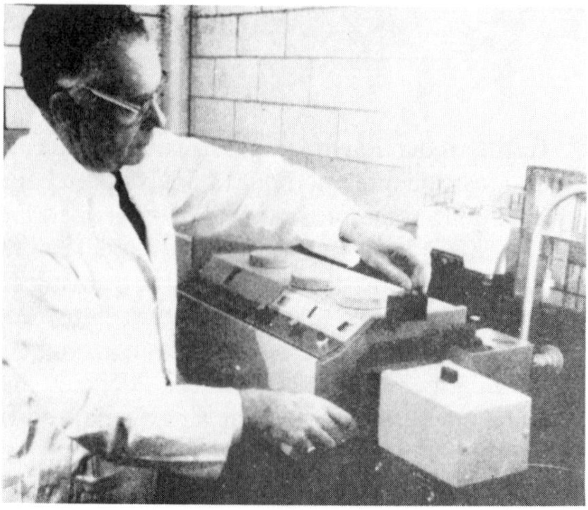

Fig. 8. Determination of 5′ nucleotide concentration in chicken breast and leg muscle broth flavor studies by ultraviolet absorption.

Fig. 9. Gaseous condensate from chicken flavor volatiles is taken from a sealed trap by means of a gas-tight syringe prior to injection into the gas chromatograph at room temperature.

Fig. 10. The chicken flavor fraction is injected into the gas chromatograph.

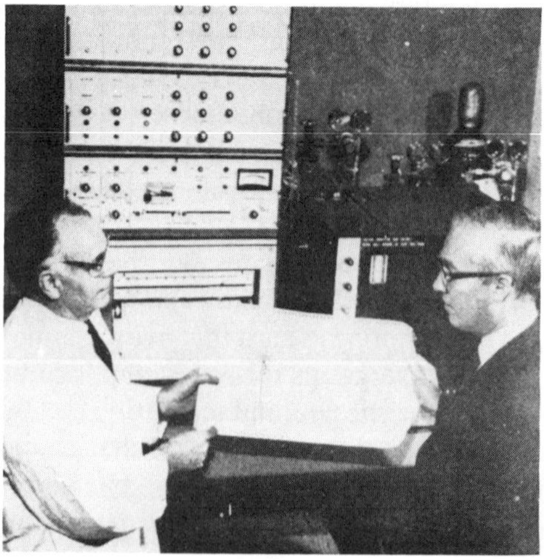

Fig. 11. The resulting chromatogram shows the retention times and peak areas of individual chemical components.

compounds in cooked chicken aroma. However, separation has proved to be much easier than the subsequent indentification of the peaks, each of which may represent either one discrete entity or several chemical entities combined. In other words, the more peaks one separates by gas chromatography, the more involved their identification may become.

Separating the volatiles is only the first step in analyzing a particular food odor. Samples of odorous materials injected into a gas chromatograph average about 1 or 2 ml of concentrated flavor volatiles. Fractionation—ideally—involves separation of this small amount of flavor compounds into one hundred or more discrete and minute component fractions. Subsequent identification of these fractions requires sensitive instruments. For example, a combination of the human nose, mass spectrometry, nuclear magnetic resonance, and infrared and ultraviolet spectrophotometry was used by Day (1965) in studies on the analysis of cheese volatiles.

As stated before, chemical methods of identification require much higher concentrations of food volatiles than one obtains by using gas chromatographic separations of odorous constituents. Accordingly, Hoff and Feit (1963) devised an ingenious syringe technique for functional group analysis by microchemical methods followed by gas chromatography. Solubility classification, functional group analysis, derivative preparation, gas chromatography, and organoleptic (taste and odor) tests have been used in combination by Minor *et al.* (1965) in making a series of studies on chicken flavor (1964, 1965). The uses and limitations of gas chromatography in flavor research have been reported by Burr (1964). Progress is being made in the analysis of food odors by applying organoleptic tests, chemical tests, instrumentation, and other physiochemical methods together with physiological studies.

PRACTICAL USE OF FLAVOR RESEARCH DEVELOPMENTS

Food flavor research is progressing on bread, wine, red meats, poultry, fish, milk, cultured dairy products, cheese, potato, onion, hops, peaches, pears and other fruits, coffee, and flavor potentiators such as monosodium glutamate (MSG) and the sodium salts of the 5′ nucleotides (Moncrieff 1965).

For centuries we have relied on the addition of salt, sugar, spices, and wood smoke to the natural flavors that occur in foods. These additives lend savory richness to certain dishes. Soya sauce as a flavoring and monosodium glutamate as a seasoning and flavor potentiator have been developed in the Orient to make vegetable protein foods tolerable to a meat eater.

Soya sauce with vinegar and spices is the base for Worcestershire sauce. Prime quality soya sauce is made from wheat and soy beans by a slow fermentation process. MSG occurs naturally in wheat, meat, poultry, and other foods, and since the early 1900s it has been manufactured by several methods (Marshall 1948). Today it is being produced by microbiological or enzyme action from low-cost sources (Kuninaka 1965).

Vanilla bean extract is another flavoring of ancient origin. Other extracts such as oil of wintergreen, spice oils, oleoresinous extracts from spices, and natural fruit extracts have also been used as food flavorings for decades. Hydrolyzed plant proteins from grain and yeast sources and the sodium salts of the 5′ nucleotides from Japan represent more recent developments that are being applied to complement or replace beef extract, which is often expensive and in short supply.

A list totalling 1023 flavoring ingredients has been compiled (Hall and Oser 1965). We may wonder why so many flavoring materials, both synthetic and natural, are needed. But let us consider one small facet of the total fruit flavor picture—strawberry flavor. Based on the annual consumption of strawberry flavoring (imitation) and the average annual production of strawberries in the United States, it has been calculated that the entire strawberry crop, if used only to provide a natural flavor extract, would yield only enough to satisfy the annual needs of a city the size of Pittsburgh. Synthetic flavorings are useful and necessary supplements to our natural fruit flavor supplies.

Fruit flavors have been worked on for several decades by organic chemists. Synthetic strawberry, raspberry, and cherry flavors have been used in candies and gelatin desserts for three decades or longer. Recently it was stated in an article by Moncrieff (1964) that the best flavors are still the natural ones, although much progress has been achieved in the synthetic flavor field. This advance in synthetic flavors is partly due to the complete analysis (chromatographic and spectrographic) of complex mixtures of natural products: for example, raspberry flavoring constituents. One key advantage of these synthetics is their stability toward oxygen in the air (see Table 1).

Synthetic flavors today are better than ever before. Still we have not succeeded in duplicating even the simplest one of the true natural flavors. Qualitative and quantitative factors combine to magnify the problem to computer proportions and perhaps beyond that. As with infinity in mathematics, we may find that we can approach natural flavor but never quite attain it. Thus, flavor chemistry may offer the food scientist a never-ending challenge.

It is easiest to synthesize imitations of fruit flavors. Vegetable flavors are harder, and butter and cheese flavors harder still, to imitate, although

TABLE 1. Fruit Aromas

Source	Compounds found to date
Pineapple	38
Banana	37
Passion fruit	4
Black currant	89
Apple	84
Pear	69
Peach	33
Raspberry	61
Strawberry	137
Grapefruit	31
Lemon	61
Lime	46
Orange	124
Grape	83

Adapted from H.E. Nursten and A.A. Williams. Chem. Ind. London, 25 (March 1967), pp. 486–497.

biochemists are producing useful cheese essences. Most difficult of all flavors to simulate are those for meat, fish, and poultry. Research on meat flavor began nearly two centuries ago when chemistry was in Europe. At that time scientists had begun studying the chemical composition of meat extract.

Beef extract, hydrolyzed vegetable proteins, casein digests, and yeast autolysate extracts are flavorings that have characteristic amino acid, peptide, protein, nucleotide, and browning reaction flavors (Hall 1948). The browning reaction or Maillard synthesis occurs in foods when either amino acids, peptides, or proteins react with reducing sugars to form brown-colored reaction products having individualistic flavors.

Each hydrolyzed plant protein is different from the other; the protein source and the manufacturing process chosen are responsible for flavor differences. Yet these products are compatible or synergistic with one another and with certain meats or meat and vegetable mixtures. In short, these are meat and vegetable flavor synergists that work with meat flavor to enrich or supplement it. Occurring as by-products of glutamate manufactured from plant protein hydrolysates, they are related to monosodium glutamate as molasses is to sugar. In other words, they are the compounds present in the mother liquor from which MSG is isolated by chemically controlled crystallization.

Pure chemical compounds that are likewise synergistic with the flavorings described above, with meat, and with each other are MSG, DSG, and DSI. DSG and DSI are abbreviations for the sodium salts of the 5′ nucleotides, disodium guanylate and disodium inosinate. Their primary function is to provide flavor enrichment by blending flavors synergistically and additively (Caul and Raymond 1964; Toi *et al.* 1963; Kuninaka and Sakaguchi 1964; Kurtzmand and Sjöström 1963.

Meat Substitutes

The secret of flavor development according to Sjöström and Cairncross (1950) is blended flavor. Of all the condiments, however, meat extract provides the truest resemblance to the mouth satisfaction indigenous to freshly prepared meat stock. In fact, there is no flavor substitute that matches real meat taste and aroma. Classical meat extract preparation and analysis by Liebig was prompted by meat shortages in Europe resulting from the Napoleonic wars (Liebig 1847). In the early 1960s there were about 3.2 billion people on earth, with 550 million consuming over 90% of the meat supply (Borgstrom 1965).

In the search for ways to close the ever-widening protein versus population gap, the Japanese have turned to fishing. A Frenchman, Champagnat (1965), succeeded in producing protein from crude petroleum by developing strains of yeast that can subsist on petroleum hydrocarbons. A soy protein matrix perfected by Boyer (1956) is flavored with beef-like, ham-like, bacon-like, and chicken-like flavors. A Purdue research team announced development of a lysine-rich mutant strain of corn in their efforts to alleviate kwashiorkor (protein deficiency disease) among infants in underfed countries (Anon. 1965). Furthermore, lysine and most of the other essential amino acids are now produced by synthesis or microbiologically. But in their present stage, none of these developments nor any combination of them can go far toward alleviating protein shortages.

Man improves the biological efficiency of grain proteins by feeding them to ruminants, thus converting them to animal protein of relatively high biological value. However, it takes 7 cal of plant carbohydrate to produce 1 cal of beef protein and 3.5 cal of plant carbohydrate to produce 1 cal of chicken protein.

Meanwhile, the natural resource holding the most serious threat to our food supply and living standard is water (Maxwell 1965). About 330 gal of water are required to provide enough wheat for one person to subsist on for 1 day; whereas 4200 gal are needed to produce only 1 lb of beef.

We must look to the Orient for guidance in making practical substitutions of vegetables for meat and in flavoring these substitute foods. Bean sprouts produced from either soy or mung beans are highly nutritious and flavorful. Furthermore, the Chinese have discovered that a combination of green soybeans with Chinese cabbage provides a complete and balanced spectrum of the essential amino acids in adequate amounts to support growth and maintenance of the human body.

Flavor satisfaction is achieved by adding soya sauce, monosodium glutamate, and the sodium salts of the 5′ nucleotides to the bland vegetables and rice that make up the Asian diet. For centuries the Japanese have used sea tangle for its glutamate effect and dried bonito for its nucleotide effect in seasoning their meals.

It was reported by Ikeda (1908, 1909) that the principal flavor component of sea tangle extract is monosodium glutamate. Today most of the MSG is produced by direct fermentation processes. The world supply, which was recently reported to be 150 million pounds per year, valued at about $80 million, comes mainly from Japan (Nagle 1965). Production in the United States is less than one-fourth of the total amount produced. When one considers that monosodium glutamate usage is at a level of one-tenth the concentration of salt used in food and that its use is restricted to protein foods, we begin to appreciate the impact of this Oriental seasoning on our American food habits. We are seasoning about 30 billion pounds of protein foods annually (about 150 lb per person per year) with MSG and the use is increasing.

The 5′ nucleotides may also be used to flavor meat substitutes. Inosinic acid, an important 5′ nucleotide, was first isolated from beef muscle in 1847 by Liebig, who named it after the Greek word meaning muscle. This nucleic acid, upon neutralizing with mild alkali, yields the flavor nucleotide disodium inosinate. It is interesting to note that this flavor nucleotide is a constituent of ribonucleic acid, which is present in the muscle and brain of mammals and fish.

Apparently, then, there are key relationships between flavor and life. It is interesting to note that compounds that contribute to life processes occurring in nature may also be isolated, purified, and neutralized to serve as food flavor potentiators.

The monosodium salt of glutamic acid is a building block of protein and the most widely occurring amino acid found in natural proteins. The nucleotide disodium inosinate occurs in the RNA of muscle and may be derived directly from RNA by acid hydrolysis, followed by neutralization with sodium hydroxide, or by enzyme action. DSI contributes an amazing synergistic action to the flavor-accentuating powers of MSG and the hydrolyzed plant proteins. Disodium guanylate (DSG), another nucleotide, is derived from yeast cells and is about 20 times as effective as DSI, but in a little different manner.

The nucleotides are effective in seasoning protein foods at concentrations in the range of one-twentieth of the level of MSG or less. A blend of nucleotides consisting of 50% DSI and 50% DSG (Fig. 12) is being mar-

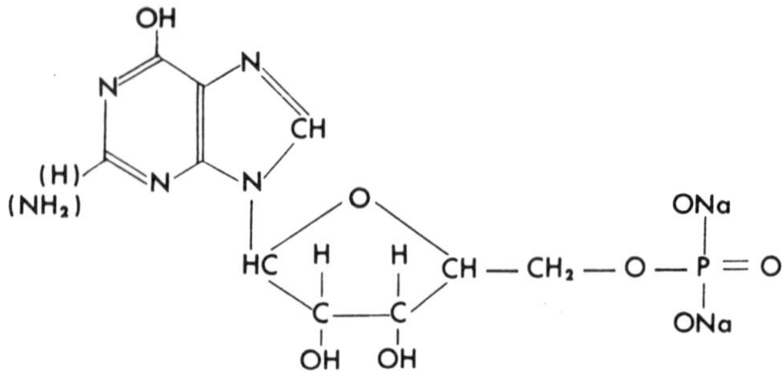

H — Disodium Inosinate

NH_2 — Disodium Guanylate

Fig. 12. Structure of sodium salts of 5′ nucleotide seasonings.

keted in the United States. This product is imported from Japan and sells for \$25 per pound; the price is dropping. At present its main use is to partially replace beef extract. By modifying and improving hydrolyzed plant protein flavors, the nucleotides achieve a meatier connotation of flavor than is possible with MSG alone. Scientists have proved that inosinic acid, the precursor of the flavor nucleotide, is one of the major active ingredients in natural beef, chicken, and fish muscle, present in the nonvolatile flavor fraction of cooked meat.

As Borgstrom (1965) says, "we live on a hungry planet where the protein gap may soon challenge our existence." He warns that complacency will spell our doom. Perhaps this is true, but the mind of man has unlocked many secrets, and more will be elucidated. Studies of the organic chemicals in sea water may reveal untapped nutritional wealth (Pratt 1965). Fertilizers offer quick results for more food. A sensible solution to the fresh water problem has been suggested by Maxwell (1965). According to Dr. Robert H. Burris, (1965) nitrogen fixation is a key biochemical process for feeding the hungry planet. A leader in the development of synthetic rubber, Dr. Archibald T. McPherson of the Institute for Applied Technology, National Bureau of Standards, believes that proteins, amino acids, and vitamins can be produced synthetically to ease the growing problem of hunger (Misc. and Savory 1965).

Scientific research and development may one day close the protein gap by applying known biochemical principles to the conversion of air, water, and carbohydrate or carbon to protein. This kind of protein when available will have to be modified in texture, appearance, taste, and aroma. For unless the synthetic product is acceptable in both nutrition and flavor, it will not be eaten (see Fig. 13).

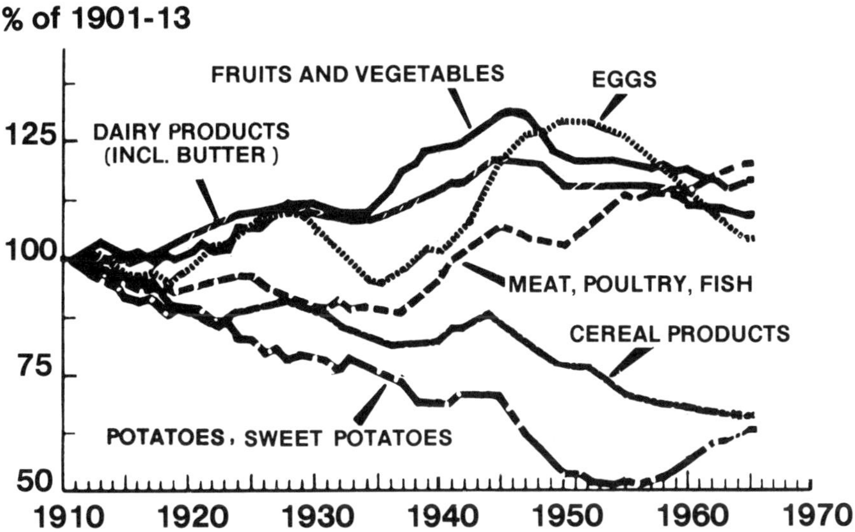

Fig. 13. Consumption of meat, poultry, and fish per capita in the United States has steadily increased since the Depression of the late 1930s, while the population has doubled.

Our flavor heritage and the current pace of flavor research augur well for the future. Flavor chemistry activity in the field of food science is destined to increase several-fold within the next two or three decades. Scientists will press on toward the distant goal of matching natural flavors with synthetic or enzyme-produced replacements as the protein gap is being closed.

Research effort in diverse fields of science may one day result in food production capabilities that will cope with the emergencies created by burgeoning population pressures. Nutrition and flavor together will then triumph over world hunger when a balance between birthrate and death rate on this planet is made to conform with total resources and food production capabilities.

FOOD FLAVORING MATERIAL STANDARDS

Various flavoring materials used in food and beverage manufacture are derived from plants. These include fruits, flowers, roots, barks, seeds, and leaves that yield herbs and spices together with their derivatives (fruit juices, essential oils, and oleoresins and extracts).

Spices

Americans are using more spices per capita than ever before. These include (a) true spices derived from aromatic tropical plants, for example, pepper, cloves, ginger, basil, cinnamon, and nutmeg; (b) herbs (leaves of temperate zone plants, for example, sage, rosemary, oregano, basil, and thyme; (c) aromatic seeds including anise, caraway, poppy, sesame, cumin, and cardamon; and (d) miscellaneous condiments such as paprika, garlic, onion, chives, shallots, celery, carrots, and spice blends.

Purchasing Spices

Spices are judged by their strength and quality of flavor. Paprika and turmeric are judged differently, by color, strength, and flavor. Inexpensive spices lacking in flavor and color attributes are not good buys as the amount of spice used in a meal is small. High quality is the best buy since it assures customer satisfaction.

Spice purity is regulated by the FDA. During World War II an influx of imitation pepper (oil of black or red pepper in a buckwheat or similar carrier) occurred. Good food requires high-quality, real pepper as its flavor is truer and more stable and provides real economy.

Storage and Packaging

Spices should be stored no longer than 6 months in tightly closed containers that minimize oxidation and exclude light. Spices are photosensitive, with light exposure causing photooxidation that results in color loss and flavor deterioration. Cardboard and glass containers are unsuitable. Metal containers with friction tops are best. Spice flavors are volatile, and air exposure should be minimal. As some are hygroscopic and readily absorb humidity, containers should be tightly sealed. Heat should be avoided, and spices should be stored at just below room temperature (60°F; 16°C).

Proper Use of Spices

When a spice can be identified in a food it has been overused. Spices should add subtle shades of flavor that blend in with the total flavor profile. They should not be used with a heavy hand. Excessive garlic or oregano can easily ruin food. A "bouquet garni" sachet of spices is often used in stews and chowders. After doing its work the bag of spices is removed.

Often the spice, in powder form, is preblended with salt or sugar to assure uniform dispersion.

Ethnic Foods

Ethnic foods such as Polish sausage, Kielbasa, have a distinctive, highly seasoned flavor. These items are acceptable to particular ethnic groups, but to others the flavoring is overdone. In some East Coast restaurants, New England clam chowder containing high levels of sage are served. Locals enjoy it, but visitors do not. In southern restaurants the levels of red and black pepper used on fish and in other foods may cause the eyes of visitors to water. Mexican foods likewise contain levels of oregano and red pepper that are intolerable to those not accustomed to them. Italian foods with high garlic content and Chinese foods with high monosodium glutamate content are other examples.

Spice Garnishes

Garnishing with spices includes paprika for color in fish, soup, potato salad, and other dishes. Cloves and cinnamon sticks enhance pears, peaches, fruit compotes, and beverages. Nutmug in cream desserts and bananas, cinnamon on toast, sesame seeds on crackers and rolls, and caraway seeds in noodles and sauerkraut are other common garnishes.

Some spice seasoning suggestions are given in Table 2.

TABLE 2. Spice Seasoning Suggestions

APPETIZERS—COCKTAILS—CANAPES

Avocado—Pepper, Onion Salt, Chili Powder.

Cranberry Juice—A tiny dash of Ground Cloves.

Cream Cheese Spread—Onion Salt, Celery Seed.

Ham Spread—Onion Salt, Celery Seed.

Smoked Salmon—Pakrika, Black Pepper.

Stuffed Celery—Paprika, for appearance and flavor.

Tomato Juice—A dash of Mace or Marjoram.

SOUPS

In all soups, celery salt, onion salt, pepper to taste, then use some of the other spices as indicated, to add the final touch of piquant flavor.

Bean—Bit of Cloves and Thyme, Mustard.

Beef—Cloves, Allspice, Garlic Salt, Laurel (Bay) Leaves; and always a dash of Nutmeg just before serving!

Chicken—Nutmeg.

Chowders—Poultry Seasoning, or Thyme.

Consommé—Ground Allspice, Bit of Thyme or Sage.

Cream Soups—(Chicken, Potato) Mace, Paprika.

Cream Soups—(Tomato, Pea) Cloves, Paprika (a dash of nutmeg in split Pea Soup is a chef's specialty)

Lamb Broth—Mace, Curry Powder.

Mulligatawny—Curry Powder, Mace, Cloves.

Oyster Stew—Light touches of Mace, Cayenne, goodly dash of Paprika.

Vegetable—Thyme, Savory, Garlic Salt.

MEATS

Beef Stew—Celery Seed, Laurel (Bay) Leaves, Pepper, dash of Nutmeg. For variety, try cooking with small amount of Pickling Spice.

Boiled Beef—Cloves, Laurel (Bay) Leaves.

Chicken—To gravy, add Onion Salt, and a bit of Mace or Nutmeg. For fried chicken, add a tablespoon of Curry to the flour in which you dip the chicken before frying—a bit of Poultry Seasoning is fine in the gravy to go with fried chicken.

Croquettes—Poultry Seasoning: Sage, or Celery Seed.

Ham—Stick whole Cloves into ham to roast or bake.

Hamburger—Onion Salt, a dash of Allspice or Poultry Seasoning. Try seasoning with Curry Powder once in a while for variety.

Lamb—Use Garlic Salt sparingly, Pepper.

Leftovers—Serve with Curry Sauce (teaspoon of Curry added to White Sauce).

Meat Loaf—Celery Salt, Onion Salt, a little Cloves, Allspice and Pepper. Garlic Salt is also liked by many. Some use just Poultry Seasoning.

Meat Patties—Poultry Seasoning gives just the right dash of flavor.

Pot Roast—Cloves, Allspice, Laurel (Bay) Leaves, Garlic Salt. (Sometime try rubbing just a little Ground Ginger on the meat before cooking.)

Roast Beef—Small amount Onion or Garlic Salt rubbed into meat before cooking.

Spareribs—Garlic Salt, Chili Powder, Laurel (Bay) Leaves, Paprika.

Sweetbreads—Dash of Onion Salt, Mace, White Pepper, Paprika.

Veal—Onion Salt, Celery Salt, Poultry Seasoning.

(Continued)

TABLE 2. *(Continued)*

FISH

Baked Fish—Sprinkle with Curry Powder before baking.
Boiled Fish—Use small amount of mixed Pickle Spice.
Croquettes, Etc.—Mustard, Onion Salt, White Pepper.
Shredded Codfish—Celery Salt, Pepper.
Shrimps—Serve with Curry Sauce.

STUFFINGS

Poultry Seasoning is all-sufficient, but if there's none available, use Onion Salt, Sage, Thyme and Pepper. Add Mustard to fish stuffings.

VEGETABLES

Baked Beans—Pepper, Mustard, bit of Allspice.
Baked Potatoes—Plenty of Paprika.
Beets—Cloves, Laurel (Bay) Leaves.
Cabbage—Onion Salt, Celery Seed, or Curry Sauce.
Canned Corn—Try it with a bit of Chili Powder.
Cauliflower—Poppy Seeds of Celery Seed, White Pepper; serve with White Sauce.
Eggplant—Allspice, Laurel (Bay) Leaves, Sage.
Fresh Corn—Paprika, Pepper.
Kale—Serve with a dash of Nutmeg.
Kidney Beans—Chili Powder, Laurel (Bay) Leaves.
Lima Beans—Dash of Cayenne, Celery Salt, Onion Salt.
Onions—Celery Seed or serve with Cream Sauce flavored with dash of Cloves.
Red Cabbage—Allspice, especially when you combine it with apples.
Rice—Serve with Curry or Tomato Sauce (see sauces).
Spinach—A dash of Nutmeg.
Squash—Cinnamon, or a bit of Squash Pie Spice.
String Beans—Spanish Style—Bay Leaf, Whole Cloves.
Succotash—A dash of Nutmeg.
Sweet Potatoes—(Mashed) dash of Nutmeg, Cloves.
Swiss Chard—Onion Salt
Tomatoes—A dash of Allspice or Celery Salt.

SAUCES

Brown Sauce for Fish—Mustard, Paprika.
Brown Sauce for Meats—Onion Salt, Garlic Salt if desired, Allspice, Pepper.
Cream Sauce for Chicken—Onion Salt, Celery Salt, Nutmeg.
Cream Sauce for Veal—Onion Salt, Celery Salt, Nutmeg and a pinch of Cayenne.
Curry Sauce—Make basic White Sauce, add Curry Powder to taste.
Mushroom Sauce—Small amount of Onion Juice, Nutmeg, and a generous amount of Paprika.
Tomato Sauce—Onion or Garlic Salt, Celery Salt, or Celery Seed, Cloves, Black Pepper.
White Sauce—Onion Salt, Mace or Nutmeg, White Pepper, Pinch of Cayenne, Paprika.

CHEESE

Cottage Cheese—Try Caraway Seeds mixed in it
Cream Cheese—Onion Salt, Celery Seed or Celery Salt.
Melted Cheese—Mustard, Paprika, Pepper.
Welsh Rarebit—Paprika, Mustard, dash of Cayenne, Black Pepper.

Source: The National Restaurant Association (undated).

Vanilla Extract Flavor Standards

Vanilla extract is made from the beans of an orchid plant. The beans grow on vines bearing pods or siliques and resemble oversized green beans. The largest vanilla bean crops are grown in Madagascar. Other producers are Mexico, Java, Tahiti, the Comoro Islands, and Réunion.

Vanilla Bean Cultivation

Cultivation of vanilla beans is very long and laborious. Hand labor is used to fecundate the flowers (November–December) by perforating the membrane that separates the pollen from the pistil. Fecundation occurs naturally when either birds or insects perforate the membrane while searching for food. Development of the pods (siliques) requires about 9 months. When the lower tips start to yellow, the beans are harvested.

Curing the Beans

Before curing, the beans are placed in straw baskets and dipped in hot water. The curing process then takes 90 days by alternate exposure to sunlight and covering with wool blankets to develop the aroma. When exudation is complete, the siliques are oiled with cocoa oil to avoid chapping during drying, dried, and branded. During the final stages the best quality siliques form a vanilla "brine" that crystalizes on the surface of the bean. Total time for processing vanilla beans is one year. The most important commercial varieties are brined vanilla, bastard vanilla, and vanilla pompona (Fenaroli 1975).

About 750 vanilla beans comprise 1 lb, and the color of properly cured beans is chocolate brown. Cured vanilla beans contain an average of 2 % of natural vanillin.

Synthetic Vanillin and Vanilla Extract

Synthetic vanillin can be obtained from coniferous trees or oil of cloves. Paper chromatography tests indicate that in addition to vanillin there are 8 organic acids present in pure vanilla extract.

Vanilla extract is prepared by chopping the beans and percolating them at 70°F in a stainless steel percolator using alcohol as a solvent. Following percolation a high quality vanilla extract is aged for at least 3 months to recover and remove suspended material that forms a sediment.

Vanilla Fold and Extract Use Standards

A vanilla fold is a legal designation of the amount of bean extractives contained in a gallon of vanilla extract. A 2-fold vanilla extract contains the extractives from 26.7 oz of beans/gal of extract, a 4-fold 53.4 oz, and so on.

Most Widely Used Flavoring

Use standards for vanilla extract are as follows:

1. For finest vanilla flavor use pure vanilla.
2. In cake-making always cream the vanilla with the shortening.
3. Add pure vanilla extract to puddings or sauces after cooking and cooling.
4. Vanilla works as a binder that blends and rounds out the flavor.
5. To make vanilla sugar, split 2 beans and add them to 3 or 4 lb of sugar in a jar. Keep sealed when not in use.

Ice Cream Flavor Standards with Vanilla[2]

In a National Ice Cream Retailers Association bulletin, Dr. C. W. England stated, "Variation in the intensity of vanilla flavor can be due to changes in the mix formula. For example, an increase of one percent in the milk-solids-not-fat will require the addition of 40 to 50 percent more vanilla flavor to produce the same flavor intensity." A similar situation occurs when the total solids content of the mix is increased. More vanilla flavor is usually necessary as the total solids content of the mix increases, regardless of whether this increase results from fat, milk-solids-not-fat, or sugars.

Effects of High Temperature and Off-taste on Vanilla Flavor

Besides having a high solids content—with sometimes unbalanced ingredients to contend with—the problem is complicated to a greater degree by employing high-temperature, short-time pasteurizing equipment that fundamentally was not intended to be used for ice cream mix. These conditions cannot be covered up by pure vanilla no matter how great an amount is used. Vanilla is naturally mild and delicate in both flavor and bouquet. There is a point in its usage beyond which more vanilla does not yield more flavor, and generally it is impossible, for this reason, to over-flavor a mix with pure vanilla. It is equally difficult to conceal undesirable off-tastes; however, some help may be obtained by the intelligent use of vanillin.

Vanillin Use Standards in Ice Cream Mix

Vanillin should never be considered as a substitute for vanilla but rather as an intensifier. There has been a myth that vanillin can be added to pure vanilla and then half of the amount of this mixture can be used to obtain the same flavor result. People applying this approach would add 1 oz of vanillin to 1 gal of vanilla extract, which normally would be used at the level of 4 oz extract per 5 gal of mix. Now, instead of using 4 oz extract to 5 gal of mix, only 2 oz of the new vanilla–vanillin mixture is used. This may save money, but certainly it will not give the same flavor result. The correct procedure would be to use the original level, namely, 4 oz extract per 5 gal of mix, with the vanillin used as a flavor intensifier to assist in overcoming masking effects of ingredients and processing procedures. Even using vanillin in this manner will not serve as a cure-all for the faults of excessive holding time in relation to the pasteurizing temperature, poor homogenization, or too long a storage time.

Lincoln once said, "What is involved is not the use of a bad thing, but the

[2]From W. Weed. 1965. The use and abuse of vanillin in ice cream. Jackson, Michigan.

abuse of a very good thing." So it is with vanillin. Use it with intelligence; do not abuse it.

NATURAL EXTRACTS

Natural extracts are prepared in the following ways:

Maceration or percolation of seeds, roots, leaves, or fruits. Examples are: vanilla, tonka, and ginger extracts.

Solution of essential oils, including lemon, lime, orange, and almond.

Concentration of fruit juices with alcohol added to prevent fermentation, principally strawberry, raspberry, cherry, and pineapple.

Use standards for natural flavor extracts are the following:

1. Store in a cool dry place away from sunlight.
2. Do not cold-shock them by storing at below 60°F (16°C).
3. Store in a dark place at 60°–70°F (16–21°C).
4. Orange, lemon, lime, and other citrus oils contain terpenes that will oxidize and turn rancid, producing horrible turpentine flavors. Since 90% of citrus oils consists of terpenes, these must be removed as completely as possible. Terpeneless oils are very expensive but are essential if high-quality flavor and long shelf-life are desired.
5. Choose reliable suppliers when purchasing natural extracts.
6. Test all shipments of flavor extracts prior to use against a standard product.

Folded Oils

Folded oils are obtained by removing the inert or undesirable fractions (terpenes) by concentrating the original extract. Generally, folded oils are limited to 10-fold and are made by distilling off terpenes under vacuum. About 90% of the terpenes present are removed for each fold. Antioxidants are added to increase shelf-life.

Concentrated Fruit Juices

Concentrated fruit juices are prepared using vacuum distillation, low temperatures, and special techniques that result in juices concentrated five- or sixfold. These fruital flavors are of great importance in flavoring beverages.

FOOD BASES

Full-bodied, high-flavor-solids food bases furnish a complete flavor system for maintaining high quality food standards. These bases are designed for use in a broad range of food products. They are used to produce stocks for soups and for seasoning instantly by dissolving 1 lb of base in 5 gal of boiling water while stirring. These are comparable in flavor to those produced by the old-fashioned stock pot method that took 7–8 hours to produce a comparable product at much higher cost.

Kinds of Food Bases

Four groups of food bases comprise the basic food flavor systems. These are meat bases and sauces, poultry bases and sauces, fish and seafood bases, and vegetable bases. The meat group consists of beef, veal, pork, ham, lamb, espagnole, glace de viande, au jus, and beef consomme.The poultry group is comprised of chicken, duck, turkey, and chicken supreme sauce. In the seafood group are shrimp, crab, lobster, clam, and a fish base. Vegetable bases are onion, garlic, and mushroom.

Food Base Ingredients

The first ingredient of a food base is the meat, poultry, seafood, or vegetable for which the base is named. Salt is used along with MSG both to season and to preserve the product. A subtle blend of spices, spice extractions, seasonings, protein and carbohydrate derivatives, and some fat or oil may be included in the formula. Use of the bases saves labor, time, equipment, and energy in the kitchen in addition to greatly reducing purchasing and inventory problems. However, it is imperative that only high quality bases be used whenever maximum customer satisfaction is desired.

Escoffier (1941) said, "Stock is everything in cooking. At least in good and well-flavored cooking. With good stock the rest of the work is easy. Without it nothing of value can be produced."

High quality food bases have 30–40% meat content with additional concentrated meat stocks and juices. Their storage life at room temperature (70°F; 21°C) is several weeks with some flavor loss. At refrigeration temperature (38°F; 3°C) they may be stored without flavor loss for at least one year.

Uses of Food Bases

Food bases are versatile and convenient to use in making complete stocks, soups, gravies, and sauces. When complemented with juices from cooked meats or poultry, enriched gravies may be made. Addition of wine further enhances these products.

Seasoning Foods with Food Bases

For seasoning foods the base is added directly at a level of 1 lb of base to 88 lb food (12.5 g/kg). In recipes containing salt an adjustment should be made eliminating 5 oz salt/1 lb base added otherwise the food will be too salty. Frozen food entreés may be flavored with the bases prior to freezing, or sauces and gravies made with chicken supreme sauce base can be added to enrich the flavor of entreés while improving their freeze-thaw stability.

Flavor Dips. Dips made with the bases together with hors d'oeuvres and salad dressings are of many flavorful varieties. Meat flavors may be extended by combining the bases with hydrated soy protein or cereals and adding these blends to chopped meats.

Baked Items. Bakery products can be flavored with the various bases to provide unique bread and biscuit flavors that are useful as meat, fish, or poultry accompaniments and snack items. Macaroni and other pasta may also be flavored in this manner by blending the base with the dough while eliminating 5 oz salt/1 lb base used. Hydrated rice prepared with broths made from the bases and dried can be rehydrated into rice soups.

Textured Vegetable Protein. An excellent extruded and textured vegetable protein product resembling meat, poultry, or seafood has been made using the food bases and a Wenger steam-extrusion machine. Shrimp and lobster analogs tasting like their seafood counterparts were developed in 1980 by Dr. John Sargent of the CRS Company of Minneapolis. Minor's food bases, used in this work, withstood the extremely high processing temperatures required in the process.

Breaded Items. In making breaded products the base can be added to breading or batter to enhance flavor. This should be especially advantageous in the making of delicately flavored breaded seafood products.

ESSENTIAL OILS

Essential oils are aromatic volatile oils derived from plants that usually carry the flavor of the plant. Terpenes and many other classes of chemical compounds may be present including acids, esters, alcohols, aldehydes, ketones, sulfides, mercaptans (thiols), lactones, and others. They are distinguished from fixed oils, such as vegetable oils, that are glycerides of fatty acids and hence saponifiable. Essential oils, except those containing esters, are nonsaponifiable. Some essential oils such as oil of wintergreen (methyl salicylate) are nearly pure single compounds. Others, for example, oil of bitter almond (benzaldehyde, hydrocyanic acid) are mixtures. From the flavoring viewpoint they are strong and convenient sources of desirable aroma.

Sources of Essential Oils

The essential oils may be concentrated in special cells within the plant or its parts. For example, citrus oils occur in the cells of the skin, whereas oil of celery may be derived from either the seed or the leaf. Yields of oils from lemon, lime, or orange skins vary to a maximum of 1%. Peppercorns yield about 10%, caraway seeds 7%, and rose petals 0.02%.

Methods of extraction include (a) steam distillation; (b) pressing (fruit rinds); (c) percolation with solvent (vanilla); (d) extraction with volatile solvents that are afterwards distilled off; (e) maceration in fixed oil or fat extraction with solvent and isolation or distilling; and (f) enfluerage, exposing odorless fats to aromatics contained in flower petals until strongly scented and then extracting with solvent.

Terpeneless oils are obtained by removal of 90% or more of the terpenes from citrus or other oils by fractional vacuum distillation. Thus the nonterpene components are concentrated five- or tenfold. Their increased stability toward oxidation is important. However, they lose some of the original flavor potency of the fruits or leaves.

Storage and handling techniques must be designed to safeguard essential oils from exposure to light, air, heat, or cold. Photochemical effects induced by exposure to light catalyze their deterioration. Oxidation of terpenes resulting from exposure to air causes objectionable turpentine odor and sticky polymeric compounds to develop. Heat accelerates resin formation. Cold shock causes the oil to separate. Accordingly, essential oils are protected by packaging them in dark-glass or tin containers and storing in the dark at room temperature (60°–70°F).

Essential oils are mainly used for flavoring foods and beverages. Some important volatile oils used in flavoring foods are shown in Table 3.

Oleoresins

Oleoresins are semisolid mixtures of the resin and essential oil of the plant from which they exude. They have pungent tastes and characteristic odors sometimes termed balsamic.

Solvent extraction or percolation followed by removal of the solvent by distillation are the processes used to separate oleoresins from spices and herbs. Ethylene dichloride is the preferred solvent for oleoresin of pepper,

TABLE 3. Characteristics of Essential Oils

Oil	Description of odor	Taste	Important components
Garlic	Pungent, sulfury	Biting	Diallyl disulfide and other sulfur compounds
Leek	Pungent, sulfury	Biting	Vinyl sulfide, thiols, aldehyde
Onion	Pungent, lachrymatory	Biting	Sulfur compounds, and allyl aldehyde
Ginger	Pungent, spicy, fragrant	Burning	Zingerone, citral
Cardamon	Fragrant, camphoric, spicy	Burning	Cinede, camphor borneol, terpineol
Pepper	Pungent, piney	Burning	Terpenes, camphor
Nutmeg	Spicy, turpentinic, lemony	Bitter	Terpenes, terpene alcohols, eugenol, esters, aldehydes
Cinnamon (bark)	Cinnamon	Sweet	85% cinnamic aldehyde
Cassia (bark)	Cinnamon	Sweet	70–85% cinnamic aldehyde
Bitter almond	Peach kernels	—	Benzaldehyde, prussic acid
Apple (skin)	Fragrance of apples	—	Acetaldehyde, amyl esters
Peach (skin)	Fragrance of peaches	—	Acetaldehyde, methyl esters, linalool, aldehyde
Lime (skin)	Lemony	—	Citrol and 4 other aldehydes, dipentene
Lemon	Lemony	—	4–5% citrol (90% cipentene)
Orange (sweet)	Orangey	—	Linalyl esters, terpineol, u-decyl aldehyde (95% dipentene)
Cloves	Fragrant, spicy, pungent	Numbing	About 85% eugenol
Coriander	Lavenderlike	—	Linalool
Celery (seed)	Celery	—	Sedanonic lactone, dipentene
Caraway	Distinctive caraway	—	50% carvone, dipentence
Dill	Like caraway	—	Carvone, dipentene, dill apiole
Sage	Spicy, herbaceous	—	Camphor, cineole, terpenes
Marjoram	Lavenderlike	—	Terpineol, esters, terpenes
Thyme	Spicy, phenolic, herbaceous	—	50–70% carvacrol

Source: Crocker (1945).

but it must be carefully removed from the finished product as it is toxic in food products except in trace amounts. For reasons of safety, hexane has replaced ethylene dichloride.

Ground pepper powder often contains filth including microbial, insect, and rodent contamination. Oleoresins overcome these problems and provide a convenient means of standardizing flavor quality and strength. They provide good stability in storage. When freshly made, oleoresin black pepper is a dark green viscous liquid with a pungent aroma. On standing, piperine crystallizes out. Hence it is necessary to warm and stir the product before using it in order to assure homogeneity and uniformity.

Propylene glycol may be added in amounts up to 20% by weight of the oleoresin. This solvent solubilizes the piperine. The resultant liquid pepper may be blended into either a salt or dextrose carrier at a concentration of 7 lb liquid pepper per 100 lb carrying media. Uniform distribution may be achieved by heating the liquid pepper and stirring to bring the oleoresin into solution. Addition to 10 lb aliquots of the carrier accompanied by thorough blending distributes the liquid pepper uniformly over each particle of carrier. The soluble pepper thus produced may be used pound for pound to replace ground pepper in a given formula.

Soluble pepper on a salt carrier or similar preparations made from other herb or spice oleoresins provide convenient sanitary, standardized flavorings for meats, salad dressings, prepared entrees, soups, and foods. Soluble ginger, soluble mace, soluble cinnamon, soluble nutmeg, and the like on a dextrose carrier are ideal for bakery products and beverages.

Important oleoresins include oleoresin pepper, oleoresin capsicum, oleoresin paprika, oleoresin celery, oleoresin vanilla, and oleoresin ginger.

Other Flavorings

Juices are important flavoring raw materials. However, they are fortified with their essential oils or with synthetic chemicals.

Research on essential oil and fruit flavors has resulted in the identification of compounds that are active flavoring ingredients. These include vanillin (vanilla), benzaldehyde (almonds), cinnamaldehyde (cinnamon), ethyl formate (artificial rum flavor), *n*-amyl acetate (bananas), octyl acetate (oranges) ethyl butyrate (pineapples), amyl butyrate (apricots), and hundreds of others. Accordingly, synthetic flavors are of major importance in the food industry.

Of more than 1100 substances now used in flavors, most have been found to occur naturally or to be closely related chemically to those already analytically identified in foods. Vanillin flavor is used three times more often than natural vanilla, synthetic strawberry flavor two times more often than natural strawberry, and synthetic Concord grape five times its equivalent in Concord-type grapes grown of all purposes.

Flavors are of two general classes: natural or true and synthetic or imitation. Natural flavors include those already discussed. Imitation flavor materials include mixtures of aromatic chemicals, either alone or blended with natural flavors. These serve as the structural materials for the flavorist who is building flavor. Table 4 shows the ingredients of an orange flavor.

Flavor ingredients may be stabilized with sodium benzoate to avoid microbiological spoilage. Chemical deterioration is most often due to their reaction with oxygen from the air. To preclude this type of spoilage, suitable antioxidants are added to the oils prior to or during processing.

TABLE 4. Orange Flavor Ingredients

Quality sought	Formulation		
Character Impact or Characterizing Flavor Notes	Orange oils	5.0	lb
	5 Fold orange oil	2.0	lb
	Terpeneless orange oil	0.125	lb
Contributor notes (not essential)	Citrus Oils	1–2	lb
Contributor Notes essential for juice character	Orange juice fortifier[1], imitation (mixture of aroma chemicals properly blended)	0.5	lb

[1]The imitation orange juice fortifier is prepared as follows:

Quality sought	Formulation		
Neutral Base present in most synthetic fruit flavors	Isoamyl acetate		
	Ethyl acetate		
	Ethyl butyrate (optional)		
	Isoamyl butyrate		
	Benzyl alcohol	49.0	parts
Primer—character impact note	Decyl aldehyde	10.0	parts
Naturalizer rounds out the composition	Orange oil(s)	20.5	parts
Toner imparts secondary notes	Ethyl anthranalate		
	Acetal		
	Ethyl formate		
	Octyl aldehyde	20.0	parts
Lifts or accentuates the flavor	Organic acid	0.50	parts
		100.0	parts

Source: Melillo (1968) re: Smith and Minor (1974).

CLASSIFICATION OF FLAVOR INGREDIENTS

In the United States flavor ingredients are generally classified as either natural or synthetic. In Europe a chemical identified in a natural material is termed nature-identical and may be used interchangeably with its synthetic counterpart in a natural flavor. Since regulations governing the use of flavor chemicals are in a state of flux, the U.S. Federal Register and the Food Chemicals Codex should be referred to regarding safety and the recommended level of use.

USDA Designations of GRAS Materials

The FDA designated three categories of GRAS materials in November 1974.

1. GRAS for intended usage, without regard to level.

2. GRAS with levels limited to historically used levels.
3. Regulated food additives having restricted use levels.

Category 2 includes products acceptable under the grandfather clause: based on widespread use prior to 1 January 1958 or prior sanction.

Physical Classification

Physical state (e.g., solid or liquid) of flavor ingredients is a criterion for their classification as shown in Table 5. There are also two general types of flavor ingredients, simple and complex. Examples of simple ingredients are chemicals such as vanillin and amyl acetate. A classification of simple ingredients by functional groups includes hydrocarbons, acids, aldehydes, ketones, alcohols, esters, and so on. Components of Natural Apple Aroma have been tabulated by functional grouping, as shown in Table 6. This system is being used by the USDA for its Scientific Literature Review in its program to verify the GRAS status of some 1000 synthetic or isolated flavor ingredients.

Flavor Carriers

Most flavors are blends of simple and complex ingredients dissolved in a suitable solvent that is compatible with the product in which they are to be

TABLE 5. Physical Classification of Flavor Ingredients

Solids	Liquids	Pastes
Crystals	Essential oils	Soft extracts
Powders	Folded	Resins (natural or prepared)
Freeze-dried	Rectified	Resinoids
Spray-dried	Terpeneless	Concretes
Dried extracts	Sequiterpeneless	Emulsions (creams)
Plated	Oleoresins	
Encapsulated flavors	Absolutes	
	Fluid extracts	
	Compounded oils	
	Alcoholates	
	Alcolates	
	Tinctures	
	Infusions	
	Distillates	
	Spirits	
	Soluble essences	
	Emulsions	
	Fractions and isolates	
	Concentrated juices	
	Single-strength juices	

Source: Fenaroli (1975).

TABLE 6. Components of Natural Apple Aroma

Hydrocarbons:	*Esters (continued):*	*Free and Esterified Acids:*
1-Butoxy-l-ethoxyethane	Ethyl butyrate	Acetic
1,-1-Diethoxyethane	Ethyl formate	Benzoic
1-Ethoxy-l-hexoxyethane	Ethyl hexanoate	Butyric
1-Ethoxy-l-methoxyethane	Ethyl 2-methylbutyrate	Formic
1-Ethoxy-l-(2-methylbutoxy)	Ethyl 2-methylpropionate	Hexanoic
-ethane	Ethyl octanoate	*n*-Hexenoic
1-Ethoxy-l-propoxyethane	Ethyl pentanoate	3-Methylbutyric
1-Methyl-naphthalene	Ethyl 2-phenylacetate	4-Methylpentanoic
2-Methyl-naphthalene	Ethyl propionate	2-Methylpropionic
2, 4, 5-Trimethyl-l, 3-dioxolane	*trans*-2-Hexen-l-yl-acetate	Octanoic
Free and Esterified Alcohols:	Hexyl acetate	Pentanoic
	Hexyl butyrate	Propionic
Butanol	Hexyl propionate	*Aldehydes and Ketones:*
Ethanol	Methyl acetate	
Geraniol	2-Methylbutyl acetate	Acetaldehyde
Hexanol	3-Methylbutyl acetate	Acetone
n-Hexenol	3-Methylbutyl 3-methylbutyrate	Acetophenone
trans-2-Hexen-l-ol	Methyl butyrate	Butanal
3-Hexen-l-ol	Methyl formate	2-Butanone
Methanol	Methyl hexanoate	Diacetyl
2-Methylbutan-l-ol	Methyl 2-methylbutyrate	Formaldehyde
3-Methylbutan-l-ol	Methyl 3-methylbutyrate	Furfural
2-Methylpropan-l-ol	2-Methylpropyl acetate	Hexanal
Pentanol	2-Methylpropyl propionate	2-Hexanone
Propanol	Pentyl acetate	2-Hexenal
2-Propanol	Pentyl butyrate	2-Methylbutanal
Esters:	Pentyl 2-methylbutyrate	3-Methylbutanal
	2-Phenylethyl acetate	2-Methylpropanal
Benzyl acetate	Propyl acetate	Nonanal
Butyl acetate	2-Propyl acetate	Pentanal
Butyl butyrate	Proypl butyrate	2-Pentanone
Butyl hexanoate	Propyl pentanoate	3-Pentanone
Butyl propionate	Propyl propionate	Propanal
Ethyl acetate		

Source: Fenaroli (1975).

used. Ethanol is the solvent that is most acceptable to regulatory agencies. However, other functional carriers that may be used include vegetable oils, propylene glycol, esters such as triacetin (glyceryl triacetate), dibutycin (glyceryl dibutyrate), and others.

General Methods of Preparation

Flavor ingredients are manufactured directly by synthetic routes or as fractions and isolates derived from natural sources or by complete recovery from natural sources. These ingredients are then compounded into finished products. Natural flavor ingredients are recovered by various unit processes including direct heating; steam molecular, vacuum, azeotropic, or fractional distillation; differential solubility; expression; chromatographic deterpeni zation, concentration; crystallization; lyophilization (freeze-drying); spray-drying; microencapsulation; and polymer-leashing (whereby flavor value is utilized, but the compound traverses the alimentary canal unchanged).

Flavors Produced by Heating Foods

Pyrazines, thiazoles, and volatile sulfur compounds form when foods are heated (as in roasting, baking, and cooking) as a result of enzymatic or non-enzymatic reactions. Maillard browning reactions between amino acids, amines or proteins, and reducing sugars occur in meat, poultry, fish, cheese, cocoa, coffee, bakery products, barley, dairy products, popcorn, nut products, potato products, rum and whiskey, soy products, vegetables, and other foods when they are heated, resulting in pyrazine formation.

Synthetic Pyrazines

Following isolation of pyrazine compounds from various foods synthetic pyrazines were produced between 1965 and 1970 and by 1975 more than 30 pyrazine compounds were included in the GRAS list of nearly 1400 GRAS approved flavoring agents.

Uses of Pyrazines

Applications for these pyrazine flavors include flavor enhancement of potato products, potato and green bell pepper flavor concentrates, peanut butter, instant coffee, cocoa, chocolate flavor, sugar syrup, cereal flakes, corn chips, margarine, beef soup base, cream cheese, bacon flavor, fondant, ice cream and milk pudding.

Volatile Sulfur Compounds

Volatile sulfur compounds occur in vegetables, meat, chicken, seafood, bread, chocolate, coffee, roasted nuts, mushrooms, pineapple, black currant milk, cheese, Japanese soy sauce, wine, whiskey, beer, and hops. Off-flavor in sun struck beer has been identified as 3-methyl-2-butene-1-thiol formed by an interaction between hydrogen sulfide sesquiterpene and other beer ingredients. Patents describing the formation of meat flavors by non-enzymatic browning reactions between hydrogen sulfide, mercaptan, cystine, and other volatile sulfur compounds; carbohydrates, aldehydes, monosodium glutamate, or hydrolyzed vegetable proteins have appeared regularly in scientific journals.

TABLE 7. GRAS Flavoring Ingredients and Usage Levels
Flavor and Extract Manufacturer's Association average maximum levels (in ppm) on which the Expert Panel based its judgments that the substances are generally recognized as safe for their intended uses

Substance	Baked goods	Frozen dairy	Meat products	Soft candy	Gelatins & puddings	Soups	Snack foods	Nonalcoholic beverages	Alcoholic beverages	Gravies	Other use categories
Acetoin acetate see 3526											
3526 2-ACETOXY-3-BUTANONE	49.3	20.0	—	47.8	20.0	—	—	20.0	20.0	—	
9-Acetoxy-1-*p*-menthene see 3566											
3-Acetoxyoctene see 3582											
3527 3-ACETYL-2,5-DIMETHYL-THIOPHENE	2.0	0.6	1.0	1.5	1.5	1.0	—	1.0	1.0	—	Milk products—0.6
Acetyl ethyl carbinol see 3550											
Acetyl methyl carbinyl acetate see 3526											
o-Acetylphenol see 3548											
Amyl ethyl carbinol see 3581											
Amyl ethyl carbinyl acetate see 3583											
iso-Amyl acetoacetate see 3551											
Amyl vinyl carbinyl acetate see 3582											
1,3-Benzenediol see 3589											
3528 1,2-BUTANEDITHIOL[a]	0.2	—	0.2	—	—	0.2	0.2	—	—	0.2	Nut products—0.2
3529 1,3-BUTANEDITHIOL[a]	0.2	—	0.2		—	0.2	0.2	—	—	0.2	Nut products—0.2
2-Butanon-3-yl acetate see 3526											
Butyl ethyl carbinol see 3547											
Campholenic aldehyde see 3592											
Carvomenthol see 3562											
Celery ketone see 3577											
3530 *m*-CRESOL	1.0	—			—	0.5	0.5	—	—	0.5	Nut products—0.5; Instant coffee & tea—0.5; Household seasonings & flavorings—0.5;

(continued)

TABLE 7. *(Continued)*

Substance	Baked goods	Frozen dairy	Meat products	Soft candy	Gelatins & puddings	Soups	Snack foods	Nonalcoholic beverages	Alcoholic beverages	Gravies	Other use categories
3531 CYCLOHEXANECARBOXYLIC ACID[b]	2.0	1		—	1.0	—	—	1.0	—	—	Fruit ices—1.0; Confectionery & frosting—2.0; Chewing gum—1.5
3532 3-DECEN-2-ONE	19		—	7.8	4.8	—	—	4.3	4.0	—	
Dallyl di-, tri-, tetra-, and penta-sulfides see 3533											
3533 DIALLYL POLYSULFIDES	1.		1.0	—	—	—	0.1	—	—	0.1	Processed vegetables—1.0; Household seasonings & flavorings—1.0
3534 1,2-DI[(1′-ETHOXY)-ETHOXY] PROPANE	330	54.9	—	137	273	—	—	62.5	54.8	—	Milk products —54.9; Processed fruit—54.9; Fruit ices—54.9 Condiments & relishes—273; Confectionery & frosting 137; Jams & jellies —273; Sweet sauce—273; Nut products —62.5; Imitation dairy products—54.9; Hard candy —137; Chewing gum —1546; Household seasonings & flavors—273

1,3-Diethylacetonyl 3-methyl-3-furyl sulfide see 3570											
cis-Dihydrocarvone see 3565											
Dihydrocuminyl acetate see 3561											
3,7-Dihydro-3,7-dimethyl-1H-purine-2,6-dione see 3591											
Dihydrojasmone see 3552											
m-Dihydroxybenzene see 3589											
Diisobutyl ketone see 3537											
1,3-Diisopropylacetonyl 2-methyl-3-furyl sulfide see 3538											
1,2-Dimercaptobutane see 3528											
1,3-Dimercaptobutane see 3529											
1,3-Dimercaptopropane see 3588											
2,5-Dimethyl-3-acetylthiophene see 3527											
3535 2,3-DIMETHYLBENZOFURAN	2.0	—	1.0	—	—	1.0	—	—	—	—	Condiments & relishes—1.0; Household seasonings & flavorings—1.0
3536 DIMETHYL DISULFIDE	16.9	4.8	2.2	9.4	8.3	—	—	4.8	2.0	—	Condiments & relishes—3.8; Sweet sauce—0.007
3537 2,6–DIMETHYL-4-HEPTANONE	5.0	2.0	—	5.0	1.1	—	—	0.8	1.1	—	
6,6-Dimethyl-3-hydroxy-2-methylenebicyclo [3.1.1]heptane see 3587											
3538 2,6-DIMETHYL-3-[2-METHYL-3-FURYL)THIO]-4-HEPTANONE	1.0	—	1.0	—	—	1.0	1.0	—	—	1.0	Nut products —1.0
3539 3,7-DIMETHYL-1,3,6-OCTATRIENE	15.2	7.7	—	15.2	4.0	—	—	2.3	4.0	—	
2,5-Dimethylphenol see 3595											
3,4-Dimethylphenol see 3596											
3540 2,6-DIMETHYLPYRIDINE	10.0	—	5.0	—	3.0	5.0	10.0	—	—	5.0	Confectionery & frostings—3.0; Nut products —5.0; Instant coffee & tea—0.15

(continued)

TABLE 7. *(Continued)*

Substance	Baked goods	Frozen dairy	Meat products	Soft candy	Gelatins & puddings	Soups	Snack foods	Nonalcoholic beverages	Alcoholic beverages	Gravies	Other use categories
3541 3,5-DIMETHYL-1,2,4-TRITHIOLANE	—	—	0.3	—	—	0.3	—	—	—	0.3	Milk products —0.3
3542 6,10-DIMETHYL-5,9-UNDECADIEN-2-ONE	10.0	10.0	—	10.0	10.0	—	—	10.0	—	—	
3,7-Dimethylxanthine see 3591											
1,3-Dipropylacetonyl 2-methyl-3-furyl sulfide see 3571											
3543 ETHYLENE BRASSYLATE	2.0	2.0	—	2.0	2.0	—	—	2.0	—	—	
Ethylene glycol brassylate cyclic diester see 3543											
3544 ETHYL CYCLOHEXANE-CARBOXYLATE[b]	0.01	0.01	—	—	0.01	—	—	0.01	—	—	Fruit ices —0.01; Confectionery & frosting —0.05
3545 ETHYL 3-HYDROXYHEXANOATE	5.0	1.0	—	—	1.0	—	—	1.0	1.0	—	Breakfast cereals —5.0; Other grains —5.0; Milk products —1.0; Fruit ices—1.0; Confectionery & frostings—1.0; Jams & jellies —1.0; Chewing gum —1.0;
3546 5-ETHYL-2-METHYLPRIDINE	1.5	—	1.0	—	—	0.5	—	—	—	0.5	Breakfast cereals —1.0; Nut products —1.0; Instand Coffee & tea—0.05;

Ethyl vinyl carbinol see 3584											
2-Furfurylidenephenyl-acetaldehyde see 3586											
Geranyl acetone see 3542											
3547 3-HEPTANOL	18.5	8.8	—	13 5	8.2	—	—	7.8	6.3	—	
Hexahydrocarvacrol see 3562											
2 Hexyl-2-cyclopenten-1-one and 2-hexylidene-cyclopentanone mixture see 3552											
3548 2-HYDROXYACETOPHENONE	0.2	—	0.1	—	—	0.1	0.2	—	—	0.1	Poultry—0.1; Condiments & relishes—0.1; Instant coffee & tea—0.1; Household seasoning & flavors—0.1
3549 6-HYDROXYDIHYDROTHEA-SPIRANE	—	0.2	—	0 2	0.2	—	—	0.05	—	—	
1-Hydroxy-2,5-dimethyl-benzene see 3595											
1-Hydroxy-3,4-dimethyl-benzene see 3596											
3550 3-HYDROXY-2-PENTANONE	10.0	10.0	—	10 0	10.0	—	—	10.0	—	—	
5-Hydroxytetradecanoic acid lactone see 3590											
6-Hydroxy-2,6,10,10-tetramethyl-1-oxaspiro-[4,5]decane see 3549											
3-Hydroxytoluene see 3530											
4-Hydroxy-2,6,6-trimethyl-bicyclo[3.1.1] hept-2-ene see 3594											
3551 ISOAMYL ACETOACETATE	166	83.2	—	10€	81.6	—	—	80.8	54.0	—	
Isoamyl 3-oxobutanoate see 3551											
3552 ISOJASMONE	2.3	1.9	—	2 5	1.9	—	—	1.6	10.0	—	
3553 ISOPHORONE	50.0	4.7	—	50 0	50.0	—	—	10.0	—	—	Condiments & relishes—1.0; Chewing gum —1.0; Household seasoning & flavors—1.0

(continued)

TABLE 7. *(Continued)*

Substance	Baked goods	Frozen dairy	Meat products	Soft candy	Gelatins & puddings	Soups	Snack foods	Nonalcoholic beverages	Alcoholic beverages	Gravies	Other use categories
4-Isopropenyl-1-cyclohexene carbinyl acetate see 3561											
4-Isopropenyl-1-cyclohexene-1-carboxaldehyde see 3557											
4-Isopropenyl-1-methyl-1-cyclohexanol see 3564											
3-Isopropenyl-6-methylcyclohexanone see 3565											
3-Isopropyl-6-methyl-cyclohexanol see 3562											
4-Isopropyl-1-methyl-3-cyclohexen-1-ol see 3563											
3554 5-ISOPROPYL-2-METHYLPYRAZINE[c]	4.0	4.0	—	4.0	4.0	—	—	4.0	—	—	
3555 2-ISOPROPYL-4-METHYL-THIAZOLE	—	—	—	1.0	1.5	—	—	1.0	2.0	—	Confectionery & frosting—2.0; Jams & jellies —2.0; Sweet sauce —1.5; Imitation dairy products—2.0; Hard candy —2.0; Chewing gum —4.0; Instant coffee & tea—2.0
3556 ISOPROPYL MYRISTATE	50.0	30.0	—	50.0	50.0	—	—	30.0	—	—	
Isopropyl tetradecanoate see 3556											
2,6-Lutidine see 3540											
3557 *p*-MENTHA-1,8-DIEN-7-AL	4.5	6.3	20.0	9.7	4.5	—	—	4.0	6.0	—	
3558 *p*-MENTHA-1,3-DIENE	21.5	11.5	20.0	17.8	12.0	—	—	12.0	10.0	—	
3559 *p*-MENTHA-1,4-DIENE	13.6	8.6	20.0	10.3	8.6	—	—	8.5	10.0	—	Hard candy —50.0; Chewing gum —25.0

3560 *p*-MENTHA-1,4(8)-DIEN-3-ONE	5.0	5.0	—	5.0	5.0	—	—	5.0	—	—	
3561 *p*-MENTHA-1,8-DIEN-7-YL ACETATE	16.0	8.0	3.0	16.0	4.0	—	—	2.0	4.0	—	
3562 *p*-MENTHAN-2-OL	14.8	7.6	—	14.8	4.1	—	—	2.2	4.0	—	
3563 *p*-MENTH-3-EN-1-OL	30.0	10.0	—	25.0	20.0	—	—	10.0	—	—	
3564 *p*-MENTH-8-EN-1-OL	47.5	20.0	10.0	37.5	20.0	—	—	14.6	10.0	—	
3565 *p*-MENTH-8-EN-2-ONE	15.7	7.3	—	14.0	4.7	—	—	2.7	4.0	—	
3566 1-*p*-MENTHEN-9-YL ACETATE	9.0	4.5	—	7.0	4.0	—	—	4.0	—	—	
3567 *p*-METHOXYCINNAMALDEHYDE	5.0	—	2.0	—	5.0	—	—	—	—	—	Milk products —2.0; Condiments & relishes—4.0; Confectionery & frosting—5.0; Jams & jellies —5.0; Sweet sauce —4.0; Household seasoning & flavors—5.0
3-Methylbutyl 3-oxobutanoate see 3551											
3568 METHYL CYCLOHEXANE-CARBOXYLATE[b]	0.1	0.01	—	—	0.1	—	—	0.01	—	—	Fruit ices —0.01; Confectionery & frosting—0.05; Imitation dairy products—0.01
Methyl disufide see 3536											
Methyldithio-1-propene see 3576											
3569 2-METHYL-3,5 or 6-ETHOXY-PYRAZINE[bc]	—	0.5	—	—	3.0	—	—	0.5	—	—	Confectionery & frosting—2.0
2-Methyl-5-ethylpyridine see 3546											
3-[(2-Methyl-3-furyl)thio]-2,6-dimethyl-4-heptanone see 3538											

(continued)

TABLE 7. *(Continued)*

Substance	Baked goods	Frozen dairy	Meat products	Soft candy	Gelatins & puddings	Soups	Snack foods	Nonalcoholic beverages	Alcoholic beverages	Gravies	Other use categories
3570 3-[(2-METHYL-3-FURYL)-THIO]-4-HEPTANONE	1.0	—	1.0	—	—	1.0	1.0	1.0	—	1.0	Nut products —1.0
3571 4[(2-METHYL-3-FURYL)-THIO]-5-NONANONE	1.0	—	1.0	—	—	1.0	1.0	—	—	1.0	Nut products —1.0
3572 5-METHYLHEXANOIC ACID[b]	10.0	—	—	—	—	3.0	5.0	—	—	—	Imitation dairy products—5.0
1-Methyl-3-hydroxybenzene see 3530											
1-Methyl-4-isopropenylcyclo-hexan-1-ol see 3564											
1-Methyl-4-isopropyl-1,3-cyclohexadiene see 3558											
1-Methyl-4-isopropyl-1,4-cyclohexadiene see 3559											
1-Methyl-4-isopropyl-2-cyclohexanol see 3562											
1-Methyl-4-isopropyl-3-cyclohexen-1-ol see 3563											
1-Methyl-4-isopropylidene-1-cyclohexen-3-one see 3560											
2-Methyl-5-isopropylpyrazine see 3554											
3573 METHYL 2-METHYL-3-FURYL DISULFIDE	0.5	—	0.5	—	—	0.5	0.5	—	—	0.5	Nut products —0.5
3574 4-METHYLNONANOIC ACID	10.0	—	5.0	—	—	2.5	10.0	—	—	2.5	Milk products —5.0; Imitation dairy products—5.0
3575 4-METHYLOCTANOIC ACID[b]	—	3.0	0.15	—	0.15	0.15	3.0	—	—	0.15	Milk products —3.0; Cheese—3.0; Confectionery & frosting—0.5
3-Methylphenol see 3530											
3576 METHYL 1-PROPENYL DISULFIDE	1.0	1.0	—	1.0	1.0	—	—	1.0	—	—	

3577 3-METHYL-5-PROPYL-2-CYCLOHEXEN-1-ONE	14.7	6.5	9.3	10.5	4.0	—	—	5.9	—	—	
3578 2-METHYL-4-PROPYL-1,3-OXATHIANE	0.1	0.1	0.1	0.1	0.1	—	—	0.05	—	—	
3579 1,4-NONANEDIOL DIACETATE	9.0	7.0	—	7.0	7.0	—	—	7.0	—	—	
3580 *cis*-6-NONENAL	1.0	0.3	—	—	0.5	—	—	0.2	0.1	—	Breakfast cereals—0.1; Fruit ices—0.3; Condiments & relishes—0.1; Confectionery & frosting—1.5; Chewing gum—1.0
trans-β-Ocimene see 3539											
3581 3-OCTANOL	4.8	4.0	—	4.0	4.0	—	10.0	4.0	1.0	—	Chewing gum—11.2
3582 1-OCTEN-3-YL ACETATE	4.8	4.0	12.0	4.0	4.0	—	10.0	4.0	—	—	
3583 3-OCTYL ACETATE	4.4	4.0	2.6	4.0	4.0	—	10.0	4.0	—	—	Chewing gum—2.6
3584 1-PENTEN-3-OL	8.8	4.3	—	5.0	4.3	—	—	3.5	2.0	—	
Perillaldehyde see 3557											
Perillyl acetate see 3561											
3585 L-PHENYLALANINE[d]	110	60.0	10.0	268	60.0	—	—	—	—	—	Milk products—66.0; Condiments & relishes—10.0; Confectionery & frosting—268; Sweet sauce—220

(continued)

TABLE 7. *(Continued)*

Substance	Baked goods	Frozen dairy	Meat products	Soft candy	Gelatins & puddings	Soups	Snack foods	Nonalcoholic beverages	Alcoholic beverages	Gravies	Other use categories
3586											
2-PHENYL-3-(2-FURYL)-PROP-2-ENAL	2.0	1.0	—	—	2.0	—	—	1.0	—	—	Confectionery & frosting—2.0
3587											
2(10)-PINEN-3-OL	1.0	1.0	—	1.0	1.0	—	—	1.0	—	—	
2-Pinen-4-ol see 3594											
Pinocarveol see 3587											
Piperitenone see 3560											
3588											
1,3-PROPANEDITHIOL[a]	0.2	—	0.2	—	—	0.2	0.2	—	—	0.2	Nut products —0.2
1-Propenyl methyl disulfide see 3576											
2-Propenyl polysulfides see 3533											
3589											
RESORCINOL	15.0	—	5.0	—	—	5.0	10.0	—	—	5.0	Condiments & relishes—5.0; Household seasoning & flavors—10.0
Tirpilene see 3558											
α-Terpinene see 3558											
γ-Terpinene see 3559											
1-Terpineol see 3563											
β-Terpineol see 3564											
3590											
Δ-TETRADECALACTONE	40.0	—	30.0	30.0	—	15.0	30.0	—	—	15.0	Fats & oils —30.0; Milk products —20.0; Cheese—30.0; Poultry—30.0; Confectionery & frosting—30.0; Imitation dairy products—40.0; Hard candy —15.0; Household seasoning & flavors—15.0

3591 THEOBROMINE[d]	1050	—	—	4020	795	—	—	—	—	—	Milk products —990; Confectionery & frosting—4020; Sweet sauces —3300
Tetradecanedioic acid cyclic ethylene glycol diester see 3543											
3,5,5-Trimethyl-2-cyclohexen-1-one see 3553											
3592 2,2,3-TRIMETHYLCYCLOPENT-3-EN-1-YLACETALDEHYDE	8.0	—	—	—	—	—	—	—	5.0	—	Condiments & relishes—5.0; Reconstituted vegetables—5.0
3593 1,2,3-TRIS [1′-ETHOXY) ETHOXY]-PROPANE	308	51.3	—	128	255	—	—	58.3	51.1	—	Milk products —51.3; Processed fruit —51.3; Fruit ices—51.3; Condiments & relishes—255; Confectionery & frostings—128; Jams & jellies —225; Sweet sauce —255; Nut products —58.3; Imitation dairy products—51.3; Hard candy —128; Chewing gum —1442; Household seasoning & flavors—255

(continued)

TABLE 7. *(Continued)*

Substance	Baked goods	Frozen dairy	Meat products	Soft candy	Gelatins & puddings	Soups	Snack foods	Nonalcoholic beverages	Alcoholic beverages	Gravies	Other use categories
3594 VERBENOL	1.0	1.0	—	1.0	1.0	—	—	1.0	—	—	
3595 2,5-XYLENOL	4.0	—	2.0	—	—	2.0	—	—	—	2.0	Nut products —2.0; Instant coffee & tea—2.0; Household seasoning & flavors—2.0
3596 3,4-XYLENOL	4.0	—	2.0	—	—	2.0	—	—	—	2.0	Nut products —2.0; Instant coffee & tea—2.0; Household seasoning & flavors—2.0

Source: Oser and Hall 1979. Reprinted with permission. Copyright by Institute of Food Technologists.
[a] Total dithiol added to any food not to exceed 1.0 ppm.
[b] Substance has not been covered in a Scientific Literature Review nor is it presently scheduled for future coverage.
[c] To be used at not more than 10.0 ppm in the finished food.
[d] To be used in cocoa substitute only.

TABLE 8. GRAS Flavoring Ingredients and Usage levels
Flavor and Extract Manufacturer's Association average maximum levels (in ppm) on which the Expert Panel based its judgments that the substances are generally recognized as safe for their intended uses

	Beverages (non-alcoholic)	Frozen desserts (ice cream, ices, etc.)	Confectionery	Baked goods	Puddings, gelatins, jams	Chewing gum	Meat, meat sauces, soups	Milk dairy products	Condiments, pickles	Other category use
iso-Amyl isobutyrate see 3507										
iso-Amyl 2-methylbutanoate see 3505										
iso-Amyl 2-methylpropanoate see 3507										
Amyl vinyl ketone see 3515										
Benzyl methyl disulfide see 3504										
3476 BIS-(2,5-DIMETHYL-3-FURYL) DISULFIDE	—	—	—	0.1	—	—	0.1	—	—	
3477 2,3-BUTANEDITHIOL	—	—	—	0.2	—	—	0.2	—	—	
3478 1-BUTANETHIOL	—	—	—	—	—	—	0.02	—	0.02	Seasonings—0.02
n-Butyl mercaptan see 3478										
3479 CANDELILLA WAX (wax from stems & branches of Euphorbia Cerifera)	30	10	15	—	—	—	—	—	—	Beverages, alcoholic—30
3480 o-CRESOL	—	—	—	—	—	—	0.5	—	0.5	Cereals—0.5, Seasoning—0.5
2,3-Dimercaptobutane see 3477										
1,2-Dimercaptoethane see 3484										
1,6-Dimercaptohexane see 3495										
1,9-Dimercaptononane see 3513										
1,8-Dimercaptooctane see 3514										
1,2-Dimercaptopropane see 3520										
S-(2,5-Dimethyl-3-furyl) thio-2-furoate see 3481										
S-(2,5-Dimethyl-3-furyl) thiosiovalerate see 3482										
3,7-Dimethyl-1,6-octadien-3-yl phenyl-acetate see 3501										
3481 2,5-DIMETHYL-3-THIOFUROYL-FURAN	—	—	—	0.2	—	—	0.2	—	—	
3482 2,5-DIMETHYL-3-THIOISOVALE-RYLFURAN	—	—	—	0.2	—	—	0.2	—	—	
3483 2,8-DITHIANON-4-EN-4-CARBOX-ALDEHYDE	—	—	—	—	—	—	0.2	—	0.2	Seasoning—0.2
Dithioglycol see 3484										
3484 1,2-ETHANEDITHIOL	—	—	—	0.2	—	—	0.2	—	—	
3485 o-(ETHOXYMETHYL) PHENOL	—	—	—	—	—	—	4.0	—	4.0	Cereals—4.0

(continued)

TABLE 8. *(Continued)*

	Beverages (non-alcoholic)	Frozen desserts (ice cream, ices, etc.)	Confectionery	Baked goods	Puddings, gelatins, jams	Chewing gum	Meat, meat sauces, soups	Milk dairy products	Condiments, pickles	Other category use
3486 ETHYL *trans*-2-BUTENOATE	3.0	8.4	16.1	20.7	5.71	—	—	—	—	Beverage, alcoholic—4.0
Ethyl crotonate see 3486										
Ethyl α-crotonate see 3486										
Ethylene dithioglycol see 3484										
2-Ethylfenchol see 3491										
Ethyl hendecanoate see 3492										
2-Ethyl-3-hydroxy-4H-pyran-4-one see 3487										
3487 ETHYL MALTOL	12.4	144	139	152	119	83	19.6	—	—	Misc.—140; Hard candy —27.9: Beverages, alcoholic—18.6
3488 Ethyl 2-METHYLPENTANOATE	5	100	500	400	—	1500	—	—	30	
3489 ETHYL 2-METHYL-4-PENTENOATE	—	1.0	3.0	—	1.0	5.0	—	1.0	—	Beverages, alcoholic—0.5
Ethyl 2-methylvalerate see 3488										
3490 ETHYL OCTADECANOATE	2.0	8.0	16.0	—	—	—	—	—	—	Beverages, alcoholic—4.0
2-Ethylpyromeconic acid see 3487										
Ethyl stearate see 3490										
3491 2-ETHYL-1,3,3-TRIMETHYL-2-NORBORNANOL	0.1	0.02	—	0.05	—	0.5	—	0.1	0.07	
3492 ETHYL UNDECANOATE	2.0	8.0	16.0	—	—	—	—	—	—	Beverage, alcoholic—8.0
Ethyl undecylate see 3492										
3493 *trans*-3-HEPTENYL ACETATE	2.0	2.0	3.0	—	2.0	5.0	—	—	—	
trans-3-Heptenyl isobutyrate see 3494										
3494 *trans*-3-HEPTENYL 2-METHYLPROPANOATE	2.0	2.0	—	2.0	2.0	5.0	—	—	—	

3495										
1,6-HEXANEDITHIOL	—	—	—	0.2	—	—	0.2	—	—	
3496										
cis-4-HEXENAL	—	—	—	—	—	—	0.2	—	0.2	Seasoning—0.2
3-Hexenyl isopentanoate see 3498										
3-Hexenyl isovalerate see 3498										
Hexenyl isovalerianate see 3498										
3497										
3-HEXENYL 2-METHYLBUTANOATE	14.0	16.0	28.7	37.0	14.7	0.57	—	—	—	Beverage, alcoholic—7.0
3498										
3-HEXENYL 3-METHYLBUTANOATE	14.0	16.0	28.7	37.0	14.7	2.6	—	—	—	Beverage, alcoholic—7.0
3-Hexenyl 2-methylbutyrate										
Hexyl isopentanoate see 3500										
Hexyl isovalerate see 3500										
Hexyl isovalerianate see 3500										
3499										
HEXYL 2-METHYLBUTANOATE	18.7	21.8	36.7	51.6	31.3	0.34	—	—	—	Beverage, alcoholic—7.0
3500										
HEXYL 3-METHYLBUTANOATE	21.5	25.0	36.7	51.7	31.3	0.23	—	—	—	Beverage, alcoholic—7.0
Hexyl 2-methylbutyrate see 3499										
3-Hydroxy-2-butanethiol see 3502										
2-Hydroxy-3-butanethiol see 3502										
2-Hydroxy-1-methylbenzene see 3480										
1-(2-Hydroxyphenyl)propane see 3522										
o-Hydroxytoluene see 3480										
Isoamyl isobutyrate see 3507										
Isoamyl 2-methylbutanoate see 3505										
Isoamyl 2-methylbutyrate see 3505										
Isoamyl 2-methylpropanoate see 3507										
Isopentyl isobutyrate see 3507										
Isopentyl 2-methylbutanoate see 3505										
Isopentyl 2-methylpropanoate see 3507										
3501										
LINALYL PHENYLACETATE	4.0	3.0	4.0	6.0	4.0	—	—	—	—	
Linalyl α-toluate see 3501										
3502										
2-MERCAPTO-3-BUTANOL	—	—	—	0.2	—	—	0.2	—	—	
3-Mercapto-2-butanol see 3502										
3-[(2-Mercapto-1-methylpropyl)thio]-2-butanol see 3509										

(continued)

TABLE 8. *(Continued)*

	Beverages (non-alcoholic)	Frozen desserts (ice cream, ices, etc.)	Confectionery	Baked goods	Puddings, gelatins, jams	Chewing gum	Meat, meat sauces, soups	Milk dairy products	Condiments, pickles	Other category use
3503 2,3 or 10-MERCAPTOPINANE	0.03	0.02	0.03	0.03	0.01	—	—	—	—	
Methialdol see 3483										
3504 METHYL BENZYL DISULFIDE	—	—	—	0.3	—	—	0.3	—	—	
2-Methylbutyl isopentanoate see 3506										
2-Methylbutyl isovalerate see 3506										
2-Methylbutyl isovalerianate see 3506										
3505 3-METHYLBUTYL-2-METHYLBUTANOATE	29.9	29.9	50.0	50.0	29.9	—	—	—	—	Beverage, alcoholic—20.0
3506 2-METHYLBUTYL 3-METHYLBUTANOATE	11.0	11.0	14.5	18.2	11.0	—	—	—	—	Beverage, alcoholic—50.0
3507 3-METHYLBUTYL 2-METHYLPROPANOATE	48.1	74.0	114	128.7	103	—	—	—	—	Hard candy 0.09; Beverage, alcoholic—21.1:
Methyl β-Hydroxycaproate see 3508										
3508 METHYL 3-HYDROXY-HEXANOATE	1.0	1.0	1.0	5.0	1.0	1.0	—	1.0	—	Beverage, alcoholic—1.0; Cereals—5.0
Methyl β-hydroxyhexanoate see 3508										
3509 α-METHYL-β-HYDROXYPROPYL a-methyl-β-mercaptopropyl sulfide	—	—	—	0.75	—	—	0.75	—	—	
3510 4-METHYL-2-PENTENAL	1.0	1.5	—	2.0	1.2	8.0	—	1.0	—	Cereals—1.5; Beverages, alcoholic—1.0
3511 2-METHYL-4-PENTENOIC ACID	—	2.0	5.0	—	2.0	5.0	—	2.0	—	Beverages, alcoholic—1.0
o-Methylphenol see 3480										
Methyl phenylmethyl disulfide see 3504										

3512										
2-METHYLTETRAHYDROTHIOPHEN-3-ONE	0.5	0.5	0.5	1.0	0.5	—	—	0.5	—	
5-(Methylthio)-2-(methylthio)-methylpent-2-en-1-al see 3483										
3513										
1,9-NONANEDITHIOL	—	—	—	0.2	—	—	0.2	—	—	
3514										
1,8-OCTANEDITHIOL	—	—	—	0.2	—	—	0.2	—	—	
3515										
1-OCTEN-3-ONE	—	—	—	2.0	—	—	1.0	—	—	
3516										
trans-2-OCTEN-1-YL ACETATE	0.01	0.05	0.1	0.15	0.1	—	—	—	—	Beverages, alcoholic—0.05
3517										
trans-2-OCTEN-1-YL BUTANOATE	0.005	0.02	0.04	0.06	0.05	—	—	—	—	Beverages, alcoholic—0.025
trans-2-Octen-1-yl butyrate see 3517										
Octyl 2-furancarboxylate see 3518										
3518										
OCTYL 2-FUROATE	5.0	10.0	20.0	—	10.0	20.0	—	—	—	
3519										
2-PHENYL-4-PENTENAL	—	—	—	—	—	—	2.0	—	2.0	
Pinanethiol see 3503										
Pinanyl mercaptan see 3503										
3520										
1,2-PROPANEDITHIOL	—	—	—	0.2	—	—	0.2	—	—	
3521										
PROPANETHIOL	1.0	1.0	1.25	0.929	1.0	—	2.2	—	—	Soups—3.0; Beverages, alcoholic—1.0
1-Propanethiol see 3521										
n-Propyl mercaptan see 3521										
3522										
o-PROPYLPHENOL	—	—	—	—	—	—	3.0	—	2.0	Seasonings—2.0
2-Propylphenol see 3522										
Propylthiol see 3521										
3523										
PYRROLIDINE	0.5	1.0	3.0	2.0	—	6	—	0.5	—	Cereals—1.5
Tetrahydropyrrole see 3523										
n-Thiopropyl alcohol see 3521										
2,4,5-Trimethyl-2,5-dihydrooxazole see 3525										
3524										
3,5,5-TRIMETHYLHEXANAL	3.0	2.0	12	20	7.0	40	—	—	—	
3525										
2,4,5-TRIMETHYL-Δ-3-OXAZOLINE	—	—	—	10	—	—	10	—	—	

Source: Flavor and Extract Manufacturers Association.

A GRAS list consisting of 88 sulfur compounds has been compiled by the Flavor Extract Manufacturers Association. These are used at extremely low levels for flavoring (usually below 1 ¼g/kg food).

Thiazole Compounds

Thiazole (sulfur) compounds have been known for nearly a century, but it was not until 1967 that a natural food system (namely, cocoa extract) revealed its presence as a nutlike odor. Soon afterwards these flavor substances were identified in boiled potato, potato chips, coffee, beer, beef broth, roasted nuts, popcorn, heated milk, shallow-fried beef, pressure-cooked beef, stale nonfat dry milk, rum, soybean milk, whiskey, and tomato.

Synthetic Thiazoles

Thiazoles have been synthesized that have odors resembling pyridine, nuts, green vegetable, green herbs, popcorn, cereal, meat, and green-tomato vine. Future applications of thiazoles as food flavors, contingent upon USDA approval for inclusion on the GRAS list of flavor ingredients, may be forthcoming.

GRAS Flavoring Ingredients and Usage Levels

The flavor and Extract Manufacturers Association has published a GRAS Flavoring Ingredients and usage levels report. This lists, for selected substances, the average maximum levels (in ppm) on which a government-approved expert panel bases its judgments that the substances are generally recognized as safe for their intended uses. This information is compiled in Tables 7 and 8.

CONCLUSION

Essential oils, oleoresins, spices, herbs, and other natural or synthetic flavorings used historically are currently being supplemented with an increasing number of new synthetic flavors based on compounds occurring in our natural food systems. When approved, these are labeled GRAS. For example, pyrazines, volatile sulfur compounds, and thiazoles useful as meat, poultry, fish, and vegetable flavorings have been approved by the USDA since 1970. Beef extract replacements have been developed using the 5′ nucleotide flavor potentiators that work synergistically to improve the performance of MSG in meats, poultry, fish, and vegetables. The flavor-potentiating value of maltol has likewise been demonstrated in bakery products and other sweet-goods. This new and enlarged spectrum of flavor capability may be traced to the application of new physicochemical analytical methods that continually reveal the presence of previously unidentified compounds in our natural food supply.

ACKNOWLEDGMENT

This material (in part) originally appeared in the *Cornell HRA Quarterly* and is reprinted here by permission. ©1966 School of Hotel Administration at Cornell University.

REFERENCES

AMOORE, J.E. 1952. Stereochemical specificities of human olfactory receptors. Perfum. Essent. Oil Rec. *43*, 321–23.

AMOORE, J.E., JOHNSTON, J.W. JR., and RUBIN, M. 1964. The stereochemical theory of odor. Sci. Am. *210*(2), 42–49.

ANON. 1959. "Charcoal-flavored" steaks without charcoal present—a real menace to consumers' health. Consumer Bull. *42*, 24–26.

ANON. 1965. In brief. The Sciences (N.Y. Acad. Sci.) *5*(4), 27.

AOAC. 1960. Official Methods of Analysis of the Association of Official Agricultural Chemists. Washington, D.C.

BARTHEL, J. 1966. Quando Manducamus. Status *2*(1), 47–50.

BEEBE-CENTER, J.G. and WADDELL, D. 1948. A general psychology of taste. J. Psychol. *26*, 517.

BEIDLER, L.M. (Editor). 1971. Handbook of Sensory Physiology, Vol. 4, Taste. Springer-Verlag, New York, Berlin.

BORGSTROM, G. 1965. The Hungry Planet. The Macmillan Company, New York.

BOUDREAU, J.C. 1980. Accounting for taste. The Sciences (N.Y. Acad. Sci.) *20*(3), 14.

BOYER, R.A. 1956. Method of preparing imitation meat products (pH control). U.S. Patent No. 2,730,448.

BREW, W.B., DORE, J.B., BENEDICT, J.H., POTTER, G.C., and SIPOS, E. 1959. Characterization of unidentified compound producing edema in chicks. J. Assoc. Off. Agric. Chem. *42*, 120.

BURR, H.K. 1964. Gas chromatography in flavor research. Food Technol. *18*(12), 60–62.

BURRIS, R.H. 1965. Snatch nitrogen from air. Sci. News. Lett. *87*, 68.

BYERRUM, R.U. 1965. The scientific revolution. Address given to graduate students, College of Natural Science, Michigan State University, September 29.

CAIRNCROSS, S.E. and SJÖSTROM, L.B. 1950. Flavor profiles: a new approach to flavor problems. Food Technol. *4*(8), 308.

CAUL, J.F. 1957. The profile method of analysis. Adv. Food Res. *7*, 1–40.

CAUL, J.F. 1958. Food acceptance. *In* Encyclopedia of Chemistry (supplement), pp. 139–143. Reinhold Publishing Corp., New York.

CAUL, J.F. and RAYMOND, S.A. 1964. Home-use test by consumers of the flavor effects of disodium inosinate in dried soups. Food Technol *18* (3), 95–99.

CHAMPAGNAT, A. 1965. Protein from petroleum. Sci. Am. *213*(4), 13–17.

CROCKER, E.C. 1945. Flavor. McGraw-Hill, New York.

DAY, E.A. 1967. Flavor of cheese. *In* Symposium of Foods: The Chemistry and Physiology of Flavors. H.W. Schultz (Editor), AVI Publishing Co., Westport, Connecticut.

DÖVING, K.B. 1967. Physiological basis of odor. *In* Symposium on Foods: The Chemistry and Physiology of Flavors. H.W. Schultz (Editor). AVI Publishing Co., Westport, Connecticut.

ESCOFFIER, August. 1941. The Escoffier Cook Book. Crown Publishing Co., New York.

FARBMAN, A.I. 1967. Structure of chemoreceptors. *In* Symposium on Foods: The Chemistry and Physiology of Flavors. H.W. Schultz (Editor), AVI Publishing Co., Westport, Connecticut.

FENAROLI, G. 1975. Handbook of Flavor Ingredients 2nd Ed. CRC Press, Cleveland, Ohio.

GESTELAND, R.C. and LETTVIN, J.Y. 1964. Smell governed by electrical process. Sci. News Lett. *86*, 328.

HALL, L.A. 1948. Protein hydrolysates as a source of glutamate flavors. Symposium on Monosodium Glutamate Vol. 1 pp. 53–61.

HALL, R.L. and OSER, B.L. 1965. Recent progress in the consideration of flavoring ingredients under the food additives amendment. III. Gras Substances. Food Technol. *19*(2), 151–197.

HENNING, H. 1924. Der Geruch. Barth, Leipzig.

HICKS, C.B. 1965. Your mysterious nose. Today's Health (October), p. 35.

HOFF, J.D. and FEIT, E.D. 1963. Functional group analysis in gas chromatography with the syringe reaction technique. Anal. Chem. *35*, 1298.

HONEYWELL. 1965. An investigation of the sense of smell through examination of individual olfactory cells. Sci. Am. *213*(6), 1.

HORNSTEIN, I. 1967. Flavor of red meats. *In* Symposium on Foods: The Chemistry and Physiology of Flavors. H.W. Schultz (Editor), The AVI Publishing Co., Westport, Connecticut.

HUTCHINGS, I.J. 1961. An introductory thought for food. Stanford Research Institute J. *5*, 2–3.

IKEDA, K. 1908. Japanese Patent 14805.

IKEDA, K. 1909. On a new seasoning. J. Tokyo Chem. Soc. *30*, 820.

JANOWITZ, H.D., HOLLANDER, F., ORRINGER, D., LEVY, M.H., WINKELSTEIN, A., KAUFMAN, R., and MARGOLIN, S.G. 1950. A quantitative study of the gastric secretory response to sham feeding in a human subject. Gastroenterology *16*, 104.

KAZENIAC, S.J. 1961. Chicken flavor. *In* Proceedings: Flavor Chemistry Symposium–1961. pp. 37–56. Campbell Soup Company, Camden, New Jersey.

KRAMER, A. 1964. Definition of texture and its measurement in vegetables products. Food Technol. *18*(3), 46–49.

KRAMER, A. 1965. The effective use of operations research and EVOP in quality control. Food Technol. *19*(1), 37–39.

KRAMER, A. and TWIGG, B.A. 1966. Fundamentals of Quality Control for the Food Industry, 2nd Ed., pp 105–154. AVI Publishing Co., Westport, Connecticut.

KUNINAKA, A. 1967. Flavor potentiators. *In* Symposium on Foods: The Chemistry and Physiology of Flavors. H.W. Schultz (Editor), The AVI Publishing Co., Westport, Connecticut.

KUNINAKA, A., KIBI, M., and SAKAGUCHI, K. 1964. History and development of flavor nucleotides. Food Technol. *18*(3), 29–35.

KURTZMAN, C.H. and SJÖSTRÖM, L.B. 1963. The flavor modifying properties of disodium inosinate. 23rd Annu. Meeting of Institute of Food Technologists, May 26–29. Paper 110. Detroit, Michigan.

LAIRD, D.A. and LAIRD, E.C. 1961. The Dynamics of Personal Efficiency, pp. 81–85. Harper & Brothers Publishers, New York.

LANGLEY, L.L. and CHERASKIN, E. 1951. The Physiological Foundation of Dental Practice. C.V. Mosby Co., St. Louis, Missouri.

LIEBIG, J. 1847. Über die Bestandtheile der Flüssigkeiten des Fleisches. Ann. Chem. Pharm. *62*, 257.

LIJINSKY, W. and SHUBIK, P. 1964. Benzo [a] pyrene and other polynuclear hydrocarbons in charcoal-broiled meat. Science *145*, 53–55.

MARSHALL, A.E. 1948. History of glutamate manufacture. *In* Symposium on Monosodium Glutamate Vol. 1 pp. 4–14.

MAXWELL, J.C. 1965. Will there be enough water? Am. Sci. *53*(1), 97–104.

McKINLEY, R.W. 1958. Odor- and taste-transfer testing. *In*: Flavor Research and Food Acceptance, pp. 94–96. Reinhold Publishing Co., New York.

MEYER, L.H. 1960. Food Chemistry, p. 160. Reinhold Publishing Co., New York.

MEREDITH PRESS. 1966. Family Medical Guide, pp. 580–581. Better Homes and Gardens, Meredith Press, New York.

MINOR, L.J., PEARSON, A.M., DAWSON, L.E., and SCHWEIGERT, B.S. 1964. Gas chromatographic analysis of volatile constituents from cooked carcasses of old and young chickens. Poult. Sci. *44*, (2) 535–543.

MINOR, L.J., DAWSON, L.E., and PEARSON, A.M. 1964. Flavor: its factors and significance. Poultry Meat *12*, 26–32.

MINOR, L.J., PEARSON, A.M., DAWSON, L.E., and SCHWEIGERT, B.S. 1965. Chicken flavor: the identification of some chemical components and the importance of sulfur compounds in the volatile fraction. J. Food Sci. *30*(4), 686–696.

MINOR, L.J., PEARSON, A.M., DAWSON, L.E., and SCHWEIGERT, B.S. 1965. Separation and identification of carbonyl and sulfur compounds in the volatile fraction of cooked chicken. J. Agric. Food Chem. *13*, 298–300.

MISC. & SAVORY. 1965. Synthetic foods forecast from coal, gas, petroleum. Food Technol. *19*(1), 60.

MONCRIEFF, R.W. 1944. The Chemical Senses. John Wiley and Sons, Inc., New York.

MONCRIEFF, R.W. 1949. A new theory of odor. Perfum. Essent. Oil Rec. *40*, 279–285.

MONCRIEFF, R.W. 1950. The salt taste. Perfum. Essent. Oil Rec. *41*, 367–371.

MONCRIEFF, R.W. 1950. The sour taste. Perfum. Essent. Oil Rec. *41*, 415–419.

MONCRIEFF, R.W. 1951. The sweet taste. Perfum. Essent. Oil Rec. *42*, 25–30.

MONCRIEFF, R.W. 1952. The bitter taste. Perfum. Essent. Oil Rec. *43*, 51–55.

MONCRIEFF, R.W. 1955. Taste, smell and molecular weight. Chemical Products *18*, 131–133.

MONCRIEFF, R.W. 1957. Stimulus for smell. Perfum. Essent. Oil Rec. *48*, 34–58.

MONCRIEFF, R.W. 1961. An instrument for classifying odors. J. Appl. Physiol. *16*, 742–749.

MONCRIEFF, R.W. 1964. Progress and problems in flavors. Manuf. Chem. *35*(9), 63–65.

MONCRIEFF, R.W. 1967. Introduction to the symposium. In Symposium on Foods: The Chemistry and Physiology of Flavors. H.W. Schultz (Editor), AVI Publishing Co., Westport, Connecticut.

NAGLE, J.J. 1965. Big gains are made by food seasoning. New York Sunday Times, Market Section, November 10, p. 9.

NRA. Undated. Spices—How to buy them—How to store them—how to use them, with cooperation of the American Spice Trade Association. Tech. Bull. 190, 2nd Rev. National Restaurant Association, Chicago, Illinois.

NEJUD, M.S. 1961. Factors involved in the mechanism of stimulation of gustatory receptors and bare nerve endings of the tongue of the rat. Ph.D. thesis, Florida State University, Tallahassee, Florida [Dissertation Abstr. *22*, 2285 (1962)].

NEWELL, G.W. 1961. Future trends in American diet. Ibid. *5*: 30–36.

OSER, B.L. and HALL, R.A. 1979. GRAS substances. Food Technol. *33*, 7, 65–73.

PRATT, C.J. 1965. Chemical fertilizers. Sci. Am. *212*(6), 62–76.

RIETZ, C.A. and WANDERSTOCK, J.J. 1965. A Guide to the Selection, Combination, and Cooking of Foods. The AVI Publishing Co., Westport, Connecticut.

SHARON, I.M. 1965. Sensory properties of food and their function during feeding. Food Technol. *19*(1), 35–36.

SMITH, A., FARMAN, A. and DAVIES, J. 1965. Absence of taste-bud papillae in familial dysautonomia. Science *147*(3661), 1040–1041.

SMITH, L.L. and MINOR, L.J. 1974. Food Service Science. AVI Publishing Co., Westport, Connecticut.

TOI, B., MAEDA, S., IKEDA, S., and FURUKAWA, H. 1963. Flavoring and preparation thereof. U.S. Patent No. 3,109,741.

VON BÉKÉSY, G. 1964. Duplexity theory of taste. Science *145*, 834–835.

VON FRISCH, K. 1964. Smell, sex, and survival in animals. Science Digest *53*, 65–72.

WANGERSKY, P.J. 1965. The organic chemistry of sea water. Am. Sci. *53* (3), 358–374.

WEED, W. 1965. Vanilla ice cream flavor standards. Personal communication.

WENGER, M.A., JONES, F.N. and JONES, M.H. 1956. Physiological Psychology. Holt, New York.

6 Standards in Nutrition

Everyone has to eat in order to live. How well one eats has much to do with how well one lives. The responsibility for assuring that people eat well rests not only with those who manage meals for their families but also with foodservice managers who prepare and serve meals away from home. About a fourth of the money spent for food in this country is spent in foodservices, and approximately 40% of all meals served are consumed away from the home. Both of these facts stress the rule that we all must be concerned about nutrition.

FOODSERVICE NUTRITION STANDARDS

Is food as nutritious when served in a foodservice operation as when it is served in the home? Do foodservices often serve food high in calories, salt, fats, and cholesterol? Do foods produced in quantity lack in minerals and vitamins? Is fast food junk food? Do many foods served outside the home contain undesirable or even harmful substances? Why do foodservices not do more to indicate the nutritional value of the food they serve? These and many other questions are asked by consumers who wish to eat foods that will maintain and promote health. Many nutritionists lament that food produced in quantity does not often meet established nutrition standards.

The United States Senate Select Committee on Nutrition has conducted hearings for a number of years to ascertain whether foodservices should be doing more to promote nutrition and protect customers. The committee is trying to determine whether foodservices should more effectively inform customers about the nutritional value of the food items it serves. The Federal Trade Commission (FTC) has also expressed concern that menus constitute an advertising medium and therefore should conform to the regulations applied to other aspects of food advertising. Should nutritional labeling laws apply to menus?

The foodservice industry has attempted to reply to these concerns. Some few foodservice managers say they are not in the business of informing the public about nutrition and do not have a responsibility to meet nutrition standards. In general, however, the industry has indicated its concern for meeting nutrition standards in the foods served and has pointed out that it will be glad to do much more in the field of nutrition when consumers ask it to do so.

Some who have tried to emphasize nutrition by serving meals that provide a high amount of nutrients relative to caloric content have discovered that their customers have not been especially interested. Foodservice personnel often report that the food served in their operations is as nutritious (or perhaps even more nutritious) than that served in the home. There are not many data to support such claims. Certainly, the nutritional value of meals served in many homes is also questionable.

Fast Foods and Nutrition

Studies by Appeldorf (1974) on the nutritional quality of fast foods, typified by McDonald's and Burger King, have shown that these foods are adequate in nutritional values if the consumer chooses the right menu, e.g., a quarter-pound hamburger, french fries, and a milk shake. Most foodservice managers claim that customers who know how to select proper food could obtain nutritionally adequate meals in their foodservice operations. They also question their responsibility to provide nutrition education for the public. In their view that responsibility does not belong to the foodservice industry.

Whether foodservice is doing its part in helping to resolve nutritional problems in this country cannot be settled here. However, the industry must pay more attention to nutrition by focusing on nutrition standards as it prepares and offers foods. Customers who are increasingly interested in nutrition want to know that they are consuming healthful foods. The governmental agencies of this country will also begin to insist that adequate nutrition standards are met. Managers, supervisors and subordinate workers in the foodservice industry will have to learn more about nutrition to discuss nutritional matters intelligently with customers.

In many commercial operations customers can select what they want, dine when they choose, and patronize whomever they wish. These facilities have lessened the ability to control which food items are consumed. The customer essentially determines the nutritional quality of the dietary intake. However, these foodservices should still assure that the menu include items offering a wide variety of nutrients.

Customers cannot expect a full complement of nutrients when they select food items that are simply less nutritious than others. Foodservices should, however, attempt to offer a wide variety of food items. Junk foods (high energy-content items that contribute few, if any, other nutrients) should not be the only food items offered.

Institutional foodservices incur other types of obligations for attaining nutritional standards. For example, hospitals and other health care facilities having great health responsibilities must be able to serve foods of maximum nutritional value as well as special dietary needs. Hospitals with adequate staffing and facilities should be able to provide almost any type of diet. Other health care facilities that lack the resources may have to limit dietary services. Many institutions have a major responsibility to serve well-balanced meals. These include prisons, schools, and other institutions in which residents essentially consume all meals on-site. Other facilities that provide only a part of the total dietary intake would assume a lesser responsibility. As a minimum, however, foods should contain all the nutrients originally contained in the food. Whenever customers have freedom of choice (of items selected, dining times, and the like), more responsibility for nutritional intake rests with the customer. Some in this group, such as school foodservices, may have a greater responsibility for nutritional education. However, since voluntary selections by students in higher grades is often permitted, the foodservice responsibility for serving nutritionally adequate meals begins with having all components of a well-balanced meal available and ends with the assuming of some responsibility for the development of nutritional habits.

NEED FOR FOOD

Food fulfills three of the basic needs of man: (1) to survive, grow, and reproduce—biological or physical needs; (2) to meet social needs—allowing people to come together with food and beverage as socializing agents; and (3) to fulfill psychological needs important to the individual.

Biological Needs

A baby may weigh only 6 lb when born, but is in reality a metabolic giant who doubles that birth weight in the first 3 months and triples it within a year. Twenty-one years later the baby may be a vigorous, healthy person weighing 180 lb. Such growth and vitality come about largely because of food.

The type of food consumed has much to do with the rate of development and health in the individual. Mental ability has also been shown to be dependent upon food. Poorly fed mothers give birth to children who have diminished brain power; offspring may even be mentally retarded. Insufficient food during infant and early childhood years will also demonstrably affect mental capacity. While effects are not so evident later in life, food undoubtedly still influences our mental processes. It also affects all our other body functions. We are what we eat. As one consumes a nutritionally adequate diet, physical and mental health improves. Good health, reproductive vigor, and living satisfaction are all associated with the physical return that food makes to the body.

Social Food Standards

Our social lives frequently revolve around food. The family gathers together for meals, and often family celebrations will center around the birthday cake or Thanksgiving or Christmas feasts. These are generally happy times, remembered throughout life.

On other occasions a gathering of friends may be enriched by serving food and beverages. Meetings, receptions, and social affairs of all kinds frequently have food and beverage as the central, unifying component. Few conventions ever conclude without a number of important events centered around luncheon and dinner activities. The luncheon table, made infamous by the three-martini businessman's lunch, is often where business negotiations occur. Without food and beverages our social and business lives would be less productive and enjoyable.

Historically, man has used food to commemorate specific events. Feasts are usually marked with the service of special foods. Food has been given strong religious significance. For example, the "body and blood" of Christ is symbolized by bread and wine. The Arab merchant who will not negotiate until the client has a cup of tea or coffee—the modern approach may be a Coke—is following an ancient custom that says, "My friend has come to deal with me; I am honored and must show my appreciation." Likewise, in ancient times the Irish met guests at the door and offered them a pinch of salt to show that they were so honored on the occasion that they would share their most precious food substance, salt.

Many foodservices profit heavily from the custom of incorporating foods and beverages into social affairs. Catering of weddings, receptions, banquets, and other events has become an important part of the income of the food and beverage departments of clubs, hotels, restaurants, and other foodservice operations.

Psychological Food Standards

Food also meets strong psychological needs within individuals. People do not go out to eat just to get filled up. They may dine out because they are tired of preparing food at home and because they are bored and want entertainment. Many profitable foodservices know this and cater to this need by featuring unusual food items. A businessman may take a client out to a very expensive restaurant knowing not only that its food and wines are good but also that the client will be favorably impressed. High quality foods and beverages have a prestige value. Some people will eat certain foods because of this factor. They use food and wine to show their cosmopolitan tastes, their affluence, and their status-consciousness.

Emotional Factors

Food is closely tied to our emotional makeup. Mother-love is supposed to arise in part because the mother feeds the child. Infants cry because they are hungry. Many people in later life over-indulge in food when they are emotionally disturbed. Food riots may occur in colleges just before exam time when the students are fed up with both the pressures of school and stereotyped, never-changing menus.

A businessman may go to his club and complain bitterly about the meal, perhaps not because the food or service is bad, but rather because he is upset over the events of the day. Many people in institutions show their disturbance at being away from familiar surroundings and family by protesting about the food (which may be of better quality than that they received at home). Some old and senile people may enter reality only when their meal is served, because food is something familiar. At mealtimes they recognize people, friends, and family. Once the meal has been consumed, many drift back into a dream world and again lose touch with reality.

Satiety Value of Food

Food has what nutritionists call a satiety value, which means that food can not only satisfy hunger but also provide an inner comfort. Often people who are emotionally disturbed overeat. In fact, some people are obese because they are emotionally upset; they eat to obtain an inner satisfaction not otherwise possible. Other people have strong psychological attachments to food. Others can get ill from eating certain foods, tasting a particular flavor or texture, or even seeing a distasteful food. Other persons have the opposite reactions; thinking about a food makes them hungry. Though they may not have an appetite, they will eat anyway because of this compulsive desire. Understanding how people react psychologically to food is valuable knowledge for those who serve food to the public.

NUTRITION SCIENCE

Nutrition science deals with the body of knowledge concerned with nourishment. The body cannot function unless it has certain chemical substances called nutrients, which are found in food. The body uses them to build bones, blood, and tissues for strength, energy, and warmth. The science of nutrition studies the identity and characteristics of nutrients and the roles they play in body functions such as digestion, absorption and use of food in the body, and elimination of wastes.

DIETETICS

Dietetics is the application of the science of nutrition. A dietitian has completed several years of study in nutrition, related scientific subjects, and other areas of concentration and practice in applying the principles of nutrition science. Many dietitians serve internships and constantly study and research to improve themselves professionally. A registered dietitian is an individual who qualifies academically as a dietitian, has passed a professional examination, is a member of the American Dietetic Association (ADA), and continues to advance professionally.

Nutrition is a young science. The roots of the study of nutritional science perhaps began when Lavoisier studied oxidation in the body in 1770. However, it was not until the early 1900s that information relating to nutrients and their functions in the body became the subject of concentrated study and research. For example Table 1 lists the 12 known vitamins and the dates of their discovery and synthesis. Except for niacin the dates are within the last 50 years. Current vitamin research is attempting to determine whether there are other vitamins and, if so, what their functions might be. Similarly, studies of minerals and the metabolic functions of the body relating to carbohydrates, proteins, and fats together with other investigations go on continuously.

TABLE 1. Known Vitamins and Dates of Discovery and Synthesis

	Discovered	Synthesized
Fat-soluble vitamins		
Vitamin A	1913	1947
Vitamin D	1918	1936
Vitamin E	1922	1937
Vitamin K	1934	1939
Water-soluble vitamins		
Vitamin C	1932	1933
Thiamin (B_1)	1921	1936
Riboflavin (B_2)	1932	1935
Niacin (nicotinic acid)	1867	1898
Pyridoxine (B_6)	1934	1939
Pantothenic acid	1933	1940
Biotin	1924	1942
Folacin (folic acid)	1945	1945
Cobalamin (B_{12})	1948	1973

Source: Stecher 1960.

THE NUTRIENTS

Nutrients are substances in food that nourish the body. They either make body substances or carry out some function in the body. The five main groups of nutrients in food are carbohydrates, proteins, fats, vitamins, and minerals. Three other factors that play a critical role in the utilization of nutrients by the body and are considered by some to be nutrients also are air (oxygen), water, and light. Alcohol, which could also be classed as a separate nutrient, is usually considered in discussions with carbohydrates or fats.

Table 2 summarizes the functions of various nutrients in the body and also indicates the calories per gram that carbohydrates, proteins, fats, and alcohol contribute. The remaining types of nutrients do not contribute energy in significant amounts.

Nomenclature

Nutrients are often identified by their chemical names. Carbohydrates, proteins, fats, and alcohol are organic compounds. When oxidized, they can produce either energy or warmth in the body. Their intake into the body is measured in grams (g); the volume of alcohol, a liquid, is often stated in milliliters (ml) or fluid ounces (oz). One milliliter of water weighs one gram. Alcohol is less dense than water, and 1 ml of alcohol weighs 0.8 g; 1 ml of alcohol contains 5.6 calories, and 1 fluid oz (about 30 ml) contains about 168 cal (30 ml/oz $\times$ 5.6 cal/ml = 168 cal/oz). The proof of alcoholic

TABLE 2. Nutrients and Their Functions

Nutrient	Functions	Kilocalories per gram
Carbohydrate	Oxidized to give energy or warmth; excess is stored as glycogen or fat.	4
Proteins	Build or rebuild cells, tissues, muscles and bones; the basic substance of the blood, lymph fluids, hormones, enzymes, and other body materials.	4
Fats	Oxidized to give energy or warmth; excess is usually stored as fat; protects and supports body organs and helps insulate and protect outer body surfaces.	9
Alcohol	Oxidized, metabolized, to give energy or warmth; excess converted to glycogen or fat and stored.	7
Vitamins	Help regulate the body; work with many enzymes, minerals, and other substances; basically protein in composition.	0
Minerals	Basic substances in blood, bones, teeth, eyes, hormones, and body constituents; work with vitamins and enzymes in regulating the body functions; help transfer nerve impulses.	0
Air (oxygen)	Oxidization of proteins, carbohydrates, fats; acts with some enzymes in their oxidative functions.	0
Water	The fluid in which most body reactions occur; helps form the blood and other body fluids; is important in body cellular functions; allows hydrolytic enzyme functions to occur; aids digestion through the metabolism process.	0
Light	Affects the function of endocrines and their production of hormones; light is known to be important in stimulating the production of sexual hormones in some animals and birds (but is not known to function this way in man).	0

spirits is defined to be twice their percentage of alcohol. Thus, the calories in 1 oz of 80-proof whiskey would be 1 × 168 cal × (80/2)/100 = 67 cal.

Food Energy Measurement

Energy in food is measured in calories. A calorie is defined as the amount of heat needed to raise 1 g of water at 4°C one degree Celsius (Centigrade). This is often called the gram-calorie. It is used in sciences such as physics and chemistry, but in biological sciences such as nutrition the unit kilocalorie is used. A kilocalorie (1000 gram-calories) is abbreviated as kcal.

The Food Standards Committee (FSC) of the European Economic Community (EEC) recommended that by 1 January 1978 the kilocalorie should no longer be used to indicate food energy values. It recommended that the kilojoule (kJ) should become the common unit to express energy value. The joule is a common unit used to measure mechanical power or energy. Thus, the recommendation was to substitute a mechanical value for a heat equivalent. A kcal equals 4184 J, and a kJ equals 0.24 kcal. The BTU is a common heat unit used in the English measurement system and equals 252 gram-calories. The BTU (British thermal unit) represents the amount of heat required to raise 1 lb of water 1°F.

The decision of the FSC has not yet been accepted in this country, but many nutritional texts do use both kilocalorie and kilojoule values.

Vitamin Standards and Potency Units

Vitamin and mineral values are usually given in milligrams (mg), micrograms (μg) or International Units (IU). An International Unit is a standard value based on the response of an animal to a given quantity of the vitamin. The IU was developed before the exact chemical nature of the vitamin was known, when the amount needed by an animal could not be determined. However, if 10 g of butter gave a certain standard growth to rats, this amount was translated into an International Unit value and used. The tendency today is to change IU values into other kinds of units. Table 3 indicates IU equivalent values.

TABLE 3. Weight Equivalents for International Units

International unit for vitamin	Weight equivalent
1 IU Vitamin A	0.344 μg vitamin A acetate, 0.3 mg retinol, or 0.6 μg of beta-carotene; a retinol equivalent (RE) is commonly used, and one RE equals 5 IU.
1 IU Thiamin	3.0 μg thiamin hydrochloride
1 IU Vitamin C	0.05 mg ascorbic acid
1 IU Vitamin E	1.0 mg alpha-tocopherol acetate
1 IU Vitamin D	0.025 μg cholecalciferol (vitamin D_3)

CARBOHYDRATES

Starches, sugars, and substances such as dextrin, pectin, gums from trees and plants, algins, Irish moss, agar seaweed, and inulin from Jerusalem artichokes are called carbohydrates. Largely composed of carbon, hydrogen, and oxygen, they are synthesized in plants that contain chlorophyll. These plants have the ability to join carbon dioxide and water together by using light energy, in the process called photosynthesis. When eaten, these carbohydrates are broken down in the body into carbon dioxide and water. Solar energy stored in them is released to be utilized for body energy or warmth.

Food Sources

Many foods are plentifully supplied with carbohydrates. Starch is found in corn, wheat, rice or other cereals; sweet potatoes or Irish potatoes; dried peas, beans, and other legumes; and items such as tapioca, arrowroot, or sago palm. The nutritive sweetener sugar is plentiful in cane or sugar beets, honey, molasses, maple syrup, and in some well-ripened fruits. Dried fruits such as raisins and dates are high in sugar. Total nutritive sweetener (sugar, honey, syrup, molasses, and so on) consumption has increased from 10% of total energy intake in the American diet in 1909–1913 to 14% in 1965.

The changing nature of the carbohydrate component of the diet has caused a decrease in fiber content (Leveille 1976). Cellulose is a fiber found in bran, vegetables, and fruits. It is a polysaccharide carbohydrate. Man lacks the enzyme needed to digest cellulose; however, some organisms do produce cellulose. Human beings need cellulose in the diet—about 5–6 g a day—to furnish bulk during digestion that will keep foods apart so that digestive agents can act on them. Bulk furnished by cellulose also helps in moving waste out of the colon.

Constipation is often caused by a failure to eat enough fruits, vegetables, and cereals that contain fiber such as bran (especially hemicelluloses). An all-vegetable (vegan) diet furnishes from 8 to 12 g of fiber a day. Although too much fiber can cause problems for some people because of irritation to the intestinal area, our diets generally are lacking in fiber. Another aide to digestion is pectin from fruits and vegetables, which reduces serum and liver cholesterol. Dairy products, meat, fish and poultry, eggs, fats, and sugars contain almost no fiber.

The average diet should get 55–65% of its total energy from carbohydrate. If less carbohydrate is in the diet, the body takes fat or protein for its energy needs.

Energy from Carbohydrates

Carbohydrates give 4 kcal of energy per gram. Thus, a man needing 2400 kcal in a day should eat slightly over 1200 kcal in carbohydrate, since approximately 55% of his total calories should come from carbohydrate sources. This is not hard to do. Foods such as bread, cereal, potato, beans, peas, and other items high in starch will furnish the major share. The rest will come from various other foods in the diet. A diet high in carbohydrate is less costly than one high in protein or fat. Using carbohydrates leaves less toxic residue in the body. Athletes do better on high carbohydrate diets; few eat diets high in fat or protein. They have learned that the high carbohydrate diet builds the largest store of reserve energy in the body and yields more energy and greater stamina.

Carbohydrate, Protein, and Fat Metabolism

All carbohydrates are broken down in the body to glucose, the only form of sugar the body can use. Glucose can also be made in the body from proteins and fats.

The necessary next step, the breakdown of glucose into energy, water, and carbon dioxide, is a very complex process. Many nutrients are involved. Necessary oxygen is transported from the lungs by the blood. The resulting carbon dioxide is absorbed in the blood and carried to the lungs where it is released. Water is absorbed and used in the body. Excess water carrying toxic wastes is eliminated as urine.

Glucogen Storage

Glucose need not end up as water and carbon dioxide immediately. The liver can change it into glycogen (also called body or animal starch) that contains high levels of energy per unit; the body stores glycogen in either the liver or the muscles. The average body stores from 900 to 1200 kcal as glycogen, as a reserve energy source that can quickly supply emergency energy. If the body has all the glucose it can use in the blood and muscles and all the glycogen it can store, excess glucose is changed into fat.

Amino Acid Synthesis

Glucose can also be used to make some non-essential amino acids (protein building blocks). Carbohydrates can also be converted into a sugar called ribose, which is used to make ribonucleic acid (RNA) and deoxyribonucleic acid (DNA). These substances are important in the regulating function of body cells. Ribose occurs at significant levels in meat, poultry, fish, and yeast.

Diabetes Mellitus

A diabetic is an individual who lacks the ability to use glucose efficiently. This condition may be caused by a failure of the pancreas to manufacture the hormone insulin, which must be present to utilize glucose. Alternatively, the body may make adequate insulin but for some reason not utilize it. If the first condition exists, the individual must take insulin injections. If the second condition is the cause, oral drugs can help the body to use the insulin properly. If a young person cannot handle carbohydrates, the reason is usually a failure of the pancreas to make insulin. Many people after age 45, especially women, fail to utilize the insulin their pancreas produces. Oral drugs are effective in this case. However, these drugs gradually lose their effectiveness; even these older individuals finally must take insulin by injection. Excessive hunger, thirst, and urine output; the accumulation of organic acids, acetones, and ketones in the blood; and weakness and a loss of body weight are symptoms of diabetes.

Controlling Diabetes

Individuals with diabetes must reduce their carbohydrate intake to below 50% of their food. The diet they must follow usually allows a specific number of carbohydrate or other food exchanges (menu variations). Thus, a diabetic may be allowed five exchanges of carbohydrate, four of protein, and several of fat, with an unlimited allowance of very low carbohydrate foods such as spinach, lettuce, celery, and leafy greens. Diabetics must balance their insulin and carbohydrate intakes. If it runs out of insulin, the body breaks down fat for energy; but, since it lacks carbohydrate to utilize the fat completely, the ketones, acetones, and other acid-producing products build up. This results in ketosis; the person can faint from an over-acid condition of the blood and can go into a coma and die. An individual who faints from a lack of carbohydrate and then revives may be given some sweet food or liquid item.

The Lactose Problem

Some people cannot digest the carbohydrate lactose found in milk. They lack the enzyme, lactase, that is needed to digest this sugar. Most individuals can produce enough lactase during infancy to digest milk, but many lose this ability as they grow older. From 60 to 80% of the people in the Near East, 70% of blacks, and 90% of Orientals as well as a large part of South and North American Indian populations lose the ability to manufacture lactase early in life. This also occurs in many Caucasians. Some people get ill when they consume as little as a glass of milk a day. Some Orientals are not able to eat butter or even margarines that contain some milk solids. Lactose can be added to milk inexpensively, but so far few dairy manufacturers do this. A few people have problems with lactose because of the simple sugar galactose that comes from lactose breakdown. Galactose is treated as a foreign substance by the bodies of those who are sensitive to it. However, soluble lactase in immunoenzyme form is now available in individual packets for those needing it to digest lactose.

Alcohol

Alcohol is often considered a carbohydrate or fat in nutrition even though it is different chemically. It gives 7 kcal/g, which makes it about twice as productive in energy as carbohydrates or proteins. Twelve ounces of 5% beer contains 120 kcal; 1 oz of 100-proof spirits yields about 100 kcal, and an average 6 oz serving of dry wine about 120 kcal. A sweet dessert wine may contain 140 or more kcal.

Alcohol breaks down in the body in a manner similar to fats. Therefore, many nutritionists are now beginning to consider alcohol as a fat rather than a carbohydrate. Anyone drinking a considerable quantity of alcohol should remember that each gram yields 7 kcal more than the 4 kcal/g provided by carbohydrates and fats. Alcohol supplies no other food-need than the need for energy.

PROTEINS

Foods containing amino acids are vital to life. Called proteins, they can come from animal or plant sources. Animal sources are milk, cheese, eggs, meat, fish, or poultry. Some vegetables such as legumes including soy beans, mung beans, lima beans, dahl, peas and others are high in protein.

Protein Requirements

The average diet should get 10–15% of its total energy from protein; about 25–50% of this protein should come from animal sources such as meat, lactoprotein (milk or dairy source), or eggs (ovo source). Thus, a young man needing 2400 kcal a day should have from 240 to 360 kcal from protein. About 60–180 of this energy should be from animal protein sources and the remainder from other proteins. As 1 g of protein yields 4 kcal, the diet should provide 60–90 g of protein, of which protein from animal sources should approximate 15–45 g daily. For example, an egg for breakfast, a cheese sandwich for lunch, and a thigh and leg of chicken for dinner provide 37 g of animal protein. If one adds a glass or two of milk and an adequate amount of cereals, fruits, and vegetables, animal and total protein needs are more than adequately met. Protein needs today may be calculated on a standard of 45 g for milk, meat, and egg products and 65 g otherwise, as the biological value of vegetable proteins is only about two-thirds that of animal proteins.

Biological Differences

Not all proteins have the same value in a diet. Animal proteins such as eggs, milk, cheese, meat, fish, and poultry have the highest value. These provide excellent protein sources of complete proteins that are effectively utilized by our bodies. Gelatin is not a complete protein. Cereals, nuts, legumes, and some other plant foods have fairly good protein, but they do not contain all the amino acids needed to completely meet the needs of the body. The proteins found in vegetables are very incomplete. However, by blending different grains we can make complete proteins, for example, soy and corn.

Alpha Amino Acids.

Alpha amino acids are organic acids having the amino group (NH_2) on the carbon atom adjacent to the carboxyl ($-COOH$) acid group, the alpha carbon. They are the basic structural units of protein and enter the body in this form. Nature provides them in optically active *levo* forms that rotate to the left on the plane of polarized light when tested in a polarimeter. The *dextro* form may be synthesized, but it is not useful in the diet, as the body will not use it. The body takes the essential amino acids and makes them up into substances such as blood, bone marrow, antibodies, hormones, flesh, collagen, and enzymes. There are about 20 naturally occurring amino acids. The body can make some amino acids if it has the right building materials. For example, it can take a glucose molecule and add an amine radical to make an amino acid. However, an essential eight or nine amino acids cannot be synthesized by the body; they must be ingested in food. Complete proteins contain all eight or nine essential amino acids as well as some nonessential amino acids in the proper ratio needed by the human body. Incomplete proteins such as gelatin lack one or more of the essential amino acids or have an improper balance of them for body needs. Growth, life, and reproductive functions depend upon the body getting these essential amino-acids in the diet. Table 4 lists the essential and nonessential amino acids.

Animal products other than gelatin furnish all essential amino acids in a proper ratio. Legumes and nuts contain all of the essential amino acids but, except for soybeans, they are not in the correct ratio. Cereals also contain all the amino acids but lack some in sufficient amounts. Fortunately, as amino acids not found in legumes are generally found in cereals, many cultures in the world have been able to exist on a cereal and legume diet. Consider, as an example the Hindu Indian people with their rice and dal or chapati

TABLE 4. Essential and Non-essential Amino Acids

Essential amino acids	Nonessential amino acids
Isoleucine	Alanine
Leucine	Arginine
Lysine	Asparagine
Methionine	Aspartic acid
Phenylalanine	Cysteine
Threonine	Cystine
Tryptophan	Glutamic acid
Valine	Glycine
Histidine[1]	Proline
	Serine
	Tyrosine

[1]Needed by infants because of rapid growth. After infancy the human body can made enough to satisfy its needs.

(wheat bread) and dal. The Chinese have done well for centuries on an essentially vegetarian diet.

It is important when considering different amino acids in various foods to recall that companion foods must be consumed at the same time. It does little good, then, to have cereal for breakfast and beans for dinner.

Biological Value

Another reason that not all proteins in the diet have the same food value is that some are not as completely digested and therefore not as well utilized in the body as others. For this reason, a large amount of some proteins in the diet will not contribute as much utilizable protein as other proteins in foods consumed in lesser amounts.

The amount of protein available to the body in food is often called the biological value (BV). The proteins in milk or eggs have the highest known BV. Almost all of these proteins are digested, absorbed, and used by the body. The highest possible BV that a protein can have is based on 100. Table 5 indicates the BV of some proteins. Table 6 shows the amount of selected proteins which is digested and utilized. Table 7 indicates the number of grams of particular protein foods needed to supply 70 g of protein.

BV may be somewhat related to the amino acid content of the protein. It is possible to take one food and supplement it with another to yield a protein value that is better than the sum of the protein values of the two foods when eaten separately. This improvement is called a synergistic effect. Thus, corn, which is low in the amino acids lysine and tryptophan gives a fairly high BV value when combined with a legume such as navy beans. A slight bit of animal protein such as beef added to bread made of white flour will increase the BV considerably, since meat adds lysine in good quantity.

TABLE 5. Nutritive Value of Proteins Determined by Different Biological Methods[1]

Method 1	Animal used	Whole egg	Egg albumin	Beef muscle	Casein	Peanut flour	Wheat gluten
Biological value	Man, adult	94	91	67	56	56	42
	Rat, adult	81	94	67	50	47	66
	Rat, growing	68	66	56	52	38	—
	Dog, adult	87	114	77	73	56	33
Protein efficiency ratio (PER) g gain in wt/g nitrogen consumed	Rat, growing	17.9	18.3	16.4	15.6	8.6	3.0
Protein depletion with or without anemia:							
g gain in wt/g nitrogen intake	Rat, adult	5.56	6.37	—	5.46	3.60	2.86
g body nitrogen gained/g intake	Dog, adult	0.49	0.30	—	0.48	—	0.22
Production ratio: plasma protein/hemoglobin	Dog, adult	86	63	30	31	27	36

Method 2	Whole egg	Spray dried skim milk	Casein (vitamin-low)	Soya bean meal	Dried brewer's yeast	Dried peas	Wheat gluten
Biological value	95	85	84	77	77	66	51
True digestibility	97	95	99	90	89	92	96
Net utilization value (Biol. value × true digestibility/100)	92	81	83	69	68	61	49
Net protein utilization	86	77	72	60	61	45	45

Source: Long (1961).

[1]Method 1: Nutritive value of six selected food protein sources. Results from a collaborative study sponsored by the Bureau of Biological Research, Rutgers University, New Brunswick, N.J.

Method 2: Nutritive value of nine protein foods determined on young rats at the National Institute for Research in Dairying.

TABLE 6. Digestibility and Body Utilization of Selected Proteins[1]

Food	Protein utilization[2]
Large egg	6.5 of 7 g
Whole egg (227 g)	7.5 of 9 g
Skim milk (227 g)	8 of 10 g
Broiled round steak (111 g)	26 of 35 g
Roast turkey (111 g)	23 of 33 g
Baked flounder (111 g)	25 of 33 g
Canned soybeans (111 g)	18 of 30 g

[1]Based on a comparison to eggs.
[2]Values are from several studies.

TABLE 7. Weight and Quantity of a Given Food Required to Provide 70 Grams of Protein

Food	Grams	Quantity
French bread	1400	70 slices
Chicken fryers	250	0.75 bird
Clams (canned)	450	2.25 cup
Cheese, Cheddar	280	10 oz
Cheese, Cottage	500	2.25 cup
Chicken chow mein	714	3.25 cup
Halibut, broiled	280	10 oz
Beef, hamburger (cooked)	300	10.75 oz
Beef, round (broiled)	255	9 oz
Beef stew	1110	4.75 cup
Lamb leg (roasted)	280	10 oz
Milk, whole	1952	2 qt
Oysters (canned)	800	14 oz
Peanut butter	250	8.5 oz
Pizza with cheese	800	28 oz
Pork loin (roasted)	300	10.5 oz
Salmon (broiled)	255	9 oz
Shrimp (broiled)	300	10.5 oz
Spaghetti and meat balls	900	9 oz
Turkey (roasted)	255	9 oz
Tuna, canned (drained)	240	8 oz

Protein Requirements

Table 8 indicates the protein needed daily by individuals of different sex, age, and state in life. Note that there is considerable variation in this need. Normal adults need 0.8 g/kg. Thus, a 130 lb (59 kg), 20-year-old woman needs about 47 g of protein daily. A 154 lb man (70 kg) would need 56 g of protein each day. A 6 oz hamburger steak yields 31 g of protein; a glass of milk provides 9 g. These two items together provide 40 g, which is a significant amount in the protein need for one day. The protein provided for

TABLE 8. Food and Nutrition Board, National Academy of Sciences–National Research Council Recommended Daily Dietary Allowances, revised 1980.[a]

		Weight		Height		Energy Needs (with range)				Fat-Soluble Vitamins			Water-Soluble Vitamins							Minerals					
	Age (years)	(kg)	(lb)	(cm)	(in)	(kcal)		(MJ)	Protein (g)	Vitamin A (μg RE)[b]	Vitamin D (μg)[c]	Vitamin E (mg α-TE)[d]	Vitamin C (mg)	Thiamin (mg)	Riboflavin (mg)	Niacin (mg NE)[e]	Vitamin B_6 (mg)	Folacin[f] (μg)	Vitamin B_{12} (μg)	Calcium (mg)	Phosphorus (mg)	Magnesium (mg)	Iron (mg)	Zinc (mg)	Iodine (μg)
Infants	0.0–0.5	6	13	60	24	kg × 115	(95–145)	kg × 0.48	kg × 2.2	420	10	3	35	0.3	0.4	6	0.3	30	0.5	360	240	50	10	3	40
	0.5–1.0	9	20	71	28	kg × 105	(80–135)	kg × 0.44	kg × 2.0	400	10	4	35	0.5	0.6	8	0.6	45	1.5	540	360	70	15	5	50
Children	1–3	13	29	90	35	1300	(900–1800)	5.5	23	400	10	5	45	0.7	0.8	9	0.9	100	2.0	800	800	150	15	10	70
	4–6	20	44	112	44	1700	(1300–2300)	7.1	30	500	10	6	45	0.9	1.0	11	1.3	200	2.5	800	800	200	10	10	90
	7–10	28	62	132	52	2400	(1650–3300)	10.1	34	700	10	7	45	1.2	1.4	16	1.6	300	3.0	800	800	250	10	10	120
Males	11–14	45	99	157	62	2700	(2000–3700)	11.3	45	1000	10	8	50	1.4	1.6	18	1.8	400	3.0	1200	1200	350	18	15	150
	15–18	66	145	176	69	2800	(2100–3900)	11.8	56	1000	10	10	60	1.4	1.7	18	2.0	400	3.0	1200	1200	400	18	15	150
	19–22	70	154	177	70	2900	(2500–3300)	12.2	56	1000	7.5	10	60	1.5	1.7	19	2.2	400	3.0	800	800	350	10	15	150
	23–50	70	154	178	70	2700	(2300–3100)	11.3	56	1000	5	10	60	1.4	1.6	18	2.2	400	3.0	800	800	350	10	15	150
	51–75	70	154	178	70	2400	(2000–2800)	10.1	56	1000	5	10	60	1.2	1.4	16	2.2	400	3.0	800	800	350	10	15	150
Females	11–14	46	101	157	62	2200	(1500–3000)	9.2	46	800	10	8	50	1.1	1.3	15	1.8	400	3.0	1200	1200	300	18	15	150
	15–18	55	120	163	64	2100	(1200–3000)	8.8	46	800	10	8	60	1.1	1.3	14	2.0	400	3.0	1200	1200	300	18	15	150
	19–22	55	120	163	64	2100	(1700–2500)	8.8	44	800	7.5	8	60	1.1	1.3	14	2.0	400	3.0	800	800	300	18	15	150
	23–50	55	120	163	64	2000	(1600–2400)	8.4	44	800	5	8	60	1.0	1.2	13	2.0	400	3.0	800	800	300	18	15	150
	51–75	55	120	163	64	1800	(1400–2200)	7.6	44	800	5	8	60	1.0	1.2	13	2.0	400	3.0	800	800	300	10	15	150
Pregnant						+300			+30	+200	+5	+2	+20	+0.4	+0.3	+2	+0.6	+400	+1.0	+400	+400	+150	*h*	+5	+25
Lactating						+500			+20	+400	+5	+3	+40	+0.5	+0.5	+5	+0.5	+100	+1.0	+400	+400	+150	*h*	+10	+50

[a]The allowances are intended to provide for individual variations among most normal persons as they live in the United States under usual environmental stresses. Diets should be based on a variety of common foods in order to provide other nutrients for which human requirements have been less well defined.

[b]Retinol equivalents. 1 retinol equivalent = 1 μg retinol or 6 μg β-carotene.

[c]As cholecalciferol. 10 μg cholecalciferol = 400IU of vitamin D.

[d]α-Tocopherol equivalents. 1 mg *d*-α-tocopherol = 1 α-TE.

[e]1 NE (niacin equivalent) is equal to 1 mg of niacin or 60 mg of dietary tryptophan.

[f]The folacin allowances refer to dietary sources as determined by *Lactobacillus casei* assay after treatment with enzymes (conjugases) to make polyglutamyl forms of the vitamin available to the test organism.

[g]The recommended dietary allowance for vitamin B_{12} in infants is based on average concentration of the vitamin in human milk. The allowances after weaning are based on energy intake (as recommended by the American Academy of Pediatrics) and consideration of other factors, such as intestinal absorption.

[h]The increased requirement during pregnancy cannot be met by the iron content of habitual American diets nor by the existing iron stores of many women; therefore, the use of 30–60 mg of supplemental iron is recommended. Iron needs during lactation are not substantially different from those of nonpregnant women, but continued supplementation of the mother for 2–3 months after parturition is advisable in order to replenish stores depleted by pregnancy.

the 20-year-old woman is 40 g provided ÷ 47 g required = 0.85 or 85% of her daily protein requirement.

If the 20-year-old woman became pregnant, she would need an additional 30 g of protein daily; if she were nursing she would need an additional 20 g of protein per day.

Infant and Illness Protein Standards

Infants need a lot of protein since they grow so quickly. In the first 6 months of life, a baby needs 2.2 g/kg daily. In the second 6 months this requirement drops to 2.0 g/kg each day. By the time the child is 4 years old, only 1.5 g/kg is needed daily.

During a long illness or after surgery, the need for protein can increase dramatically. For example, burn patients need a tremendous amount of protein and other nutrients since the body losses are great from a burn injury.

Protein Standards for Laborers

Some people think that those who work at hard manual labor need more protein. They do not. They may, however, need more calories since they have a greater energy expenditure. Athletes such as distance runners actually have more stamina or lasting power if they are on a high carbohydrate rather than a high protein diet.

Cost of Animal Protein

Animal protein is our highest-priced staple food. Many people on low incomes must restrict the amount of animal protein they purchase and thus may not get enough quality protein. Some concern has been voiced about the amount of saturated fat in meat. Research has been continuing to reduce the fat and cholesterol content of beef, milk, butter, cheese, and ice cream (Trenkle and Willham 1977). Animal fat blended with safflower oil gives a less saturated fat; however, the fat is softer and greasier.

The cost of meat is also the subject of research. New cattle breeds such as beefalo (a cross between the buffalo and Charolais and Hereford cattle) may bring about lower costs because larger, leaner animals are produced in a shorter period of time with less expensive feed sources. The use of different kinds of feeds, drugs, hormones, and other products may also assist in producing more meat in a shorter time; but these methods and substances should be investigated carefully to assure that they do not produce products harmful to the public health.

Mariculture

Perhaps the seas, lakes, and streams can be used more to produce needed good quality protein. The Food and Agricultural Organization (FAO) of the United Nations conducts a wide number of projects in undeveloped countries to show individuals how to raise fish in small ponds (Brown and Gratzek 1980). In the United States the raising of catfish has been extremely successful. The mariculture (ocean cultivation) of the edible blue mussel promises to give 1000 lb more meat per acre of coastal water than our prairies yield per acre in beef. Table 9 gives a comparison of the nutrients in 100 g of T-bone steak and blue mussels. Producing the blue mussel is economical and not difficult.

TABLE 9. Nutrients in Blue Mussel and T-Bone Steak

Nutrients	Blue mussel (100 g)	T-bone steak (choice) (100 g)
Energy	95 kcal	395 kcal
Protein	14.4 g	14.7 g
Fat	2.2 g	37.1 g
Carbohydrates	2.2 g	0
Calcium	88.0 mg	8.0 mg
Phosphorus	236.0 mg	135.0 mg
Iron	3.4 mg	2.2 mg
Thiamin	0.16 mg	0.06 mg
Riboflavin	0.21 mg	0.13 mg

Source: Hurlburt 1974.

Meat Analogs

The use of soy bean products and other analogs high in high quality protein is increasing, and undoubtedly this trend will continue as the cost of meat rises. The fact that these cereal or legume proteins are low in fat is helpful in reducing calories and cholesterol in the diet.

The market has accepted foods containing soy protein when they possess flavor attributes similar to those of meat. The relative flavor acceptability of both simulated and natural beef and ham loaves was organoleptically tested in a workshop of foodservice executives at Michigan State University (Minor 1972). The formulas used for the simulated meats are given in Fig. 1. Prejudice may have influenced the results. Several inexplicably low scores for the simulated products and the refusal of one panelist to taste the simulated meat loaves indicated that there was probably some predisposition to favor the natural meat loaves prepared for the comparison.

Simulated Beef Loaf

Ingredient	*Amount*
Prepared soy protein fiber	1½ cups
Beef base	1 tsp
Hot water	2 Tbsp
Consomme base	1 tsp
Corn oil	2 Tbsp
Egg white	1 egg white
Brown sauce aid	1 tsp

METHOD: First combine beef base with hot water, consomme base, and brown sauce aid. Then combine this with soy protein fiber and add egg white and corn oil. Blend thoroughly. Place in a small loaf pan (6 in. × 3 in. × 3 in.). Bake 1 hour at 325°F.

Simulated Ham Loaf

Ingredient	*Amount*
Prepared soy protein fiber	1½ cups
Ham base	1½ tsp.
Hot water	2 Tbsp
Red food color (liquid)	4 drops
Egg white	1 egg white
Corn oil	2 Tbsp

METHOD: First combine ham base with hot water and food color. Then combine all ingredients and place in a small loaf pan (6 in. × 3 in. × 3 in.). Bake 1 hour at 325°F.

Beef Loaf (Control)

Ingredient	*Amount*
Stewing beef, ground*	1½ cups
Hot water	2 Tbsp
Beef base	1 tsp
Consomme base	1 tsp
Whole egg	1 whole egg

*Ground through a medium plate. Purchased locally, fresh.

METHOD: Premix hot water, beef base, and consomme base. Then combine all ingredients. Place in a small loaf pan (6 in. × 3 in. × 3 in.). Bake approximately 1 hour at 325°F.

Ham Loaf (Control)

Ingredient	*Amount*
Smoked canned ham (ground)*	1½ cups
Hot water	2 Tbsp
Ham base	½ tsp
Whole egg	1 whole egg

*Ground through a medium plate.

METHOD: Premix ham base and hot water first. Combine all ingredients. Place in a small loaf pan (6 in. × 3 in. × 3 in.). Bake 1 hour at 325°F.

Scoring the samples: A panel of 33 untrained judges scored the samples using a hedonic scale (0–9; extremely poor to excellent range).

The results of the tests were as follows:

	Beef Meat Loaf		*Ham Meat Loaf*	
	Simulated	*Natural*	*Simulated*	*Natural*
Range	8 to 2	9 to 5	8 to 3	9 to 6
Mean	4.41	6.25	6.25	7.74

Key: 9 or above, excellent; 8, very good; 7, good; 6, fairly good; 5, fair; 4, just passed; 3, poor; and 2 or below, very poor.

Fig. 1. Formulas and preparation methods for simulated meats.

Future Protein Sources

Undoubtedly, further research will find ways to improve some of these analogs and reveal other new or unexploited protein sources and combinations to increase our options. The use of single-cell proteins from yeasts, bacteria, and other fast-growing, fairly high protein organisms and attempts to develop cereals with all the essential amino acids in satisfactory ratio (a cultivar of corn already exists) will allow us to produce more protein using fewer resources.

The Need for Protein

If infants, children, and adolescents do not get enough good quality protein they will not grow normally. These individuals and others will also lack good blood and sufficient antibodies to fight disease and may experience other disorders such as fatigue, irritability, and a lack of energy. If an infant or child lacks protein, the disease kwashiorkor appears. This can occur even though the intake of carbohydrate and some other foods may be adequate. Kwashiorkor is generally found in underdeveloped countries among children between the ages of 6 months and 3 years; the second year is the most vulnerable, as the child is being weaned and is making the transition from breast feeding or formula to solid foods. Often diarrhea, infection, or some other health problem triggers the onset of the disease.

Vegan Diets

All vegetable diets (vegan diets) may lack a protein that carries vitamin B_{12}. Vitamin supplementation may be necessary to prevent pernicious anemia and other blood problems. Some vegetarian foods may be adequately fortified with vitamins and other nutrients. People on lacto-vegetarian or ovo-vegetarian diets usually consume enough vitamin B_{12} to meet body needs. However, even these diets may need supplementation.

LIPIDS (FATS AND OILS)

Fats and oils belong to a group of substances called lipids. Other lipids in the body are fatty acids, phospholipids, sterols, and lipoproteins. Fats usually come from animals, and oils come from vegetables; together they comprise the greatest amount of lipids consumed in food. Whereas from 1909 to 1913 only 32% of total caloric intake in the American diet was derived from fat, this level rose to in excess of 40% in 1965.

Table 10 shows the fat content of seven representative food classes.

TABLE 10. Fat Content of Seven Representative Food Classes

Percentage fat	Food class
90–100	1. Salad, cooking oils, fats, lard
80–90	2. Butter, margarine
70–80	3. Mayonnaise, pecans, macadamia nuts
30–50	4. Broiled choice T-bone and porterhouse steaks, spareribs, broiled pork chops, goose, cheddar and cream cheeses, potato chips, french dressings, chocolate candy
10–20	5. Broiled choice round steak, broiled veal chop, roast turkey, eggs, avocado, olives, chocolate cake with icing, french-fried potatoes, ice cream, apple pie
1–10	6. Pork and beans, broiled cod, halibut, haddock, and many other fish, broiled chicken, crabmeat, cottage cheese, beef liver, milk, creamed soups, sherbet, most breakfast cereals
Less than 1	7. Baked potato, most vegetables and fruits, egg whites, chicken consomme

Source: Deaman 1975.

Foods high in lipids include fats and oils, butter, margarine, mayonnaise, and sausage. Some foods such as bacon, potato chips, french fries, doughnuts, and cheese are also quite high. Fruits and vegetables are usually low in fat. Avocados are an exception; they have more fat in them (37%) than does cheddar cheese (32%).

Energy Standards

A lipid contains 9 kcal/g, over twice the amount in carbohydrates and protein (which yield 4 kcal/g and 2 kcal/g more than in pure alcohol. Fats and oils are the most potent high-energy foods one can eat. Only two lipid constituents are known to be essential, the essential fatty acids, linoleic and linolenic acids. If they are lacking in the diet of infants, skin lesions and rashes and other disorders will result.

Hydrogenation

Fats and oils are called triglycerides because they are made up of three fatty acid esters joined to a glycerine radical (glycerides). Some fats and oils are called saturated because all the carbon bonds in the fatty acid chains are completely filled with hydrogens or other substances. This will be shown in the structural formula, $-\overset{|}{\underset{|}{C}}-\overset{|}{\underset{|}{C}}-$. An unsaturated fat or oil has one or more of the carbons in the fatty acid chain connected to another carbon in the chain with a double bond, shown as $-\overset{|}{\underset{|}{C}}=\overset{|}{\underset{|}{C}}-$. A monounsaturated fatty acid has only one double-bonded pair of carbon atoms; a polyunsaturated fatty acid has two or more.

An unsaturated fat or oil can be made saturated by a process called hydrogenation. The unsaturated product is put into an airtight chamber, heated, and put under pressure and powdered nickel is added. Hydrogen gas is then bubbled up through the liquefied oil, which absorbs hydrogen, with the nickel as a catalyst. This increases the saturation level of the oil by producing a fat or shortening. When the desired saturation is achieved, the process is stopped; the nickel is filtered out and the product agitated, cooled, and solidified.

Soybean oil blended with other vegetable oils is hydrogenated in this manner to make solid or liquid vegetable shortenings. Many other kinds of fats or oils may be hydrogenated to make them more solid or more plastic (semi-solid) in consistency. Fats are also hydrogenated because a saturated fat or oil is more stable toward oxidative rancidity than an unsaturated one.

Margarine brands advertised as made from unsaturated vegetable oil may be a safflower and soybean oil blend. The vegetable oils are partially hydrogenated to reduce the unsaturation and to produce the desired melting point. When purchasing margarines that may be made of polyunsaturated products it is wise to read the label. If the fat or oil is hydrogenated, the label must say so. Winterized or chill-proofed cottonseed oil is made by chilling and separating the foots that precipitate upon chilling. This type of oil is the preferred salad oil.

Cholesterol

Cholesterol is a waxy, fatty substance that collects as plaques in the arteries of the body, where it can cause arterial and heart problems. It is also an essential ingredient that the body uses to make bile, sex hormones, and other substances. The problem occurs when cholesterol adheres to the inside of the arteries and finally narrows them so that the heart must labor harder or clogs them up. Such clogging, unless diagnosed and treated, can cause a stroke or heart attack. The clogging of the arteries, called atherosclerosis, is characterized by a high ratio of low-density triglycerides in the blood serum. Saturated fats and oils are thought to bring about higher cholesterol and low-density triglyceride levels in the blood; unsaturated fats and oils do not. Thus, many people having high blood pressure or heart problems may be on diets limiting both cholesterol and saturated fats in the diet. Weight loss and exercise help to alleviate this condition, and high-fiber diets with pectin are also helpful.

Whether limitation of saturated fats or cholesterol can reduce cholesterol in the blood has not been completely proven. The body manufactures 70% of the cholesterol in the average American. Some people make a liberal supply in spite of consuming very little cholesterol in the food they eat. Certain authorities think that the tendency to run a high or normal blood cholesterol may be a hereditary condition. However, most authorities now recommend a diet low in cholesterol and low in saturated fat but high in fiber for people with heart or high blood pressure problems.

Dairy Products and Cholesterol

Nutritional values of dairy foods are highlighted in USDA figures published in January 1978. Dairy foods contributed 11.1% of total energy available in the U.S. food supply in 1977. They provided 75% of the calcium, 39% of the riboflavin, 35% of the phosphorous, 22% of protein, 22% of the magnesium, 20% of the vitamin B_{12}, 13% of the vitamin A value, 11% of the vitamin B_6, 9% of the thiamin (vitamin B_1), as well as almost all the vitamin D intake and significant amounts of niacin. Milkfat, including that in butter and all other dairy foods, represented less than 7% of the total caloric intake of the nation and less than 16% of total fat intake (National Food Review 1979).

Dairy products and eggs have been targeted by the media and some scientists as being dangerous because of their cholesterol contents. Other scientists contend that with a balanced diet and exercise cholesterol buildup is controllable even when dairy products are in the diet.

Body Cholesterol Level Standards

The average American has 250 mg cholesterol per 100 ml of blood serum. Ninety percent of the people of the world, eating different diets than the United States citizen does, have levels of between 100 and 150. They seldom die of a coronary heart attack.

Plasma Lipoproteins

Plasma lipoproteins, detectable by an electron microscope, are carriers of fats combined with proteins. Attached to each of these particles is cholesterol, divided among three different kinds of lipoprotein particles.

1. Low-density lipoprotein (LDL). Some people born with high levels of LDL die in their teens of heart attacks; Western people have high LDL levels more often than do primitive people, and women develop high levels less frequently than do men.
2. Very low density lipoprotein plays a minor role in carrying cholesterol in the blood stream.
3. High density lipoprotein (HDL) is the eliminator of excess cholesterol via the liver. Even though it makes up a small proportion of the lipoproteins,

evidence is accumulating that high levels of HDL help protect against heart disease.

Jacobson Food Scorecard

Jacobson (1977) developed a Food Scorecard that assesses plus points for protein, key vitamins and minerals, starch and fiber, naturally occurring sugar, and unsaturated fat. Foods get minus points for sugar and corn syrup added by the manufacturer and for saturated fats. Minus points are also given if fat exceeds 20% by weight on a dry basis. The highest scorers are:

1. Vegetables: collard greens, frozen (126); kale with stems and midribs (118); broccoli, frozen (116); turnip greens (111); spinach, frozen (104).
2. Meats: beef liver (172); chicken liver (158); liver sausage (104); chicken breast (62); tuna fish (55).
3. Fruits: cantaloupe (99); watermelon (74); orange (68); strawberries (50); and grapefruit (45).

VITAMINS

The word vitamin comes from the words vital and amine; the latter word indicates protein. At one time all that scientists knew was that certain micro protein substances were essential to life.

Vitamins are body-regulatory substances that do specific jobs in the body. The body cannot synthesize them in sufficient quantity with, perhaps, the exception of vitamin K. Vitamins A and D can be made in the body when certain substances necessary to form them are supplied in food.

There are now 12 substances called vitamins; others may yet be discovered or proven necessary. Table 11 indicates the natural sources of some of these vitamins.

FAT-SOLUBLE VITAMINS

Some vitamins are soluble in fat but not in water. They are often found in vegetable oils and animal fats. The human body can absorb these vitamins and store them. When an excess of fat-soluble vitamins is stored, it may become toxic.

Vitamin A

Vitamin A is found only in animal tissues. However, plants contain carotenes and cryptoxanthins (carotenoids) that the body can manufacture

TABLE 11. Natural Sources of Vitamins

Vitamin	Milk group	Meat group	Vegetable group	Bread group
I. *Water-soluble*				
Thiamin	Milk	Eggs, lean meat, liver	Fruits, legumes, yeast	Cereal grain, embryos
Riboflavin	Milk, cheese	Liver, eggs, meat	Leafy vegetables	Wheat germ
Niacin	—	Liver, kidney, lean meat, eggs, fish	Peanuts, yeast, green leafy vegetables	Bran
Pyridoxine	Milk	Liver	Yeast, legumes	Cereals
Pantothenic acid	Milk	Liver, kidney, eggs	Yeast	Wheat germ
Biotin	—	Kidney, liver, heart, egg yolk	Peanuts, cauliflower, mushrooms	
Folic acid	—	Liver, kidney	Dark green leafy vegetables, lima beans, nuts, lentils	Whole grain cereals
Vitamin B_{12}	Milk, cheese	Meats, scallops, sole, haddock, eggs	Peas, soybeans, beets, carrots	Wheat, oats, corn
Vitamin C	—	—	Citrus fruits, alfalfa, cabbage, green and red peppers, potatoes, raw turnip, tomatoes, pineapple	
II. *Fat-soluble*				
Vitamin A	Cream, butter	Fish, liver, oils, eggs	Carotenes, apricots, leaves of green plants	
Vitamin D	Evaporated milk, fortified fresh milk, fortified margarine	Fish liver oils, salmon, sardines, herring, liver, egg yolk		
Vitamin E	—	Egg yolk, meat	Lettuce, spinach, legumes	Cereal, seed oils
Vitamin K	—	—	Alfalfa, spinach, cabbage, kale, carrot greens, tomatoes	

Compiled from Stecher 1960.

into vitamin A. Vitamin A values are often stated in International Units (IU) but milligram (mg) values are also frequently used. One IU of vitamin A is equal to 0.344 μg of vitamin A acetate, 0.3 μg of retinol, or 0.6 μg of beta-carotene. Thus, if a person needs 5,000 IU of vitamin A a day, the equivalent would be 1.72 mg of vitamin A acetate, 1.5 mg of retinol, or 3.0 mg of beta-carotene.

Sources of Vitamin A

Vitamin A is found in milk fat; butter and cheese have a good amount. Some foods such as margarine are fortified with vitamin A and contain substantial amounts. Vitamin A is also plentiful in cod liver oil and some other fish oils and in animal liver. Polar bear liver is so high in vitamin A that it can be toxic to those who consume it. Green leafy, and yellow or orange vegetables contain a lot of carotene (provitamin A) which the body converts into vitamin A. Yellowish fruits such as canteloupe, apricots and mangoes also contain carotenes.

Function of Vitamin A

Vitamin A is needed for good eyesight. Insufficiency can lead to night blindness or to a disease called dry-eye or xerophthalmia, which can end in blindness. Growth does not occur if vitamin A is lacking, and it is needed to build bones and teeth. Body infections are controlled if vitamin A is present. It keeps the mucous membranes of the body in good order and helps prevent the spread of infections in these membranes.

Vitamin D

The chemical names for the two types of vitamin D are cholecalciferol (D_3) and ergocalciferol (D_2). The latter is found in plants such as yeast and fungi, while the former occurs in animal tissues. Vitamin D is related to the sterols.

Vitamin D Variability in the Body

Vitamin D can be made under the skin of the body if ultraviolet rays from sunlight or sun lamps strike ergosterol. This substance becomes ergocalciferol (D_2). If these rays strike 7-dehydrocholesterol just under the skin, cholecalciferol (D_3) is formed. Darker skins prohibit the penetration of the ultraviolet rays in the skin and lower the amount of vitamin D produced. A fair-skinned person who gets deeply tanned manufactures less vitamin D than before tanning; black races make less vitamin D than do Orientals. Black children often develop rickets (a bone disease) because they do not make much vitamin D. People living in urban areas where the sun seldom reaches the street and where there is a lot of overcast or smog may need vitamin D supplements.

Function of Vitamin D

Vitamin D mobilizes calcium and phosphorus to build bones and teeth and helps to maintain them. Vitamin D must be present in the intestines in order for calcium to be absorbed. It may also be involved in cell growth. Elderly people lacking vitamin D begin to lose calcium from their bones. Finally the bones become so fragile they easily break.

Food Sources of Vitamin D

Good sources of vitamin D are egg yolk, irradiated milk, seafood, seafish, butter, fortified margarine, liver, and fish liver oils. It is possible to get too much of the vitamin, which can cause hypervitaminosis. Some nutritionists warn mothers not to give their children cod liver oil, since they may get enough vitamin D in fortified foods.

Vitamin E (Tocopherol)

At one time it was thought that vitamin E was necessary for fertility; it became known as the fertility vitamin. The name, tocopherol, means "to bear a child," from the Greek words *tokos* (childbirth) and *pherin* (to carry). Vitamin E is plentiful in most vegetable oils, and there is seldom a lack in the diet. Its main job is to act as an antioxidant to protect substances that would be destroyed in the body if they were oxidized. The nerve cells contain vitamin E; however, we do not know its function here. Noxious gases in smog such as carbon tetrachloride, alloxan, methyl cholanthrene, and hydrocarbons joined with nitrogen are thought to be destroyed in the lungs when vitamin E is present. Some of these gases may be cancer-producing; if so, vitamin E may be useful for heavy smokers. Claims that vitamin E cures some heart problems, stops aging, is good for muscle dystrophy, and the like have not been proven.

Vitamin K

Of the several forms of vitamin K, perhaps the most common is a synthetic form called menadione. There is usually no lack of vitamin K, as it is manufactured in the intestines. Its main job is to help blood to clot. Moldy clover, alfalfa, and other leguminous plants develop a substance that destroys vitamin K in the body. Some other substances such as coumarin (formerly used in artificial vanilla) also destroy vitamin K. Aspirin can reduce its effectiveness in the body.

Phlebitis, a disease in which blood clots form in the arterial and venous systems, is often treated by giving coumarin or other substances antagonistic to vitamin K, to help to liquefy the blood clots. Hemophilia or bleeder's disease is not related to a deficiency of vitamin K.

WATER-SOLUBLE VITAMINS

Most of the water-soluble vitamins belong to the vitamin B complex, a group of related vitamins. Vitamin C is the only vitamin in this group that is not in the B complex. Water-soluble vitamins are not stored in the body and should be supplied daily or at least frequently in the diet.

Vitamin B_1 (Thiamin Hydrochloride)

For a long time it was known that a water-soluble substance in certain foods would cure beriberi and also encouraged growth. The identification in 1921 of vitamin B_1 was heralded as a major step forward in nutrition science.

Function of Vitamin B_1

Thiamin is an important vitamin that helps to stabilize the nervous system. It is needed to utilize carbohydrates, help to change the amino acid tryptophan into niacin, and make ribonucleic acid (RNA) and deoxyribonucleic acid (DNA). Thiamin may help pyridoxine (vitamin B_6) to change amino acids into glucose or glucose into amino acids. Vitamin B_1 promotes a good appetite, muscle tone, and a positive mental attitude. A lack of thiamin may show in a palpitating heart. When thiamine levels are low, one can experience depression and even more serious mental problems. Thiamin is also necessary to promote fertility and lactation. The need for thiamin often is decided by the amount of energy used, as thiamin is necessary to convert carbohydrates into energy, carbon dioxide, and water. Alcoholics have a greater need for vitamin B_1.

Sources of B_1

Brewer's yeast and wheat germ are good sources of thiamin. Pork is a rich source, and other meats are fair sources. An adequate quantity of animal products supplies a fair amount of thiamin. Most dry legumes, nuts, and seeds have good quantities. Irish potatoes, leafy greens, peas, green beans, and other fresh legumes such as black-eyed peas contribute significant amounts. Whole-grain or enriched cereals are also good sources.

Vitamin B_2 (Riboflavin)

As a dairy worker poured out whey from a pail, he noted an irridescent thin film on the top. This fluorescent substance was isolated and found to possess beneficial effects when consumed. It was initially called vitamin G, but when it was found to be related to the B vitamins, its name was changed to vitamin B_2 and then to riboflavin.

Riboflavin is a fairly stable vitamin, but sunlight or ultraviolet rays destroy it. When glass milk bottles were used they were sometimes tinted green or brown to make them opaque to the rays and to help prevent destruction of riboflavin.

Function of Vitamin B_2

Riboflavin acts in the body in many ways. It works with niacin and thiamin to produce energy. It is also active in changing tryptophan into niacin and helps the body utilize tryptophan in other ways. In ariboflavinosis, symptoms include cracks in the lips and a swollen, very red tongue. When dogs lack riboflavin their tongues change to a purplish black color, which gave rise to the term black tongue for ariboflavinosis. If the shortage continues, skin deterioration occurs, and the individual develops a hard, scaly condition called shark skin. Blood abnormalities may appear, the liver may fail to function properly, and nervous disorders may arise. Vision is impaired and light distresses the eyes.

Sources of Vitamin B_2

Good sources of riboflavin are milk, yeast, organ meats, and milk products. Meat, fish, eggs, leafy greens, and whole or enriched cereals are other good sources.

Niacin (Nicotinic Acid) and Its Functions

The ancients identified the disease pellagra, but they did not know that a food substance, now called niacin or nicotinic acid, could cure it. Niacin often interacts with enzymes in the body as a coenzyme. One of these removes hydrogen substances from compounds in the body. It also helps build or break down fats and glucose. Niacin itself also helps in cell and tissue respirations. Some forms of niacin help extend or swell the capillary system, which can be an effective treatment for high blood pressure.

The body can make niacin from tryptophan, using 60 mg of tryptophan to make 1 mg of niacin. Therefore the amount of tryptophan in food is considered when estimating how much niacin a person gets. One may hear then of the niacin value of foods rather than just the amount of niacin present.

Sources of Niacin

Niacin is found in organ meats, brewer's yeast, tuna fish, meat, poultry, some nuts, and enriched or whole grains. Milk and its products contain a small amount of niacin and also a good quantity of tryptophan. Vegetables such as legumes contain fair amounts of niacin or tryptophan.

Vitamin B_6 (Pyridoxine)

Two forms of pyridoxine exist in animal tissues; one is found in vegetables. Vitamin B_6 works in the body mainly by changing amino acids into proteins or proteins into amino acids, since it has the ability to add or to remove the amino group (NH_{2}-). Vitamin B_6 can also remove or add either carboxyl (—COOH—) or sulfhydryl (—SH) radicals. Thus, it is active in making chemical changes in the body. Sometimes a lack of pyridoxine is mistaken for a lack of niacin because the symptoms are similar.

Functions and Sources of Vitamin B_6

Vitamin B_6 joins with phosphates and other substances to make over 50 enzymes in the body. A lowered amount can cause skin lesions, convulsions, and anemia. Mother's milk has enough pyridoxine for infant growth but cow's milk does not; infant formulas may need supplementation to furnish what the child needs for growth. Growth can stop in children if vitamin B_6 is lacking. Pyridoxine is involved in the metabolism of fats and the manufacture of blood. It may be helpful in forming histamines, serotonin, and other body substances. Good sources are meats, fish, poultry, liver, vegetables, and whole grain cereals.

Folacin (Folic Acid, Folate or Folinic Acid)

The word folacin comes from foliage, because this vitamin is plentiful in green plants. It is concerned with conversion of carbon substances in the body. It can change the amino acid phenylalanine to tyrosine, cystine into methionine, and glycine into serine. It helps make choline, which may be a B-complex vitamin. It can change many substances containing nitrogen into other nitrogen-containing substances. It is important in making blood. If it is lacking, anemia may develop.

Biotin

The word biotin comes from the Greek word *bios* (life) and from the word vitamin. It helps to metabolize amino acids, proteins, carbohydrates, and fats in the body. It can add or remove carbon dioxide from body substances, which makes it helpful in utilizing fatty acid and other carbon chains in food. It is essential for the production of energy in the body.

Since the body makes some of the biotin it needs, few deficiencies are seen. Good food sources are organ meats, chicken, yeast, eggs, milk, most fresh vegetables, and some fruits.

Vitamin B_{12} (Cobalamin)

Cobalamin comes from the words cobalt and amine, indicating that it is a vitamin that contains the mineral cobalt. It is essential in the diet to prevent pernicious anemia. It is also thought to work in changing carbohydrates into energy, and it may play other roles in digestion. It works with folic acid to change methionine into choline and to produce red blood cells. It may also have a role to play in the use of fat and protein in the body. It is found in liver, brewer's yeast, meat, fish, poultry, and dairy products. Whole grain cereals may contain some but are not generally good sources. Vegetarian diets may lack cobalamin. Animal proteins are the best sources of vitamin B_{12}.

Pantothenic Acid: Function and Sources

Pantothentic acid is important in converting carbohydrates to energy. It also helps make cholesterol, the substance choline, some fatty acids, red blood cells, and other body substances. Insufficient quantities can cause a change in levels of ascorbic acid and cholesterol. Riboflavin and pantothenic acid frequently work together. Organ meats are high in pantothenic acid; whole grain cereals and egg yolks provide high amounts. Milk is a good source, and two cups of milk a day (16 oz) provide all that one needs.

Vitamin C (Ascorbic Acid)

The term limey was applied to British sailors because a British naval surgeon discovered in 1847 that lemons, limes, and other citrus fruits prevented and cured scurvy, the disease often called the sailors disease. In 1932 Doctors King and Waugh of the United States and Szent-Gyorgyi of Hungary discovered that the substance responsible for the cure was ascorbic acid. It is called vitamin C or antiscorbutic acid.

Function of Vitamin C

Besides preventing scurvy, vitamin C helps make collagen, the initial structure of bones and teeth. Collagen also helps bind tissues together.

Wound healing occurs because collagen knits the flesh together. If an individual lacks vitamin C, stitched areas from old wounds may break apart. The nutrient also helps vitamin D make bones and teeth. With insufficient quantities, tissues become extremely fragile; bleeding may occur, which is one of the basic signs of scurvy. Sometimes bleeding gums show up as an early sign of the deficiency. Vitamin C helps to metabolize amino acids and iron and aids in making the hormones thyroxine and adrenaline. The pituitary gland needs vitamin C to function; without it tryptophan cannot be converted into serotonin. Vitamin C may also help in the clotting of blood. Infections can be controlled by vitamin C. If the nutrient is liberally supplied in the diet, Pauling (1976) states, colds and other pulmonary infections will be reduced. Others, however, say that taking massive doses does not help. The evidence is not clear, and it is probably best to follow USRDA recommendations at this time.

Sources of Vitamin C

Good sources of vitamin C include tomatoes, citrus fruits, canteloupe, berries, tropical fruits (excluding bananas), leafy green vegetables, cabbage, sauerkraut, and potatoes (if the latter are baked or consumed in fairly large amounts).

Potential Vitamins

There are some substances that may be vitamins since they seem to have vitaminlike activity in the body. Choline, discovered in 1949, is thought to be one. It can be made from the amino acid methionine. It may be a catalyst in the making of some hormones and in helping nerve impulses to travel. It may help in metabolizing fatty acids and amino acids. It is known to prevent fat accumulation in the liver. It is plentiful in foods, and there should be no insufficiency in a normal diet. Myo-inositol is another substance that may be a vitamin. Plants and fungi require it; the human may not. If it is needed it functions in the manufacture of body cells, especially those of the brain. It is found in grains, organ meats, yeast, wheat germ, and whole grain cereals.

MINERALS

Only 4% of the body is composed of minerals, but these nutrients perform important functions much like those of vitamins. Both are called micronutrients. Minerals are constituents of important parts of the body such as bones, teeth, and blood.

Minerals are inorganic substances. Some are metals such as iron, copper, and sodium. Others are nonmetals such as carbon, sulfur, and chlorine. Fourteen minerals are needed by the body, and at least three others may be. Some minerals are found in the body in minute (trace) quantities, but we do not know whether they are there because they have a function or simply by accident.

Functions of Minerals

Minerals perform specific body functions. Some ionize well, which gives them good chemical activity. Ions have the ability to carry electrical charges. A mineral that ionizes well can help transfer nerve impulses and do other things. Water is attracted to minerals, which makes minerals important in pulling water from or into cells. Cell metabolism often is dependent upon this transfer or upon the osmotic capability of minerals to combine with water. Sodium and potassium are, respectively, the principal ions in extracellular and intracellular fluids of the body.

Minerals and Alkaline–Acid Balance

Minerals are important in maintaining a proper alkaline–acid reaction in the body. The body has a neutral pH, about 7.0. The body must maintain this neutrality precisely; if it is not controlled, the individual dies.

Minerals and Essential Body Acids

Some minerals are present in body acids. Sulfur is found in sulfuric acid; phosphorus is found in phosphoric acid; chlorine is an important component of hydrochloric acid. Meat, fish, poultry, eggs, cereals, and some nuts produce body acids. A few fruits such as cranberries, plums, and prunes are also acid in the body. Spinach, rhubarb, coffee, tea, and cocoa also become acids. Many cereals contain high levels of phytic acid, which interferes with iron absorption and may contribute to iron deficiency.

Organic acids in lemon juice turn to alkalis in the body. Vegetables, milk, and most fruits are alkalizers. The phosphates in vegetables and plants become alkaline. Animal phosphates become acid.

Since the alkali–acid balance is very delicate, individuals should not try to influence it. Normally individuals have sufficient stores of acid or alkali materials to help the body maintain a neutral balance.

Copper and iron help make blood. Some minerals act to stabilize the level of fluids in the body, and others join enzymes and vitamins so that they can do their work. Iron is an effective metal that picks up oxygen in the lungs, carries it through the body in blood, and then helps to transport carbon dioxide back to the lungs.

Table 12 lists the various minerals in the body, Table 13 lists the main functions of vitamins and minerals, and Table 14 indicates essential functions of minerals in the body.

TABLE 12. Inorganic Elements Present in Measurable Amounts in the Human Body

	Metals	Nonmetals[1]
Essential	Calcium	Phosphorus
	Magnesium	Chlorine
	Sodium	Sulfur
	Potassium	Iodine
	Manganese	Fluorine[2,3]
	Iron	Selenium[2,3]
	Copper[2]	
	Zinc	
	Cobalt[3]	
	Molybdenum[2,3]	
Probably essential	Molybdenum[2,3]	Barium
		Bromine
	Strontium	Fluorine[2,3]
	Chromium	Selenium[2,3]
Nonessential	Aluminum	Arsenic[4]
	Lead[4]	Boron
	Nickel	Silicon
	Rubidium 20–40 ppm[5]	

Source: Crampton, E.W. and L.E. Lloyd 1959. National Research Council 1964.

[1]The major components of the soft tissue of the human body are carbon, oxygen, hydrogen and nitrogen. These are not included in the listing because they exist in organic compounds.

[2]Can be toxic if present in greater than optimum amounts.

[3]Classification differs according to source.

[4]Highly toxic

[5]ppm = parts per million

General Functions of Inorganic Elements:

1. Part of skeletal structure (Ca, P, F, etc.).
2. Maintenance of the colloidal state of body matter and regulation of some of the physical properties of colloidal systems—viscosity, diffusion, osmotic pressure (Na^+, Cl^-, Ca^{2+}, K^+).
3. Regulating acid-base equilibrium—buffers (eg. $H_2PO_4^-/HPO_4^+$; H_2CO_3/HCO_3^-).
4. As a component or activator of enzyme and/or other biological units or systems.

Calcium

Functions of Calcium

The mineral in greatest quantity in the body is calcium. It has four main jobs: (1) building and maintaining bones and teeth, (2) promoting muscle function and tone, (3) working to produce blood and other body fluids, and (4) helping maintain a proper body pH. An adult needs about 0.8 g/day, but

TABLE 13. Functions of Vitamins and Five Important Minerals

	Bones and teeth	Prevention of anemia	Blood clotting	Resistance to infection	Healthy gums	Healing of wounds	Night vision	Protection of moist tissues	Salt level	Thyroid function	Healthy nervous system	Energy
Water-soluble vitamins:												
Thiamine											X	X
Riboflavin											X	X
Niacin											X	X
Pyridoxine											X	X
Pantothenic acid											X	X
Biotin											X	X
Folic acid		X									X	X
Vitamin B_{12}		X									X	X
Vitamin C				X	X	X						
Fat-soluble vitamins:												
Vitamin A							X	X				
Vitamin D	X											
Vitamin E											X	X
Vitamin K			X									
Minerals:												
Calcium	X		X									
Phosphorus	X											
Iron		X										
Sodium									X			
Iodine										X		

Source: Smith and Minor 1974.

TABLE 14. Essential Metals in Body Functions

Metal	Amount present	Distribution	Effect of deficiency
Ca	1050 g, in 70-kg man 1.5% total body weight	99% in bones and teeth 10 mg/100 ml blood serum Weight ratio of Ca/P in bones is 2/1	Drop in blood Ca produces hyperirritability Tetany, death

Functions

Formation of bones and teeth (approximately 1% of bones Ca exchanged daily)
Blood clotting
Regulation of cell fluids in osmosis
Reduces irritability of nerve and muscle cells
Enzyme activator important in fat catabolism, glycogen formation (carbohydrate storage), release of chemical energy for cell work

Recommended Daily Amounts

0.8 g for adults and children under 9
1.4 g for teenage boys, 15–18 yr
1.3 g for teenage girls, 15–18 yr
Need increases during pregnancy
Need Vitamin D to aid in absorption
Best sources: milk, cheese

Metal	Amount present	Distribution	Effect of deficiency
Mg	35 g in 70-kg man 0.05% total body weight	Similar to phosphorus 70% in skeleton 2.5 mg/100 ml blood serum	Drop in blood Mg produces vasodilation producing a decrease in blood pressure Hyperirritability Tetany, death

Functions

Depresses nervous irritability
Activator of many enzymes, particularly important in carbohydrate metabolism

Recommended Daily Amounts

Not established
Requirements probably 2–300 mg/day for adult male; may be more
All-milk diet for extended period or alcoholism can produce deficiency

Metal	Amount present	Distribution	Effect of deficiency
Na	105 g in 70-kg man 0.15% total body weight	93% in extracellular fluid (i.e., plasma, interstitial fluids) Present entirely in ion form	Nausea, vomiting, vertigo, mental apathy, exhaustion, cramps, respiratory failure

Functions

Maintains osmotic equilibrium between extracellular and intracellular fluid
Maintains normal pH in blood
Muscle contractility
Conduction of nerve impulses

TABLE 14. *(Continued)*

Metal	Amount present	Distribution	Effect of deficiency
		Recommended Daily Amounts	
Not established since deficiencies rarely encountered Sodium may be restricted in certain disease conditions—diarrhea, vomiting or excessive perspiration may deplete sodium			
K	245 g in 70-kg man 0.35% total body weight	Almost entirely within cells Present entirely in ion form	Muscle weakness Poor intestinal tone with distention Cardiac abnormalities Eventual failure of respiratory muscles
		Functions	
Maintains osmotic pressure regulation and acid-base balance within cell Stimulating effect on muscle irritability Enzyme activator important to energy release and storage			
		Recommended Daily Amounts	
Minimum need probably about 0.8—1.3 g/day, about the amount in the usual U.S. diet			
Mn[1]	0.2 g in 70-kg man 0.0003% of total body weight	Primarily in liver; also in skin, muscle, bone	Inhibits normal reproduction and sexual development in animals
		Functions	
Activator of enzymes concerned with carbohydrate, protein and fat metabolism			
Fe	4.5 g in 70-kg man 0.004% total body weight	75% in hemoglobin Remaining 25% primarily in liver; some in bone and spleen	Anemia
		Functions	
Essential for formation of normal red blood cells Energy production in cells Acts in enzyme systems as a component of the enzyme or an activator			
		Recommended Daily Amounts	
Men 18 yr and older: 10 mg/day Women 18–55: 15 mg/day Boys and girls 9–15: 15 mg/day Best sources: lean meat, liver, eggs, dried beans, molasses			
Cu	0.1 g in 70-kg man 0.0002% total body weight	Blood, liver, kidneys, heart, brain	Anemia Other specific disorders in farm animals

(continued)

TABLE 14. *(Continued)*

Metal	Amount present	Distribution	Effect of deficiency
		Functions	
Helps in absorption of iron from gastrointestinal tract Enzyme system in hemoglobin formation Enzyme activator in other systems			
		Recommended Daily Amounts	
Minimum intake about 2 mg/day Ordinary diets provide 2–5 mg			
Zn[1]	Small	Liver, bones, epidermal tissue and blood	Unknown
		Functions	
Part of enzyme important in reaction causing CO_2 transportation and release by blood Activator of other enzymes Seems to increase action of two female reproductive hormones			
Co	—	Vitamin B_{12}	—
		Functions	
Essential for formation of Vitamin B_{12} since humans cannot form this molecule but must use it pre-formed. The need for cobalt is closely associated with the need for B_{12}. Enzyme activator (?) may be B_{12} function.			
		Recommended Daily Amounts	
Cannot use free cobalt but need it only in form of vitamin B_{12}			
Mo	—	—	—
		Functions	
Component of enzymes			
Si	—	—	Affects bones and teeth of rats and guinea pigs
Cr	—	—	Growth factor in experimental animals
Ba	—	—	Affects bones and teeth of rats and guinea pigs
P	700 g in 70-kg man 1.0% total body weight	80% in bones and teeth 35–45 mg/100 ml blood; mostly in red blood cells Present in all tissue, particularly nervous tissue	Unknown

TABLE 14. *(Continued)*

<table>
<tr><th>Metal</th><th>Amount present</th><th>Distribution</th><th>Effect of deficiency</th></tr>
<tr><td colspan="4">Functions
Formation of bones and teeth; about 1% of bone phosphorus is exchanged daily
Form compounds that store chemical energy
Buffer systems in blood and urine: ($H_2PO_4^-/HPO_4^=$)
Important in carbohydrate and fat metabolism—participates in absorption of sugars from intestines and reabsorption of glucose from kidney tubules</td></tr>
<tr><td colspan="4">Recommended Daily Amounts
Not established
If calcium and protein intake are adequate, phosphorus intake will be also</td></tr>
<tr><td>Cl</td><td>105 g in 70-kg man
0.15% total body weight</td><td>Primarily extra cellular tissue
Some in red blood cells and other tissue cells</td><td>Unknown</td></tr>
<tr><td colspan="4">Functions
Osmotic pressure regulation
Chief anion of gastric juice
Exchanges with HCO_3^- in red blood cell during time CO_2 being carried by blood
May have some bearing on activity of salivary enzyme</td></tr>
<tr><td colspan="4">Recommended Daily Amounts
Not established. Normally ingested in adequate amounts as NaCl</td></tr>
<tr><td>S[1]</td><td>175 g in 70-kg man
0.25% total body weight</td><td>Widespread</td><td>Unknown</td></tr>
<tr><td colspan="4">Functions
Occurs almost entirely as component of organic compounds; especially protein
$SO_4^=$ in blood
Not an enzyme activator</td></tr>
<tr><td>I</td><td>0.03 g in 70-kg man
0.00004% total weight</td><td>60% in thyroid gland, remainder in blood</td><td>Thyroid enlargement (goiter)
Lower basal metabolic rate
Poor cold toleration
Mental symptoms</td></tr>
<tr><td colspan="4">Functions
Essential for formation of thyroid hormone and thus essential for maintenance of normal basic metabolic rate</td></tr>
</table>

(continued)

TABLE 14. *(Continued)*

Metal	Amount present	Distribution	Effect of deficiency
		Recommended Daily Amounts	
Not established. Good sources: seafood, water, iodized salt			
F	—	Bones and teeth	Increased number of dental caries
		Functions	
Part of structural molecule of bones and teeth			
		Recommended Daily Amounts	
1 ppm in drinking water			
Br			
		Function	
Some growth increase found in experimental animals when diet supplemented			
Se			
		Function	
Biological catalyst			

Source: National Research Council, 1964.
[1]Recommended daily amounts not established.

growing youths, infants, pregnant or lactating women, and some others may need more. Normally, if one drinks two glasses of milk a day, one has adequate calcium in the diet.

Sources of Calcium

Milk and its by-products are good sources of calcium along with molasses, canned fish with bones soft enough to eat, leafy green vegetables, broccoli, citrus fruit, legumes, meats, and whole or enriched cereals.

Phosphorus

Function of Phosphorus

The word phosphorus means light-bearer, a name the Greeks gave it because it fluoresced with a greenish glow in the light. It works with calcium in making bones and teeth. It also helps in the break down glucose into energy, forms important body fluids, and makes phospholipids. Phosphates found in milk and vegetables are better utilized than those found in flesh products. Phosphorus is needed to produce the main energy source, ATP (adenosine triphosphate), which serves as the battery of the body.

Sources of Phosphorus

Milk, meat, vegetables and many other foods are good sources of phosphorus. If a normal diet is consumed there should be no lack of this mineral.

Potassium

When wood burns, an ash is left. This residue used to be called pot-ash because many fires were built for cooking in pots. It was saved by farmers and combined with surplus hog fat to make soap by boiling it with water. As pot-ash is rich in potassium, this term was used to name the mineral. Potassium belongs to the alkaline family and works closely with sodium in many body functions. It is a good conductor of electricity, and it is important in muscle function. If too much potassium is lost from the body, as can occur if one takes diuretics for high blood pressure, muscle cramps result. A heart seizure or heart attack can also occur. Because astronauts in space lose a lot of potassium, their diets are purposely made high in potassium. Good sources of potassium are meat, fish, poultry, fruits, vegetables, and whole-grain cereals. It is fairly plentiful in other foods, and few diets lack it. The intake should be about 3 g/day.

Sulfur

The amino acids methionine, cystine, and cysteine, which make hard protein substances in the body such as hair and nails, contain sulfur. This nutrient is also found in thiamin, pantothentic acid, biotin, and insulin. It is important to build compounds that help release energy. If the protein in the diet is adequate, the amount of sulfur is usually adequate also.

Sodium

Sodium is highly active chemically and ionizes well in many compounds. With chlorine it forms NaCl, the common table salt, sodium chloride. Salt is the major source of sodium and chlorine in the body.

Function of Sodium

Sodium is a strong alkali that acts to keep the body pH level correct. It is a good conductor of electricity and is important in nerve transfer, muscle contraction, and muscle relaxation. It helps control the amount of fluid held in the body. Sodium helps cells to function by pulling fluid from them. The nutrient is helpful in digestion since it helps the body absorb glucose. This mineral is also important in blood-clotting.

Edema and Sodium

Too much sodium can interfere with the use of oxygen and may also cause edema (a puffiness or swelling caused by excess body fluid retention). Dietary salt is reduced when one has heart, high blood pressure, kidney, or other health problems. Most people consume too much salt. Doctors are now advising mothers to prepare an almost salt-free diet for babies so they will not grow up wanting as much salt as is normally consumed. The average American diet contains from 6 to 18 g of salt per day; this contributes from 2.3 to 6.9 grams of sodium. To roughly estimate the amount of sodium from salt, divide the number of grams of salt consumed by three. Actually the percentage of sodium in sodium chloride is

$$\frac{23 \text{ (atomic weight of sodium)}}{58 \text{ (molecular weight of NaCl)}} \times 100 = \text{about } 40\%.$$

Sodium Losses

Sweating can cause a high loss of sodium. Those who lose a lot of fluid this way may need extra salt. The World Health Organization of the United Nations says a worker can lose five liters of sweat in an 8 hr shift and still not need extra salt, but when losses are greater extra salt may be needed. Salt depletion is a part of heat exhaustion as evidenced by weakness, dizziness, nausea, and even collapse. It is recommended that a liter of water be used per gram of sodium consumed.

High Sodium Foods and Pharmaceuticals

Cured meats, cheese, pickles, sauerkraut, potato chips, and many other foods are high in salt. Sodium may also be plentiful in some drugs such as aspirin, sweeteners, and alkalizers. Its concentration is high in baking powder and soda. Some root vegetables such as beets may contain enough sodium that individuals on low-sodium diets may not eat them. Hard water when treated by zeolite to replace calcium and magnesium with sodium may also have to be avoided; and, in some cases, foods may not even be cooked in this softened water, but rather may require unsoftened water to prevent the absorption of too much sodium.

Chlorine

Chlorine is a substance often used to purify water. Thus, with the salt and water consumed some individuals may get a lot of chlorine. Chlorine is needed to make hydrochloric acid, an important substance in the highly acid stomach juices. The chlorine shift is an important chemical reaction in the body that helps to transfer oxygen to the cells. Chlorine acts with ptyalin and mucin, digestive enzymes, secreted in fluids of the mouth.

Magnesium

The hard enamel of teeth gets its hardness because it contains a lot of magnesium. The mineral is also used in the body to produce energy, to transfer nerve impulses and give strength to bones and teeth. If magnesium is lacking, nervous disorders appear. It is thought to trigger the release of thyroxine, the hormone that increases the speed at which cells operate. A lack can cause convulsions or tetany. Faulty cardiac function may also occur. Magnesium sulfate serves as a laxative. It draws moisture into the intestines, which gives a looser stool. Magnesium is a common substance in chlorophyll (the green substance in plants). Anyone eating enough green leafy vegetables will get enough magnesium. It is also found in good quantities in meat, milk, whole grains, cocoa, nuts, soybeans, and potatoes.

Iron

Iron is an important part of the millions of blood cells in the body. Each cell has about a 4 month life; it then goes to the spleen where it is broken down. The iron is retained in the body and used to make new blood cells.

Functions and Use of Iron

Anemia occurs if iron is lacking in the body. Males need about 10 mg a day in the diet; fast-growing youths should have 18 mg a day. Women should have 18 mg a day except during pregnancies and lactation when they should consume more. Supplementation may be needed to provide the required amount. Infants need about 6 mg a day for the first 2 months of life, 10 mg for the next 4, and about 15 mg daily from 6 months to three years. Older children should have about 5 mg a day. People living at high altitudes need more iron because more blood is needed to get all of the needed oxygen from the rarefied air. In some mines at very high altitudes in South America only native Indians can work because other people cannot produce the amount of blood needed to capture the oxygen required.

Sources of Iron

Good sources of iron are organ meats, molasses, red meat, egg yolk, clams, oysters, leafy greens, legumes, nuts, dried fruits, and enriched bread or whole-grain cereals. The iron in many fruits, vegetables, and cereals is not utilized as well by the body as iron obtained from animal products.

Manganese

The body uses manganese to help utilize glucose and to release amino acids from food in the digestive tract. It is used to make cholesterol, bile, and fatty acids. It also helps the body store thiamin. Manganese poisoning occurs when too much of the metal is present in the body. Miners in manganese mines are often disabled because of it. As most foods contain the mineral, few diets lack it.

Copper

Copper helps make blood but does not become a part of it. It is found in some enzymes and is thought to be helpful in respiratory functions. Deficiencies may cause osteoporosis and bone irregularities suggestive of scurvy in infants recovering from marasmus. It plays an important role in taste perception. It may be needed to produce elastin, a connective tissue. The mineral also may help maintain the nervous system. It is helpful in converting inactive forms of vitamin C into the active form of the vitamin in the body. A lack of copper can cause anemia, skeletal defects, gray or depigmented hair, faulty hair structure, degeneration of the central nervous system, cardiovascular lesions, and loss of taste acuity. Wilson's disease (a liver disorder) results from copper deficiency in the body. Copper exposed in cooking utensils destroys ascorbic acid and causes fats to undergo oxidative rancidity, which ruins flavor.

Few adults fail to get enough copper. Milk is low in copper; children getting a large part of their nutrients from milk may lack sufficient intake. Good sources of copper include clams, oysters, cereals, nuts, legumes, liver, shellfish, grapes, wine, cocoa, tea, avocado, and some whole-grain cereals. Meat and other animal proteins contain fair quantities.

Iodine

Goiter is caused by a lack of iodine. A goiter is an enlarged thyroid gland that makes thyroxine. The gland enlarges because it works overtime trying to produce enough thyroxine for the body. If the soil on which animals graze and crops are grown contains enough iodine, the food from such areas will furnish adequate iodine. However, a wide section of land extending from the Great Lakes to the Pacific Northwest lacks iodine and is called the goiter belt, since so much goiter used to appear in residents, especially women, of that area. Its residents can now obtain enough iodine from iodized salt containing a small amount of potassium iodide. If salt contains this additive, the label on the package must say so.

Human Defects

A low intake of iodine during pregnancy can cause the birth of a cretin—a mentally retarded child with thick lips, a thick tongue, and a coarsened expression. Cretins are lethargic, have husky voices, and get infections frequently. Some children may be born deaf or mentally retarded when the mother lacks iodine.

Adults lacking iodine can develop myxedemia, a disease somewhat related to cretinism. There is a slowing in the intellect, increased weight, a weakened heart, a loss of hair, and a loss of appetite. The hands and feet enlarge, the skin coarsens and may darken. The lips become thick and the nose enlarged. Too much iodine may causes hyperthyroidism. The individual is then irritable and has a high heart rate.

Iodine is involved in the production of cholesterol and proteins. It helps change carotenes into vitamin A and assists the body in using carbohydrate. Sulfa and other drugs can cause its depletion from the body. Members of the cabbage and turnip families contain a pregoitren that interferes with iodine absorption. Cooking destroys this pregoitren.

Cobalt

Cobalt is found in vitamin B_{12}. Of itself it is not really essential in human nutrition. It is plentiful in the cabbage and turnip families, potatoes, leafy greens, pears, lettuce, and buckwheat. Enough may come from polluted air in certain areas to supply the needs.

Zinc

Zinc is involved in the release of energy and in the functioning of some enzymes. Those individuals with sickle-cell anemia lack zinc. The metal may assist in carrying dioxide to the lungs and in the formation of insulin in the pancreas. Young men and women lacking zinc do not develop sexually. The administration of zinc corrects this. If zinc is lacking, poor thiamin utilization occurs. When adquate meat is in the diet, a sufficient intake of zinc generally results. Vegetable diets may be lower in zinc than those that include meat, and the body does not utilize this zinc as well. Diets high in fiber containing phytic acid may cause zinc loss and zinc deficiency.

Fluorine

Many communities put fluorine in the drinking water to make strong bones and teeth. Fluorine may also be helpful in warding off calcification of the arteries. Some people may take fluorine in tablets as a rinse for the mouth. If a toothpaste contains fluorine, enough may be swallowed to furnish what is needed.

Seafoods contain considerable fluorine. Dry tea has from 75 to 100 ppm; a teaspoon (about three grams) gives from 0.225 to 0.300 mg. Plants grown in soil containing fluorine may contain enough to supply what is needed in the food people eat. Some hard waters have 10 ppm, which supplies all the fluorine one needs if the water is consumed. Glacier water (gletscher wasser) that flows through rocks picks up fluorine in such excessive amounts that tooth enamel can be affected.

Chromium

While the body contains only a trace of chromium, that trace is essential for the use of glucose. A deficiency can cause a diabetes-like condition. Chromium is thought to work with insulin. It is found in dairy products, peanuts, meat, brewer's yeast, molasses, brown and raw sugar, and whole-grain cereals.

Trace Minerals

Some minerals like strontium, nickel, tin, lead, silicon, mercury, molybdenum, selenium, aluminum, cadmium, titanium, gold, silver, boron, and vanadium may be needed by the body, but we do not know all the functions they perform. Studies have shown that animals need some of these minerals, but scientists have not yet found the same needs for human beings. For instance, molybdenum is thought to be helpful in some oxidations in the bodies of animals; it is also found in the nucleic acids and may have a function there. Selenium in some animals helps detoxify the products of oxidized fats, prevents liver damage, and acts as a biological catalyst. If animals get too much selenium, they develop a disease called the blind staggers, evidenced by lameness and blindness. Children getting too much selenium develop gum and dental problems.

OTHER INPUTS

Oxygen

The body receives most of its oxygen from the air via the blood and some small amount may come from the breakdown of body substances. Oxygen is necessary for the metabolism of carbohydrates, proteins, and fats to provide calories. Enzyme reactions involving biological oxidations manipulate oxygen to produce many essential functions. We use more air than all other nutrients combined to oxidize (burn) our food and provide energy.

Water

Water is essential as the medium in which practically all metabolic reactions involving nutrients occur. It is necessary for most body chemical reactions that build, destroy, or convert protoplasm. Nutrients are dissolved in water so that they may pass through the intestinal wall and into the blood stream. Water is also important as the medium in which energy is created. It carries wastes out of the body and helps to regulate body temperature. Coffee, tea, fruits, fruit juices, and vegetables and meat are all good water sources.

Standards for Water Intake

Most of the excess water in the body is eliminated in the urine, but some is lost as vapor in the breath and by sweating. Individuals should consume six to eight glasses of water (or the equivalent) each day. This averages about a liter of water for every thousand kilocalories consumed. People drinking hard water may get valuable minerals and other nutrients from it; they can also get harmful ones when, for example, minerals such as sodium or selenium are present in great quantities.

Water Pollution and Treatment

Our municipal water supplies are deteriorating with increasing environmental pollution. Dual and triple treatments are gradually replacing primary (single) treatment, which was formerly adequate.

Alcohol

Energy Content

Pure (100%) alcohol yields 7 kcal/g, which in combination with the mixers and other ingredients added to alcoholic beverages can contribute a considerable number of calories. Table 15 shows the caloric yields. Sweetened carbonated beverages give around 12 kcal/oz.

Standards for Alcohol Use

Since alcohol provides little other than calories and may cause body damage, its use should be limited. Some individuals should avoid alcohol completely because of potential health problems.

TABLE 15. Caloric Yields of Beverages

Product	Number of kcal
Beer, 12 oz	150
Wine, dry or dinner, 3.5 oz	85
Wine, sweet or dessert, 3.5 oz	140
Spirits, 80-proof, 1.5 oz	95
Spirits, 86-proof, 1.5 oz	105
Spirits, 90-proof, 1.5 oz	110

Source: USDA 1975. Handbook No. 456 (Calculations) and Hamilton and Whitney, 1980.

The average consumption of alcohol in this country is 210 kcal/day, the equivalent of about 6½ gal a year of 80-proof whiskey. Individuals who get most of their calories from alcohol can develop severe malnutrition. Alcohol can also damage the liver; in many cases, those who consume 25% or more of their calories in alcohol develop cirrhosis of the liver, which eventually can cause death. Alcohol is harmful to the growth of young people, and teenagers are highly susceptible to alcohol addiction. When it is taken during pregnancy, abnormal babies or ones with a predisposition to use alcohol may be born. Many male alcoholics are sterile because alcohol destroys vitamin A, which is needed for complete sexual function. The tendency of alcohol to force zinc from the body may help contribute to a delay in the sexual maturation of young people. Alcoholism may interfere with the digestion and absorption of fats.

Racial Variations in Alcohol Tolerance

Some races are affected more by alcohol than others, perhaps for genetic reasons. Europeans and Russians can consume high levels of alcohol before being influenced. American Indians, Orientals, and some others have a low threshold for alcohol tolerance. Drug tolerance, including alcohol, increases in direct proportion to body weight. A lighter-weight individual has proportionately less alcohol tolerance than a heavier one.

Roughage (Fiber)

Dietary fiber increases the bulk of the feces and helps in their elimination from the body. It also keeps food apart during digestion so that digestive agents can work effectively. The average American eats less fiber today than in the past, which many authorities feel is injurious. While the average intake of fiber is less than 4 g/day, it is recommended that the intake be from 12 to 20 g/day. Some African tribes with high fiber diets eliminate their stools in about 35 hours. Most Americans on low fiber diets require 90 hours to preform this function.

High fiber diets overcome constipation straining that may lead to colon pressure that will cause the out-pouchings of diverticulosis, hiatal hernia, and heartburn. Abdominal pressure may cause pressure on leg veins and the anal area, resulting in varicose veins and hemorroids. Smaller slow-moving stools may harbor cancer-producing chemicals (carcinogens) that result from bacterial action in the bowel. The lengthened retention time allows more time for these chemicals to act on the colon membrane.

A little less than an ounce of wheat bran taken daily caused a weight loss in 25 healthy adults when used for five weeks. Fiber may help reduce elevated blood fat levels that cause arterial plaques that may cause heart attacks and strokes. Pectin and other gums occurring in fiber have reduced cholesterol levels when fed to healthy men.

Diabetic patients fed fiber-rich foods often require less insulin because blood sugar levels decrease. Adding fiber to the diet also reduces bile cholesterol, which is believed to cause gallstones.

Bowel irritation is now being treated in England and European countries with high fiber diets.

Rich fiber sources include old-fashioned slow-cooking oatmeal and whole wheat, shredded wheat and all bran, bakery items made with whole wheat flour, sesame and sunflower seeds, raspberries and blackberries, and fruits and vegetables in this order: carrot, apple, brussels sprout, eggplant, spring cabbage, orange, pear, green bean, lettuce, pea, onion, celery, cucumber, broad bean, tomato, cauliflower, banana, rhubarb, potato, and turnip.

Fiber Intake Standards

It is not necessary to consume a lot of high fiber foods. New bread products containing sawdust (advertised on the market as containing powdered cellulose or other fibrous substances) provide 7% fiber, four to five times more than ordinary whole wheat bread. Some individuals taking such preparations may get too much fiber. Diets following the Basic Four plan (explained later) usually provide adequate fiber. It is also advisable that one have some whole-grain cereal that contains bran or other fiber. Table 16 shows the fiber yields of certain foods. Excessive intakes of phytic acid from fiber may cause body losses of iron, calcium, and zinc. Leveille (1978) recommends some increase in fiber and decrease in fat in the U.S. diet. Americans have been getting 4–5 g of fiber per day, and a level of 12–20 g/day is now recommended.

DIGESTION, ABSORPTION, AND NUTRIENT UTILIZATION

Food generally cannot be utilized in the same form in which it is consumed. Some items such as sugar, water, minerals, alcohol, and amino acids

TABLE 16. Fiber Yields from Selected Foods

Food item	Fiber yield
6 g leafy vegetables, celery or carrots	1.2 g
100 g hole-grain cereal	3.0 g
1 potato, 5 oz (140 g)	0.6 g
1 orange, apple, or pear	1.0 g
1 slice whole-grain bread	1.6 g
Total	7.4 g

Source: IFT Expert Panel 1979. Reprinted with permission. Copyright 1979 by Institute of Food Technologists.

do not need conversion to be digested, absorbed, and used; most others do. In order for food to be absorbed by the stomach or intestines, both chemical and mechanical processes are necessary.

Digestion is an involved process in which foods are broken down into substances the body can absorb. The remainder is eliminated as waste. Absorption is another involved process in which nutrients are brought from the intestines into either the blood or the lymphatic system. Some nutrients are so large that special processes are needed for them to be absorbed. Nutrient utilization is another involved, complex process. The human body is a chemical laboratory that man cannot duplicate. Some of the best biochemical laboratories cannot produce some of the reactions that occur in the body; several of these activities are not even understood. The way human bodies finally use nutrients is a fascinating study.

Digestion

The chemical and mechanical breakdown of food begins when food is chewed and carbohydrates begin to be broken down by a salivary enzyme (ptyalin). The saliva also moistens the food and adds a slippery agent called mucin.

The Digestive Enzymes of the Stomach

After being swallowed, the food goes down the esophagus into the stomach. Force is needed to push food through the alimentary canal. This force is provided by peristaltic movement—a twisting, churning action by muscular tissue in the canal walls. The upper part of the stomach is largely a storage area doing little to digest food. The lower part mechanically churns the food, adding digestive juices that begin to break the food down into basic chemical components. These juices contain the protein-splitting enzymes pepsin, trypsin, and erepsin and the fat-splitting enzyme, lipase. Amylolytic enzymes that attack carbohydrates and much hydrochloric acid that works to hydrolyze protein, fat, and carbohydrate are also present. The food stays in the stomach from 3 to about 7 hours, by which time it has become a thick liquid mixture called chyme. To this point, however, only partial digestion has occurred and very little food has been absorbed. Some sugar, water, and alcohol can be absorbed; but the function of absorption is left largely to the small intestine.

Absorption in the Small Intestine

From the stomach the chyme is ejected into the duodenum, the upper part of the small intestine. Some absorption now begins to occur. Gradually the chyme works down into the duodenum, bile and other digestive agents change the chyme to an alkaline pH. This favors the digestion of fats and some other substances. Bile emulsifies fat, and then pancreatic lipase and other enzymes can break the fat down into fatty acids, glycerol, or di- or monoglycerides. Proteins are reduced to peptides and then into amino acids. Carbohydrates yield simple sugars. Bacterial action may assist in the breakdown but only to a limited degree and then only in the lower part of the small intestine. Bacterial action in the colon may also occur, but this is usually undesirable and is not helpful since the colon absorbs few nutrients. It may absorb some water and soluble minerals and vitamins but is primarily a storage area. As the food moves through the jejunum, the middle part of the small intestin, and into the ileum, the last part of the small intestine, digestion continues but absorption is the primary task.

Undigested food, unabsorbed end products of digestion, bile pigments, and waste products leave the small intestine and enter the colon to be eliminated. Good elimination is favored by the presence of fiber and water.

Metabolism

Anabolism is a metabolic process in which complex nutrients are built with the addition of energy. Catabolism is the opposite process, where complex chemicals are broken down into simpler chemicals that the body can reuse or discard. Anabolism and catabolism are combined into what is called metabolism. The liver plays an important role in anabolism and also helps in the catabolism process. The kidneys largely break down nitrogenous substances and eliminate the waste in the urine. The spleen breaks down worn-out blood cells and sends the iron back for use in the body.

Most of the metabolism goes on in the cells. They are constantly at work absorbing nutrients or eliminating waste products so that the body can do its work. The processes of metabolism occur because of the presence of many enzymes, vitamins, minerals, coenzymes, and other substances such as hormones.

Energy from Glycogen via Glucose

The metabolic processes are very complex. The liver takes glucose that comes from the digestive system and turns it into fat or glycogen, or it breaks these products down into glucose. In order for glucose to release energy, water, and carbon dioxide it must go through a very complex breakdown called glycolysis and the Krebs cycle. Amino acids may be built into proteins, or proteins can be broken down into amino acids. Glucose from amino acids may be changed into fat for body storage. Glucose may be made into nonessential amino acids or amino acids may be broken down and made into glucose and glycogen (animal starch) for use as energy. Fats may be broken down into fatty acids, glycerol, phospholipids, or lipoproteins. Amino acids may be made into blood, antibodies, hormones, enzymes, flesh, cartilage, or collagen.

Since the body can only use glucose, all carbohydrate substances must be changed into glucose and fats; amino acids must also be changed into glucose before they can be used for energy. Oxygen needed for metabolism is brought from the lungs by the blood. When the oxidation process is complete, carbon dioxide is absorbed by the blood and carried to the lungs for elimination. The body can use the water resulting from glucose breakdown, or it can eliminate it as urine.

Glycogen: The Energy Reservoir

Fat, glycogen and, to a limited extent, blood glucose and amino acid stores are the energy reserve. The amount of glucose that the blood, liver, and body can store is small, as are the available reserves of amino acid. Thus the body can run only a limited time on these sources. However, the body can convert glycogen (sometimes called body starch) into glucose. The ordinary person stores from 900 to 1200 kcal in glycogen. Fat also can be broken down for energy. Although excess body protein can be converted into glucose for energy, it is not desirable. In starvation, long illnesses, and other situations, body protein is broken down and the body deteriorates.

Functions of Glucose

Glucose is used for energy in the body. It can be made into other substances such as ribonucleic acid (RNA) or deoxyribonucleic acid (DNA), which are very important cellular regenerators. It can be given an amine radical and made into an amino acid. Glucose can combine with some body substances to make new ones. The role of glucose, however, is largely that of an energy source.

Absorption

Absorption of nutrients into the body is a very complex process. Some highly soluble substances can pass through the alimentary canal wall into the blood or lymph system by diffusion. Many, however, have to be carried through by active transport while others are transferred by osmosis or other means.

The interior of the small intestine is coated with a mass of very fine fingerlike projections called villi that make the surface look as if it were covered with fur. These villi so greatly increase the surface area of the small intestines that the surface area in the average adult is almost equal to that of a basketball court. The villi are very selective and absorb only specific nutrients. Large nutrients that are difficult to absorb may be picked up by the villi and slowly surrounded until they are inside the intestinal wall. Some other nutrients are covered with a medium that allows them to slip through the alimentary canal.

Nutrient Distribution Centers

The pathway of the nutrient after absorption into the body is also very selective. Lipids and some other nutrients are picked up by the lymphic system and carried by the lymph ducts to the main circulatory system. Other nutrients such as sugar, many minerals, vitamins, and amino acids are picked up by the capillaries and carried to the liver via the portal vein. These nutrients may also be distributed by the liver to places they are needed in the body.

ENERGY STANDARDS

Energy is the basic nutrient requirement of the human body. It comes before all else, even though other nutrients are vital to life. The need for energy can be divided into three categories: (1) basic metabolic needs, which include all the essential body functions such as breathing, blood circulation, and metabolism; (2) the supply of energy for activity, food digestion, and assimilation; and (3) personal needs such as age, sex, and hormone and metabolic makeup.

1. Basal metabolism is the energy expenditure when the body is at complete rest with no digestion or other extraneous body functions going on. It is

what the body needs to keep operating the essential functions. If one eats a light evening meal, rests well, and then takes a metabolic test (which measures energy expenditure) in the morning at complete rest the basal metabolic rate can be ascertained.

2. Energy is needed for activities; individuals do not remain at complete rest all the time. They work, play, read, eat, dance, and do other things. This activity requires more energy than needed for the basal rate. As activity increases, the energy need increases. Table 17 indicates the calorie expenditure per hour for specific activities.

3. Personal needs affect energy needs, which vary with body size and makeup, the climate or room temperature, amount of clothing worn, and the physical condition of the body. A pregnant or lactating woman needs more energy; an ill person may also. The hormone makeup of the person, the age, and many other factors make a difference in the amount of energy needed. When the temperature is below 14°C (57°F) or above 38°C (100°F) or when physical activity increases, energy needs become greater. For every kilogram of body weight a certain amount of energy is required. Thus, a large or heavy person needs more energy than a small or light one. The amount of body surface exposed is a factor; thus, a tall, thin person loses more body heat than a shorter, compact one and needs more energy; the amount of fat covering the body affects energy needs since it insulates the body. For this reason women, who have more of a fat covering over the body than men, need less energy. Older people have a slower metabolic rate than younger ones and so need less energy, but their need for other nutrients does not decrease. In fact, some old people may need more nutrients than younger ones because they cannot digest, absorb, or use the nutrients in the diet as well.

TABLE 17. Energy Needs Per Hour for Selected Activities

Activity	Energy
Sleeping	1.0 kcal
Washing or dressing	2.3 kcal
Showering or bathing	2.8 kcal
Making bed	3.6 kcal
Eating	1.3 kcal
Sitting	1.5 kcal
Standing at work	4.0 kcal
Just standing	1.3 kcal
Swimming	8.0 kcal
Studying	2.5 kcal
Walking 2.25 mph	3.0 kcal
Going upstairs	13.0 kcal
Going downstairs	2.5 kcal

Source: National Research Council 1964.

Basal Metabolism Standards

The basal metabolic need for energy can be estimated. One can add to this figure the various energy requirements for activity and personal needs to arrive at an estimate of how many kilocalories are used in 24 hours. The following is the way to calculate a 24-hour basal metabolic rate:

For men under 50:	24 kcal or 100 kJ/kg of body weight
For women under 50:	22 kcal or 90 kJ/kg of body weight
For men over 50:	22 kcal or 90 kJ/kg of body weight
For women over 50:	19 kcal or 80 kJ/kg of body weight

If the body weight is known in pounds, divide by 2.2 to find it in kilograms. Thus, a 132-lb woman weighs 60 kg (132/2.2 = 60). If 22 years old, this woman would have an estimated basal requirement of 22 × 60 or 1320 kcal a day or 5400 kJ (90 × 60). A 154 lb 65-year-old man would have an estimated basal rate of 154/2.2 × 22 or 1540 kcal or 6300 kJ (90 × 70).

OUR NUTRITIONAL STATUS

Surveys of the nutritional status of our population groups usually show that we are not a well-fed nation, especially among the lower income groups. Poor nutrition is not restricted to these groups, however; many who have adequate funds for foods that meet nutritional needs do not buy them, either because we do not know what is needed or because we decide to consume less nutritious diets. Certainly, a better understanding of what nutrients are and what they do would help to better the nutritional status of both low and high income groups. Many people have market baskets that show a poor selection of food at a higher cost than would be the price of a more nutritious selection.

Modern Stress and Excessive Caloric Intake

The life styles of today coupled with media advertising pressures have been blamed for part of the poor nutrition problem. This is probably true. Americans are eating more snacks and fast foods that may be high in some nutrients but totally lacking in others. So many foods today are prepared to the almost finished or finished state that one has little choice in what is to be consumed. Many years ago we would make a decision about adding sugar or salt to our food. Today many of the foods we eat already contain these ingredients (cereals, fruits, ice cream), and we have no choice. The same is true with fats; in the past we ate far less fats and oils—less than 35% of our total energy need compared to 45% or more today—because one could decide whether or not to add them. The hamburger, milk shake, french fry, or other meal offerings of the drive-in restaurant have been accused of being nonnutritious, a meal that many eat frequently. Studies have shown that many fast food meals are not as poor in nutrition as reputed (Appeldorf 1974). Good selection of other foods consumed in other meals can make such fast foods quite adequate nutritionally. A high intake of candy bars, cereals containing over 50% sugar, soft drinks, and other such foods offers many calories but few other nutrients.

Effects of Poor Nutrition in the United States

The health and productivity of millions of Americans are being affected by their nutritionally inadequate diets (HEW 1971). This is evidenced in the form of impaired physical and mental development, premature death, lowered resistance to disease, and reduced response to therapies aimed at overcoming disease. Evidence indicates that good nutrition could reduce respiratory, digestive, and infectious conditions resulting in restricted activity by 10% (31.6 million cases annually); cardiovascular disease, cancer, diabetes, and osteoporosis by 10% (2.2 million annually); premature deaths by 5–10%, (90–180 thousand annually). A reduction of $5 billion (5%) in annual health care costs and a saving of $2.5 billion in wages could be realized by better nutrition. Annual earnings of $500 million lost by 125,000 premature deaths could be saved and, projected to lifetime savings, could total $7 billion. The complete elimination of smoking would save the United States an additional $25 billion/yr and greatly improve the overall health of its citizens.

Achieving Calorie Nutrient Balance

One of the aims in achieving a good diet is to get the maximum number of other necessary nutrients for the energy consumed. If one does this carefully it is possible for a 1000 to 1200 kcal diet to contain all the nutrients one needs in a day. At the turn of the century a 3000 kcal diet was probably needed. The more sedentary U.S. adult of today may need less than 2000 kcal. The Food and Nutrition Board of the National Academy of Science/National Research Council (NAS/NRC) has recently revised its Recommended Daily Dietary allowance (see Table 8). If less energy is consumed it is difficult to get all the nutrients the average person needs; supplementation becomes necessary.

Achieving Adequate Nutrition

Almost every country in the world along with many health agencies has independently established what each considers an adequate diet. While these are closely parallel, they do differ. Some give total daily needs based on age, sex, and activity; others such as the World Health Organization (WHO) and Food and Agricultural Organization (FAO) state nutrient needs per 1000 kcal consumed. The amounts of nutrients needed vary; Japanese, Pakistanis, and some other races small in stature need fewer calories and thiamin; some requirements are based on minimums because of the small amount of food per person in that country. The requirements stated for people in the United States are higher than for many others and are about 1.5 times what is known as the world-wide minimum requirement.

U.S. Standards for Nutrients

Our daily requirement of vitamin C is given as 45 mg. It is known that 30 mg is adequate (the British use 30 mg and find it completely adequate), but we wanted a safety factor in our standards. We even have different standards depending upon the intended use of the standard. For instance, our Recommended Daily Dietary Allowance (RDA) is to be used to indicate the needs of various individuals in guiding food intake. However, we also have the U.S. Recommended Daily Dietary Allowances (USRDA), which are used on package labels to tell how much of the daily need a portion yields. Normally the RDA established by the Food and Nutrition Committee of the National Research Council of the Academy of Sciences is considered the standard, and there is a movement to have the U.S. government revise the USRDA to reflect world-wide standards. Table 18 shows how some nutrient standards vary depending upon the country or agency compiling them.

TABLE 18. Comparison of International Dietary Standards for Energy and Selected Nutrients

	United States		Canada		FAO	
	Male	Female	Male	Female	Male	Female
Energy (kcal)	2700.0	2000.0	2850.0	2400.0	3200.0	2300.0
Protein (g)	56.0	46.0	50.0	39.0	46.0	39.0
Calcium (g)	0.8	0.8	0.5	0.5	0.4–0.5	0.4–0.5
Iron (mg)	10.0	18.0	6.0	10.0	10.0	18.0
Vitamin C	45.0	45.0	30.0	30.0		
Thiamin	1.4	1.0	0.9	0.7	1.3	0.9

Source: Runyan (1976).

Note: The FAO standard designed for use in many developing countries includes a high recommendation for energy. This reflects the greater physical activity of people in developing countries compared to the average American. The FAO standards for essential nutrients are in general lower than the U.S. standards.

The Basic Four

Calculating the nutritional needs using the RDA is difficult for the ordinary person and, because foods vary so much in their nutritional content, making such a calculation is often inaccurate. Therefore, more simple systems that use portions to be consumed according to food groups have been devised that bypass the detailed calculation of nutrients. These systems indicate that, if a selection of foods is made each day as indicated, adequate nutrition should be achieved.

The most useful plan of this kind, called the Basic Four, divides foods into four major groups: (1) the milk group, (2) the meat group, (3) the cereal group, and (4) the vegetable and fruit group. If a person selects the right number of portions of foods from each of these groups every day, adequate nutrition should be achieved. Table 19 lists the RDA as revised recently by the National Research Council. Note that it is based on age and sex and to some extent, on status in life situations. Figure 2 indicates the Basic Four; extra energy is obtained by eating extra carbohydrates, fats, or other foods. Table 19 shows an American annual food intake as compared with 15 years ago.

Food Group	Number of Servings	Minimum recommended daily size of serving for people age 7 or older
1. Breads and cereal products, enriched or whole grain	4	1 slice bread, 1 cup flaked cereal ⅓–⅔ cup cooked cereal 1 muffin or roll, 1 pancake ½ hamburger bun
2. Meat and meat alternatives	4 oz. cooked meat	Equivalents (not including fat or bone) to 1 oz. meat: 1 egg, 1 oz nuts, 2 tbsp peanut butter, ½ cup cooked dried legumes (e.g., baked beans), 1 oz cheese (not included in the milk group serving), ¼ cup cottage cheese (not included in the milk serving).
3. Milk and milk products	2 (age 18 and up) 4 (age 8 to 11) 2 (age 7 to 10)	1 cup milk or light cream 1½ oz hard cheese 1 ⅓ cups cottage cheese
4. Vegetable and fruit group		
Dark green and and deep yellow fruits	1 every other day	If whole, 1 medium If raw, ⅔ to 1 cup If cooked, or juice, ½ cup
Good vitamin C sources[1]	1 good or	
Fair vitamin C sources[2]	2 fair	
Other fruits and vegetables	variable: to total of 4	

Source: Runyan 1976.

[1]Good vitamin C sources are oranges, green peppers, broccoli, grapefruit, brussels sprouts, cantaloupes, and strawberries.

[2]Fair vitamin C sources are asparagus tips, raw cabbage, baked potato (in the skin), cauliflower, tangerine, and tomato.

Fig. 2. Outline of the basic four food group plan.

TABLE 19. American Yearly Food Intake Today and 15 Years Ago

	Consumption today (lb)	Consumption 15 years ago (lb)	Change in Consumption[1]
Apples	15.8	21.1	--
Beans (green)	5.9	4.2	++
All meats	188.0	159.5	++
Butter	4.5	6.9	--
Margarine	11.3	9.6	+
Cheese	14.5	8.0	++
Chicken	41.1	30.8	++
Citrus fruits	27.1	34.0	-
Coffee, Tea, Cocoa	13.2	15.2	-
Dairy products	343.0	393.0	-
Eggs	36.4	44.7	-
Fish	15.0	13.7	+
Grains	138.0	148.0	-
Ice cream	17.6	18.7	-
Melons	21.3	26.9	-
Milk	244.0	330.0	--
Peanuts	0.41	0.45	-
Potatoes	118.0	107.7	+
Sugar	121.5	107.7	+
Turkey	8.8	6.8	++
Vegetables	97.8	102.2	-

Source: National Food Review 1979.
[1]increase less than 25% = +; increase greater than 25% = ++; decrease less than 25% = -; decrease greater than 25% = --.

Food Production Advances by Developing Nations

Many developing countries have more highly efficient and coordinated food strategies than the United States because of their need to maintain economic and political stability. We have been able to feed most of our populace very well, despite a lack of coordination among production, manufacture, trade, and distribution policies. Action to improve coordination may gain impetus when we recognize that abundance, even in the United States, is not limitless.

Depletion of Prime Farm Land in the United States

Developers are taking 1,000,000 acres of prime and 2,000,000 acres of less productive but still useful farm land out of production each year. Within the next decade we will find that our economy can no longer sustain wasteful practices that have become a way of life in this country so richly blessed with natural resources. Topsoil depletion on the remaining land will limit the return that we now obtain from the use of fertilizers.

NUTRITIONAL LABELING

In 1973 the Food and Drug Administration (FDA) established a nutritional labeling system that requires package labels to state the amount of nutrients per serving in the food. The use of the system is voluntary unless somewhere on the label a nutritional claim is made or implied. The total energy, grams of protein, carbohydrate, and fat per serving are to be listed along with the size of the portion. In addition, the percentage of USRDA of the following should be listed: protein, vitamin A, vitamin C, vitamin B_1, vitamin B_2, calcium, and iron, as shown in Table 20. If the serving contained less than 2% of the requirement for a day the space where the amount was to be listed could be filled with an asterisk (*) or zero (0). In addition 12 other nutrients could be listed, which were: Vitamins D, E, and B_{12}, pyridoxine, biotin, pantothenic acid, folic acid, phosphorous, iodine, magnesium, zinc, and copper. Other nutrients may be listed by the manufacturer when permission for their inclusion is granted by the FDA.

TABLE 20. Standard Recommended Daily Allowances (RDA) for Nutrition Labeling[1]

	Nutrients/day	Nutrients/1000 kcal
Energy	2800 kcal	
Protein	65 g	23 g
Vitamin A	5000 IU	1780 IU
Vitamin B_1	1.5 mg	0.53 mg
Vitamin B_2	1.7 mg	0.61 mg
Vitamin C	60 mg	21.4 mg
Calcium	1000 mg	357.0 mg
Iron	18 mg	6.4 mg

Source: Hansen 1973.

[1]Allowances for the individual nutrients used in this table were derived from the published food labeling recommendations of the FDA, Fed. Regist. *37*, 6497A, March, 1972.

Nutritional labeling should not be confused with ingredient labeling. Regulations for the latter require that all noncommon foods list the names of ingredients in the order of their decreasing concentration in the food.

Although nutrient labeling does not tell how much of a specific ingredient is in a food, it does tell what is in the food. Individuals needing more information than is listed on the label in either ingredient or nutritional labeling can obtain it by writing to the company that produces the food.

Example of a Nutritional Label

Figure 3 is a label providing nutritional information on the contents of one serving of evaporated milk. Note that the label panel is headed, Nutrition Information. In addition, the size of each portion and the number of por-

INGREDIENTS: MILK, DISODIUM PHOSPHATE AND CARRAGEENAN (STABILIZERS), VITAMIN D_3.

NUTRITION INFORMATION
PER ½ CUP PORTION

PORTIONS PER CONTAINER: 3¼

CALORIES 170
PROTEIN .... 8 GRAMS
CARBOHYDRATE .... 12 GRAMS
FAT ....10 GRAMS

PERCENTAGE OF U.S. RECOMMENDED DAILY ALLOWANCES (U.S. RDA):

PROTEIN	20	NIACIN	*
VITAMIN A	4	CALCIUM	30
VITAMIN C	*	IRON	*
THIAMIN	2	VITAMIN D	25
RIBOFLAVIN	20	PHOSPHORUS	25

*CONTAINS LESS THAN 2% OF THE U.S. RDA OF THESE NUTRIENTS

FOR INFANTS, ADDITIONAL VITAMIN C AND IRON SHOULD BE SUPPLIED FROM OTHER SOURCES.

Fig. 3. Nutritional value label from a can of evaporated milk

tions in the package are indicated. Some labels list the nutrients provided by portion and then indicate the additional nutrients obtained in a portion whenever milk or some other common ingredient is added.

The Nutrition Labeling Law

The Nutrition Labeling Law, passed in 1973, requires that foods claiming nutritional value be labeled as shown in Fig. 3. The terminology was described in 1974 by the FDA as follows:

1. *Foods* are products containing less than 50% of the United States Recommended Dietary Allowances (USRDA).
2. *Dietary Supplements* are items containing 50 to 150% of USRDA of the above nutrients and possibly others included by the manufacturer with FDA approval.
3. *Over-the-counter drugs* are products that contain more than 150% of USRDA.

RDA Calculations

Calculation of the RDA for infants, children, males, and females at various ages together with the needs of pregnant and lactating females may be made for most raw and processed foods using the following references and aids:

1. *Recommended Dietary Allowances* (NAS/NRC 1980)
2. *Handbook of the Nutritional Content of Foods* (Watt and Merrill 1963 and 1975)
3. *Nutritional Data* (Heinz 1972)
4. *Food Values of Portions Commonly Used* (Bowes and Church 1980)
5. *Nutrition Labeling* (FDA 1974)
6. *Nutritive Values of American Foods* (Adams 1975)

Fortification

The processing of food may cause a loss of nutrients. For instance, thiamin and iron are lost, along with other nutrients, when rice is polished. Cereals lose a number of nutrients when they are made into flour or meals. Other foods also lose elements in processing, which lessens their nutritive value. It is remarkable, however, that more nutrients are not lost when one considers the chance for oxidation, trim, heat destruction, and other losses that exist. Table 21 shows the variation in vitamin content that can exist in 100 g of fresh and canned green beans. Mineral losses also occur as a result of heat processing (Elkins 1979).

TABLE 21. Vitamin Differences in Raw versus Canned Green Beans

	Experimental values[1]		Handbook No. 8 values[2]	
Vitamins	raw	canned	raw	canned
Carotene (μg/100g)	413	138	360	174
Thiamin (mg/100g)	0.05	0.016	0.08	0.03
Riboflavin (mg/100g)	0.13	0.064	0.11	0.04
Niacin (mg/100g)	0.44	0.21	0.5	0.3
Ascorbic acid (mg/100g)	14.8	4.0	19	4

Source: Elkins 1979. Reprinted with permission. Copyright 1979 by Institute of Food Technologists.
[1]Average of three packs after 12 mo of ambient storage.
[2]Watt and Merrill 1963.

Some foods must be enriched with added nutrients to replace those lost in processing. Table 22 indicates how cereals should be enriched. Some processors may enrich foods to encourage customers to purchase their products. Added nutrients may include proteins, vitamins, minerals, and amino acids.

Milk and Cream Standards

Revised standards of identity for milk and cream became effective 15 December 1973. As a result, fortification of low fat and skim milk with

TABLE 22. Standards for Enrichment of Cereal Products: Minimum and Maximum Amounts of Required and Optional Nutrients Specified for Foods Labeled "Enriched"[1 2]

	Required nutrients										Optional nutrients			
	Thiamin		Riboflavin		Niacin		Iron		Calcium		Calcium		Vitamin D	
Cereal product	Min. (mg)	Max. (mg)	Min. (mg)	Max. (mg)	Min. (mg)	Max. (mg)	Min. (mg)	Max. (mg)	Min. (mg)	Max. (mg)	Min. (mg)	Max. (mg)	Min. (IU)	Max (IU)
	Per Pound of Product													
Bread, rolls, and buns, white	1.1	1.8	0.7	1.6	10.0	15.0	8.0	12.5	—	—	300	800	150	750
Cornmeal; corn grits	2.0	3.0	1.2	1.8	16.0	24.0	13.0	26.0	—	—	500	750	250	1000
Cornmeal, self-rising	2.0	3.0	1.2	1.8	16.0	24.0	13.0	26.0	—	—	500	1750	250	1000
Farina	2.0	2.5	1.2	1.5	16.0	20.0	13.0	([3])	—	—	500	([3])	250	([3])
Flour, white	2.0	2.5	1.2	1.5	16.0	20.0	13.0	16.5	—	—	500[4]	625[4]	250	1000
Flour, self-rising	2.0	2.5	1.2	1.5	16.0	20.0	13.0	16.5	500	1,500	—	—	250	1000
Macaroni products; noodle products	4.0	5.0	1.7	2.2	27.0	34.0	13.0	16.5	—	—	500	625	250	1000
Rice, milled	2.0	4.0	1.2[5]	2.4[5]	16.0	32.0	13.0	26.0	—	—	500	1000	250	1000
	Per 100 g of Product													
Bread, rolls, and buns, white	0.24	0.40	0.15	0.35	2.20	3.31	1.76	2.76	—	—	66	176	33	165
Cornmeal; corn grits	0.44	0.66	0.26	0.40	3.53	5.29	2.87	5.73	—	—	110	165	55	220
Cornmeal, self-rising	0.44	0.66	0.26	0.40	3.53	5.29	2.87	5.73	—	386	—	—	55	220
Farina	0.44	0.55	0.26	0.33	3.53	4.41	2.87	([3])	—	—	110	([3])	55	([3])
Flour, white	0.44	0.55	0.26	0.33	3.53	4.41	2.87	3.64	—	—	110[4]	138	55	220
Flour, self-rising	0.44	0.55	0.26	0.33	3.53	4.41	2.87	3.64	110	331	—	—	55	220
Macaroni products; noodle products	0.88	1.10	0.37	0.48	5.95	7.50	2.87	3.64	—	—	110	138	55	220
Rice, milled	0.44	0.88	0.26[5]	0.53	3.53	7.05	2.87	5.73	—	—	110	220	55	220

Source: Agricultural Handbook No. 456, USDA, 1975, Washington, D.C.

[1]Information here, except for rice and self-rising cornmeal, from Federal Register of Dec. 20, 1955, and information for rice and self-rising cornmeal from Federal Register of Aug. 27, 1957 and Aug. 10, 1961, respectively, and became effective for the latter on Jan. 27, 1962.

[2]Standards for enrichment provide for inclusion of calcium and vitamin D within stated limits as optional ingredients for products here, except self-rising cornmeal and self-rising flour; for these items calcium is required as indicated.

[3]No maximum level established.

[4]When acidified with monocalcium phosphate at specified range of 0.25–0.75% of the finished product, calcium levels may range from 680 to 1165 mg. per pound (150–257 mg per 100 g).

[5]Requirement for riboflavin stayed pending further hearings.

vitamin A is now mandatory; Vitamin D fortification is optional. Emulsifiers, stabilizers, nutritive sweeteners, carriers for vitamins A and D, and flavors have become optional ingredients in most milk and cream products.

Food Enrichment Procedures

Foods may be enriched with soy protein to increase the protein value. The Federal School Lunch Program permits the addition of up to 25% of hydrated soy protein to ground beef meat patties to reduce meat cost while maintaining nutrition. Some institutional foodservices fortify foods in preparation to increase nutritional values. Thus the state institutions of New York, California, Texas, Iowa, and others have developed recipes that add nutritional foods including soy flour, nonfat dry milk, and dried fruits to the lunches served to increase the nutrient levels of their recipes.

Technology of Fortification

At a workshop convened by the National Academy of Sciences Committee on Food Protection (1975) the technology of fortification was considered. Topics included the following:

1. Differences in process and storage losses, particularly for vitamins in foods that are (a) frozen, (b) refrigerated, (c) dried (hot air vs. freeze-dried), and (d) thermal processed
2. Where nutrients are degraded, presently what is known concerning breakdown products
3. The effect of the fortifying nutrient on the product itself and in some cases on foods prepared from the product fortified. For example, iron fortification often causes protein instability not only in the original canned product but also in food preparation when dishes are prepared from iron-fortified materials; organoleptic (odor, taste, color, texture) changes may be caused particularly by added minerals and B vitamins.

Lachance says, "fortification policies must be consistent with the ever-changing uses of food" (Lachance 1978).

Dangers of Overfortification

The fortification of some foods with nutrients such as fats oils or sugar is often criticized. These ingredients generally contribute only energy and few other nutrients. The trend to overfortify foods is also critized. Some contain 100% or more of the RDA of certain nutrients. Some authorities claim that no food should contribute more than a third of the RDA of any given nutrient. Otherwise, hypervitaminosis, allergies and other disorders may occur.

Standards for Developing New Foods

It is important when developing new foods to consider not only nutritional values but also flavor and texture so that the food will find acceptance. If a flavor is not good, simply increasing its nutritional values may not bring about the desired results of adequate nutritive value and good taste and odor.

Soy Protein in Ground Beef Patties

Soy protein that is textured and flavored is being used to supplement meat. Soy protein is the closest to meat in ratio and quantity of amino acids and therefore is an excellent substitute. It is also low in fat, which meat other than some poultry and fish may not be. Since the price of meat, especially beef, has risen so high, many food manufacturers are utilizing soy protein to reduce costs while maintaining a high nutrient level.

Ground beef patties now may contain up to 25% of hydrated soy protein concentrate. Soy has a slight cereal or beany flavor detectable above 20% of soy hydrate level. If a high quality of food base is added, the flavor acceptability is improved. Because of their strong seasoning contents, pizza, chili, and other highly flavored dishes can be made with 100% textured soy protein without any detectable flavor difference.

Food Analogs

Food scientists have prepared nutritious soy products resembling cheese, beef, ham, poultry, nuts, coconut, lobster, shrimp, and other analogs that are difficult to tell from the natural food. Should development and acceptance continue, the meat industry and other food manufacturers may undergo a transformation rivaling that which occurred when margarine was developed to compete with butter. In 1940, people used 17 pounds of butter and two pounds of margarine per person per year. In 1971 the yearly use was five pounds of butter and 11 pounds of margarine. Recent research on comparative digestibility favors butter, which revelation may reverse the trend. Oilseed, single-cell protein from bacteria, algae, or fungi treatment of food plant wastes are being studied as possible substitutes.

Nutrient Standards

Recent action taken by the FDA is aimed at improving the nutrient content of some foods by requiring nutrient value standards as part of the Standards of Identity. Standards of Identity have been promulgated to indicate exactly what food should be. If a name of a product is used, the contents of the product must conform to the Standards of Identity as published under that name. The quantity of iron and vitamin A specified for bread, enriched flour, and milk were increased. An index of nutritional quality (INQ) has been used to define the material in foods in terms of a nutrient density. The INQ is included in the Standards of Identity. Nutrient density is defined as the ratio of the nutrient composition of food to nutrient requirements of the human (Hansen 1973). Its purpose is to provide a better method of judging nutritional value of a food when compared to others of the same kind. For example, three brands of stew, chop suey, or other products may be compared if they are all labeled in accordance with the nutritional labeling regulations.

Nutrient Density

Nutrient density is a ratio of the nutrient content supplied by 1000 kcal of a food or menu item containing the nutrient, to the recommended dietary allowance RDA/1000 kcal of that nutrient for that sex, age, weight, and height as given in Table 9.

$$\text{Index Nutrient density (INQ)} = \frac{\text{nutrient content of a given food in g/1000 kcal}}{\text{RDA of that nutrient in g/1000 kcal}}$$

An INQ above 1.0 for a nutrient indicates that an amount of a particular food satisfying the total energy requirement, for example, 1000 kcal, also supplies more than the required amount of the nutrient. Thus 1000 kcal of fluid milk contains 54 g of protein, whereas 25 g is the RDA for protein/1000 kcal. The INQ of milk is 54 g/25 g = 2.2. Conversely, a nutrient with an INQ less than 1.0 requires either supplementation by other foods with that nutrient or consumption of the food in excess of caloric needs (Wyse *et al.* 1976). The nutritional quality of any foodstuff or food combination can be evaluated by this method. The percentage of foods from Handbook No. 8 (Watt and Merrill 1963) with an INQ of 1.0 or higher is shown in Table 23.

Nutrient Profile

Table 24 presents a computer print-out of a nutrient profile for a cheddar cheese, bread, and salad combination that furnishes 300 calories of energy, or 15 % of a 2000 kcal daily need. Figure 4 represents the nutrient profile of a food item. It shows that a standard portion of chicken casserole provides high amounts of protein and niacin and adequate amounts of iron relative to their respective INQ's. To insure a balanced meal, foods high in calcium, riboflavin, thiamin, and vitamins A and C should complement the casserole. Uses of INQ include (1) planning and designing new foods for overall nutritional adequacy, (2) evaluating current food fortification practices, and (3) determining enrichment and restoration policy in foods.

TABLE 23. Percentage of Foods with Index of Nutritional Quality of 1.0 or Higher

Food classification	Number of foods	Protein[1]	Calcium	Phosphorus	Iron	Vitamin A	Thiamin	Riboflavin	Niacin[2]	Vitamin C
Fruits	307	3.0	14.2	11.9	41.7	44.7	38.0	20.9	22.6	79.5
Vegetables	414	81.3	60.3	92.2	86.3	63.9	82.8	73.7	79.0	93.0
Grains and grain products[3]	547	36.3	10.3	47.1	28.6	2.8	40.7	12.2	26.7	2.7
Nuts, soybeans and seeds	65	73.9	32.2	86.2	56.9	6.2	58.6	32.3	33.7	9.1
Meat, fish and egg products	921	91.7	8.2	87.1	57.2	13.8	36.5	58.0	82.4	6.3
Milk products	57	84.2	85.8	85.8	0.0	61.4	20.9	84.1	0.0	5.3
Sweets and sugars	80	12.5	18.6	30.8	21.1	0.0	2.6	15.0	11.3	1.3
Fats and oils	35	9.1	11.3	11.2	2.7	22.8	0.0	8.6	0.0	8.7

Source: Hansen *et al.*, 1979.

[1]Protein calculated on a standard of 45 g for milk, meat, fish and egg products, 65 g otherwise.

[2]Preformed niacin

[3]Includes pies, cakes, and cookies.

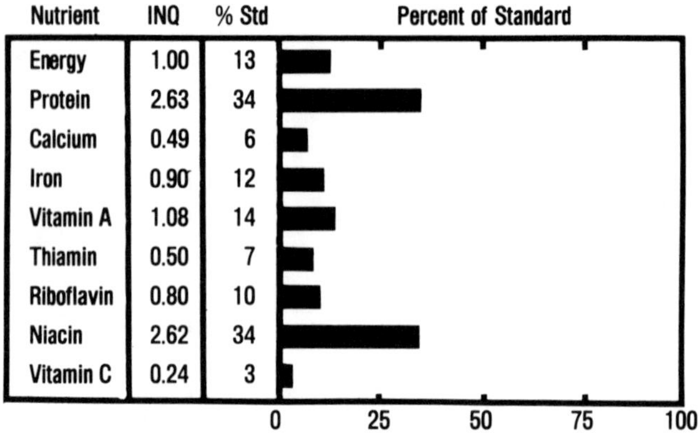

Fig. 4. Nutritional profile of a food item. Standard portion of chicken casserole provides high amounts of protein and niacin and adequate amounts of iron.
From Hansen et al. 1979.

TABLE 24. Computer Read-out of a "Nutrient Profile" for Cheddar Cheese, Bread, Salad

Nutrient	Amount	INQ	STD	0% 50% 100%
ENERGY	303.13 kcal	1.00	15	BBBCCS
VITAMIN A	3203.60 IU	5.28	80	CCCCS *SSSSSSSSSSSSSSSSSSSSSSSSS
VITAMIN C	27.94 mg	3.07	47	SSSSS *SSSSSSSSSSSSS
THIAMIN	0.22 mg	1.42	22	BBBBB*SS
CALCIUM	295.79 mg	2.17	33	BBCCC*CCCCCSS
IRON	2.81 mg	1.16	18	BBBCS *S
POTASSIUM	439.06 mg	0.58	9	BSSS *
SODIUM	479.17 mg	1.05	16	BBBCC*
CHOLESTEROL	29.22 mg	0.55	8	CCC *
FAT-TOTAL	15.29 g	1.29	20	BCCCC*SS
SATURATED FATTY ACIDS	5.99 g	1.39	21	BCCCC*CCS
UNSATURATED FATTY ACIDS	2.64 g	0.88	13	CSSSS *

Source: Hansen *et al.* 1979.
*Composite profile for 28g of CHEDDAR CHEESE (C), 25g each of whole wheat and enriched white flour BREAD (B) and a SALAD (S) composed of ½c each iceberg lettuce and spinach. 1 tomato wedge. 1 tsp of corn oil, and 1 tsp of vinegar.

The composite analysis is based upon the following daily intake values:
Energy 2000 kcal. Vitamin A 4000 IU. Vitamin C 60 mg. Thiamin 1 mg. Calcium 900 mg. Iron 16 mg. Sodium, 3000 mg. Potassium 5000 mg. Cholesterol 350 mg. Fat-Total 78 g. Saturated Fatty Acids 28.5 g. Unsaturated Fatty Acids 20 g.

State Variances

Pressure is being brought upon 19 states that do not follow the federal standards for enrichment of foods in an attempt to make them conform to the standards. Citizens of these states show a high incidence of anemia, rickets, and goiter which have largely been eradicated in states that follow the federal standards.

Some nutritionists feel that amino acid supplementation for bread and cereals by the addition of lysine would be desirable. Soy would be a much closer analog to meat if it were enriched with methionine. Ironically, poultry, animal, and pet foods have been enriched in this and other ways for several years. Cereal diets for export to malnourished people are similarly fortified.

Food Improvements by Plant and Animal Breeding

Another way of increasing the nutritional value of food is by improving the strains of animals or plants. High lysine corn has been developed by plant breeders. It is now being combined with flours to improve their nutritional values. A new cereal called triticale, a cross between rye and wheat, has been developed. It is much higher in protein and other nutrients than many other cereals. Crossbreeds of cattle and buffalo are being developed, with a cross between Hereford and Charolais cattle and the buffalo. Advantages of beefalo include the ability to mature more rapidly than cattle with greater meat yields, greater resistance to diseases and cold weather, better flavor than beef, and more valuable hides for leather.

Protein and Land Conservation

Studies show that a diet high in vegetables can improve health if it is adequate in protein and vitamin B_{12} along with other nutrients. Americans have consumed far more meat than they need and, in consequence, have had an intake of too much fat plus more protein than needed to support nutrition. Consuming less meat and more vegetables, fruits, and cereals may yield health benefits in the future. It may also extend our ability to feed people. About 21 pounds of non-animal protein such as that found in grass or grains can be produced on the same acreage needed to produce a pound of beef protein. Though it takes less land to produce lamb, mutton, pork, chickens, and rabbits (in that order), such a diet alteration may mean a big increase in the amount of food available for people of the world.

Label Information Demands of Consumers and the FDA

Consumers today are better informed on nutrition subjects than at any other time in U.S. history. Meanwhile, the media are used by the FDA to seek support from Congress and the food industry to list on labels any ingredients that may affect consumer health or safety.

Manufacturers of food products prefer to retain some leeway in labeling. For example, at the present time seasoning and flavoring are blanket-listed and each component does not have to be listed on the label. Coca-Cola and some other foods and beverages require no ingredient listing for the consumer.

1. Reducing calorie and protein intakes
2. Increasing use of protein from poultry and fish
3. Decreasing meat protein usage
4. Sugar and salt reduction
5. Increase in complex carbohydrate and fiber in the U.S. diet

These changes are aimed at reducing obesity, hypertension, heart attacks, and strokes, the major causes of premature death in the United States.

Unfortunately, we may no longer take our abundant food supply for granted. During the past 50 years we have experienced a farm food production revolution. Now, the energy crunch, fertilizer shortages, depleted topsoil, and costs threaten the future of our farms and food supplies.

Research and development of single-cell proteins from agricultural residues, algae, sugar from wood, and protein from sugar by biotechnology microbiological methods may soon supplement farming (King and Orrego 1981). Mariculture (Brown and Gratzek 1980) will undoubtedly flourish, too, as mankind struggles to continue existence in a hungry and ever-changing world.

Nutrition is replete with controversies that heighten interest in the subject. Some topics are fiber and sugar and salt in the diet; whole grain cereal products and enriched or fortified products with vitamins and minerals; cholesterol and atherosclerosis, heart attacks, and strokes; liquid protein diets; the protein-sparing diet; the fluoridated water issue; hyperactivity and food additives; federal regulations; saccharin a mild carcinogen; acne; vitamin C and colds and influenza.

Pressure by the FDA is increasing to force manufacturers and processors to list all ingredients, state their functions and reveal their concentrations on the label. Obviously this is tantamount to having them reveal formulas that are in private domain and may have taken many years to develop. Competitors would then avail themselves of the data at no cost to them.

Consumers will be required to pay the increased costs of product analysis and labeling that such changes in the existing laws will entail together with the cost of hearings held by the FDA. Results of the hearings are published as they are obtained in the FDA Consumer and Federal Register.

CONCLUSION

We Americans are among the best fed people of the world. Our food supply is adequate, although pockets of hunger where poverty persists still plague us and probably always will. Recent White House Nutrition Conferences and meetings of the National Academy of Sciences/National Research Council Nutrition Committee have established guidelines for megavitamin therapy; the low-carbohydrate diet; the U.S. diet and the world food shortage; jogging; and many more. This is a healthy situation that stimulates research. We can expect that our life spans will be lengthened and our quality of life improved as research in nutrition continues to improve our lifestyle.

REFERENCES

ADAMS, C.F. 1975. Nutritive Value of American Foods. USDA Handbook No. 56, Washington, D.C.

ALTSHUL, A.M. 1970. Interface between government and technology. Food Technol. *24*(3), 18.

AMERICAN CHEMICAL SOCIETY. 1973. Symposium: Nutrition and Public Policy: The Issues Research Report, Audio Chemistry and Public Affairs Committee, Division of Agriculture and Food Chemistry, American Chemical Society, Washington, D.C.

ANON. 1973. Nutrition labeling. Nutr. Rev. *31*(1), 36.

ANON. 1974. Standards of identity. Nutr. Rev. *32*(1), 29.

APPELDORF, H. 1974. Nutritional analysis of foods from fast-food chains. Food Technol *28*(4), 50.

AREHART-TREICHEL. 1974. School lights and problem children. Sci. News (April 20).

BOWES, A.D. and CHURCH, C.F. 1970. Food Values of Portions Commonly Used. J.P. Lippincott Co., Philadelphia.

BROWN, E.E. and GRATZEK, J.B. 1980. Fish Farming Handbook. AVI Publishing Co., Westport, Connecticut.

CANADA. 1975. Dietary Standards for Canada. pp. 70–71. Department of National Health and Welfare Department of Public Printing and Stationery, Ottawa.

CHEM, L.F. and LACHANCE, P.A. 1974. An area of concern: The nutritive profile of fast food meal combinations. Food Prod. Dev. *8*(8), 40.

CRAMPTON, E.W. and LLOYD, L.E. 1959. Fundamentals of Nutrition, pp. 205–260. W.H. Freeman Co., San Francisco.

DEAMAN, G.E. 1975. A Primer on Four Nutrients. FDA Consumer. HEW Publication No. FDA-752026. U.S. Dept. Health, Education, and Welfare, Washington, D.C.

ELKINS, E.R. 1979. Nutrient content of raw and canned green beans, peaches, and sweet potatoes. Food Technol. *33*(2), 66–70.

FDA. 1973. Part 100. Nutritional quality guidelines for foods. Fed. Regis. *38*(49), 6969.

FDA. 1974. Nutrition labeling: terms you should know. HEW Publication No. (FDA) 74-2010. U.S. Dept. Health, Education and Welfare, Washington, D.C.

GARARD, I.D. 1974. The Story of Food. AVI Publishing Co. Westport, Connecticut.

GENERAL FOODS. 1979. Nutrition information can work for you. General Foods Consumer Center, White Plains, New York.

GROTTA-KURSKA, D. 1974. Here's what you should know about vegetarianism. Today's Health *52*(10), 18.

HAMILTON, E.M. and WHITNEY, E. 1980. Alcoholic beverages. Nutrition Concepts and Controversies. Appendix, pp. 565–566. West Publishing Co., St. Paul, Minn.

HANSEN, R. 1973. An index of food quality. Nutr. Rev. *31*(1), 1.

HANSEN, R.G., WYSE, B.W. and SORENSON, A.W. 1979. Nutritional Quality Index Foods. AVI Publishing Company, Westport, Connecticut.

HARTLEY, J.A. 1974. Beefalo. Elks Mag. *53*(4), 11.

HEINZ, H.J. 1972. Nutritional Data. Heinz U.S.A., Pittsburgh, Pennsylvania.

HEW. 1971. Ten-state nutritional survey in the U.S. 1968–70. Center for Disease Control, Public Health Service and Mental Health Administration, Atlanta, Georgia.

HURLBURT, C.G. and HURLBURT, S.H. 1974. Blue Gold: Mariculture of the Edible Blue Mussel (*Mytilus edulis*). C.G. Hurlburt, Duxbury, Massachusetts.

IFT EXPERT PANEL ON FOOD SAFETY AND NUTRITION. 1979. Dietary fiber. Food Technol. *33*(1), 35–39.

JACOBSON, M. 1977. Food Scorecard. Center for Science in the Public Interest, Washington, D.C.

KING, J. and ORREGO, C. 1981. Biotechnology. McGraw–Hill Yearbook of Science and Technology, McGraw–Hill Book Company, New York.

KRITSCHEVSKY, D. 1979. Nutrition and Heart Disease. J. Food Technol. *33*(12), 39.

LABUZA, T.P. 1973. Effects of dehydration and storage. Food Technol. *27*(1), 36.

LaCHANCE, P.A. 1970. The "new" proteins. Food Technol. *24*(3), 33.

LaCHANCE, P.A. 1978. Fortification policies must be consistent with the ever-changing uses of food. Food Prod. Dev. *12*(4), 30.

LaCHANCE, P.A., MOSKOWITZ, R.B. and WINAWER, H.H. 1972. Balanced nutrition through food processor practice of nutrification. Food Technol. *26*(6), 30.

LaCHANCE, P.A., ARVIND, S.R. and MALTAS, J. 1973. Effects of reheating convenience foods. Food Technol. *27*(1), 36.

LEVEILLE, G.A. 1976. Dietary fiber. Food and Nutrition News *47*(1).

LEVEILLE, G.A. 1978. Recommendations for rational changes in the U.S. diet. Food Technol. *32:*(8), 75–76.

LITCHFIELD, J.H. 1977. Single-cell proteins. Food Technol. *31*(5), 175–179.

LIVINGSTON, G.E., ANG, C.Y.W. and CHANG, C.M. 1973. Effects of food service handling. Food Technol. *27*(1), 28.

LONG, C. (Editor). 1961. Biochemists Handbook, pp. 1122–1123. D. Van Nostrand Co., New York.

LUND, D.B. 1973. Effects of heat processing. Food Technol. *27*(1), 16.

MILLER, B.F. and KEANE, C.B. 1972. Encyclopedia and Dictionary of Medicine and Nursing, p. 161. W.B. Saunders Co., Philadelphia.

MINOR, L.J. 1966. Food flavor. Cornell Hotel Rest. Admin. Quart. *6*(3).

MINOR, L.J. and MINOR, R.E. 1972. Meat analog experiments workshop. Mich. State University, Hotel and Rest. Dept., East Lansing, Michigan.

MISKIMIN, D., BOWERS, J. and LACHANCE, P.A. 1974. Nutrification of frozen preplated school lunches is needed. Food Technol. *28*(2), 52.

NAS/NRC. 1964. Recommended Dietary Allowances Publ. No. 1046. 6th ed. National Academy of Sciences–National Research Council, Washington, D.C.

NAS/NRC. 1980. Recommended Dietary Allowances, 9th ed. National Academy of Sciences–National Research Council, Washington, D.C.

NATIONAL FOOD REVIEW. 1979. NFR6. Natl. Econ. Analysis Div. of Econ. and Statistics and Coop. Service, U.S. Dept. Agric. Washington, D.C.

PAULING, L.C. 1976. Vitamin C, the Common Cold, and the Flu. H. Freeman, San Francisco.

RUNYAN, T.J. 1976. Nutrition for Today. Harper & Row, Inc., New York.

SMITH, L.L. and MINOR, L.J. 1974. Food Service Science. AVI Publishing Co., Westport, Connecticut.

SOCIETY FOR THE ADVANCEMENT OF FOOD RESEARCH. 1974. Conference: A View of the Food Service Industry. Skokie, Illinois.

STECHER, P.G. (Editor). 1960. The Merck Index. Merck and Co., Inc., Rahway, New Jersey.

TRAGER, J. 1972. The Bellybook, Grossman Pub., New York.

TRENKLE, A. and WILLHAM, R.L. 1977. Beef production efficiency. Science *198*, 1009–1015.

USDA. 1975. Agricultural Handbook No. 456. U.S. Dept. Agric., Washington, D.C.

USDA. 1977–1978. National Food Consumption Survey. U.S. Dept. Agric. Washington, D.C.

USDA. 1978. Nutrient Content of the National Food Supply. National Food Review (January). U.S. Dept. Agric., Washington, D.C.

WATT, B.K. and MERRILL, A.L. 1963. Composition of Foods. Agriculture Handbook No. 8, U.S. Dept. Agric., Washington, D.C.

WATT, B.K. and MERRILL, A.L. 1975. Handbook of the Nutritional Contents of Foods. Dover Publications, Inc., New York.

WOOD, P. 1979. New York on the run: Excerpt from Run to Health. N.Y. Times Mag. (October 7), pp. 110–114.

WYSE, B.W., SORENSON, A.W. WITTWER, A.J. and HANSEN, R.G. 1976. Nutritional quality index identifies consumer nutrient needs. Food Technol. *30*(1), 22.

7 New Food Product Development Standards

A question often asked by the public is "Why do we need more new products?" Some of the factors that have contributed to new product activity are the following. (1) The development and growth of the retail supermarket, which has created a great demand for packaged food in nonperishable and convenient states; (2) The changed eating habits of Americans, who are eating away from home more than ever before. About one of every three meals consumed is eaten away from home. In larger cities the rate can be as high as 50% (NRA 1981). This trend has resulted in the development and growth of institutional markets. It has been estimated that the institutional trade serves as many as 50 billion meals a year. (3) The changing pattern of employment of women in this country has decreased the time that the homemaker has to devote to cooking. On the average the homemaker is spending 2½ hours a day less time in the kitchen now than a decade ago and approximately one-third of the cooking that used to be done at home is now done by either the foodservice industry or the processed food industry.

More than half the food products available today did not exist 25 years ago, and approximately 25% have made their appearance during the last decade. These facts together with the relatively high mortality rate of new products shows us why so much emphasis must be placed on new product development.

The definition of new product has to be dynamic, and the dynamics will be contributed by imagination, convenience, and technology. The changing nature of the definition can be illustrated by the following examples. At one time each represented a new product.

Removal of inedible parts by trimming
Conversion of perishable commodities to nonperishable items by canning, freezing, dehydration, and the like
Supplementation of deficiencies in natural food (thus contributing to wholesomeness)
Preparation of partially or fully cooked food
Convenience in packaging, portion control, and cleaning of dishes
Fabricated foods, wherein the ingredients are combined on the basis of functionality and may or may not resemble any naturally occurring food

As one can see from this list, the principal concept involved in new product development is providing convenience. Occasionally a new product is really new—an entirely different concept and entity with its own unique texture, flavor, or individuality. An outstanding example is the high-quality food bases that save time and labor in the kitchen but retain freshness.

Important Factors in Developing Products

From a capital and corporate business standpoint the primary motivating force behind new product development is the expansion of the market for products and eventual profits. However, additional factors to be considered are consumer needs, acceptability to the consumers, is the product different?, does the product fit into the existing operation?, competition, and availability of raw product, location of the plant, and availability of labor. These factors are fairly self-explanatory and need no further discussion.

The decision by an individual or a corporation to enter into the area of new product development should be well thought out, and it is always a good idea to seek the advice of management consultants and marketing experts. Many challenges are encountered in new product development, including (a) providing convenience and nutrition, (b) anticipating possible government restrictions or controls, (c) market changes, (d) profitability versus inflation, (e) possible impact of new technologies, (f) demographic effects, (g) domestic and foreign competition, and (h) value of the product to the consumer.

STEPS IN THE DEVELOPMENT OF A NEW PRODUCT

1. *Idea.* Probably the most important part of new product development, the idea serves as the nucleus for the steps to follow and the eventual

success of the product. The idea may come from a number of sources—from customers, from research and development groups, or from top executives of the company. Whatever the source of the idea, most companies have a new product development committee that constantly screens ideas for promise and feasibility. Several of the factors discussed earlier play an important role in the selection of the idea to be developed further. Generally the decision will require a commitment of time, personnel and capital and, in most companies, it is an executive decision.

2. *Product Development.* This stage includes the development of the prototypes for the eventual new products. The development stage involves formulation with consideration for consumer appeal, flavor, and texture. Great advances in food science have changed this area from the science of food mixology (as it was originally) to the science of food functionality. Many problems that arise during development need the expert attention of scientists and technologists alike.

3. *Taste Paneling.* Two types of test panels are used in product development. One is a small panel of company personnel who are trained to judge minute differences. The other is a much larger panel of the consumers who represent the potential buyers of the product. Attention should be given to age, sex, background, ethnicity, and family income in the selection of this type of panel.

4. *Sampling.* Once the product has been approved by the consumer panel, it is generally important to obtain a reaction from a greater number of people. Families are usually chosen representing three income levels: upper, middle, and low. A sample of the product is left with families chosen from each level, and they are asked to fill out a questionnaire that concerns the properties of the product and its acceptability. Opinion varies among researchers about whether to ask the test family the question "Will you buy this product?" Experience reveals that most people when asked this question want to be helpful and say yes, which is at times really not a true answer. If the reactions from this broader survey are good, the personnel in production are alerted about the possibility of a new product on the horizon.

5. *Shelf Life, Product Safety, and Nutritional Quality.* Keeping quality and shelf stability are very important for acceptance of the product by the consumer. The safety of the product is of paramount importance, because no tolerances can be afforded by the producer. With present knowledge, the safety checks will include microbiological aspects and hazardous chemicals such as pesticides and antibiotics. The nutritional quality of the product will have to be checked to ensure public confidence. The storage stability of flavor, color, and texture plays an important role in the shelf life of the product. Long shelf life, like that of canned or frozen products, is the goal; but realistically a storage time of three weeks for refrigerated products is

considered fairly good. Irradiated fresh foods that save energy and do not require refrigeration are being introduced (Anon. 1981).

6. *Production.* The production of a new product generally proceeds in steps from a rather small-scale kitchen type of operation to small and large pilot plants and eventually to the establishment of one or more full-scale production facilities. The extent and size of pilot plant facilities and production facilities will be governed primarily by the extent of the market testing that is planned. The decisions at these stages are expensive, mistakes are costly, and only conservative estimates should be used for planning.

7. *Packaging.* A statement generally made is that if the package fails to do an effective job, the chances are excellent that the product will be a failure. However, the reverse is not necessarily true. The packaging is not only a covering material for the product; it represents an effective sales program within highly impersonal merchandizing tactics. The basic roles of a package are (1) to protect the product, (2) to inform the customer of its content and how to use it, (3) to display the product, (4) to provide convenience, and (5) to appeal to the customers. Actually, the package has become a psychological tool to attract the approval of the customers. For example, plastic is preferred over glass in the kitchen.

8. *Market Testing.* Once the product is developed, given a name, and packaged, the developer is ready to test the whole concept to assess whether it has an adequate market potential. The market testing can be conducted nationally, regionally, or in selected areas. The channel will depend on the production facilities, the marketing budget, the degree of exposure desired and, last but not least, the confidence in the probable acceptance of the product. The best approach in many instances is to do wide testing since if the project is successful a competitive edge will be provided. A failure, however, could mean a big loss. The testing of the product in selected areas has been widely used with good success. However, some of the hazards involved here are (1) competitors will find out about the product and will have an easier time catching up; (2) selection for the appropriate test market or markets—for example, ethnic foods find better acceptance when marketed properly; and (3) self-sabotage. For instance, a favorable response in the market may be obtained through aggressive selling (overselling); but, when the marketing pressures are lifted, the sales may be disappointing.

Judging the Chances of Success

When developing a new product the developer follows various development stages that lead to either the mortality or the eventual sale of the product. These are:

Screening the idea for practicality and value by research and development and top management with the help of an experimental outline

Developing a preliminary business analysis

Studying possible regulatory limitations

Determining possible infringement on product or process patents and copyrights

Follow-up experimentation with pilot plant production when assured of the availability of raw materials and equipment needed to produce the product

Determination of the production space and utility requirments

Economic feasibility study of the project

Complete market testing

Commercialization

Market development

Problems that arise at any of these stages may lead to abandonment of the project. Consider the fact that less than 2% of new product ideas are successful. Success requires senior management involvement. Legal and financial advice are essential. Research and development (R&D), manufacturing, marketing, finance, and distribution support are essential to new product development success. Each area must be explored and thoroughly researched.

When approvals by R&D, manufacturing, and senior management, including the legal and finance directors, have been obtained, the product is turned over to marketing, and not before. Test marketing may show success in one region and not in another for demographic or ethnic or distribution reasons. All of this experience must be channeled into marketing planning. Any weak link in the food product development chain may cause failure of the project.

Product development time is a critical factor. Competitors may reach the market with a similar item when your project is at midstream. Several years of development time are usually required to achieve success with a new product; the cost can be staggering, and the pitfalls many.

NEW FOOD PRODUCTS

New Egg Products

Some egg products are modified from those generally made in kitchens to introduce convenience while others are entirely new concepts.

Frozen French toast. This product contains half an egg per slice and is sold already cooked and frozen. The only preparation required by the consumer is to heat the product in the toaster for several minutes. High-protein bread is used to prevent buckling in the center when grilling before freezing.

Hard-cooked egg roll. This item enjoys great success at the institutional level. The roll is prepared by sealing one end of a polypropylene tube, filling it with four large eggs that have been broken out of their shells, and then clipping it shut. The rolls are cooked in water at 90°C for 20 min. Two-day-old eggs are best for this product, since they are old enough for the albumen to be firm after cooking and fresh enough so that the yolk will center in the roll.

New Poultry Products

Chicken sticks. This product is made from raw stewing chicken. The ground meat is mixed with a binder and seasonings, formed, and then frozen. The frozen product is dipped into an egg batter and then rolled in corn flake crumbs.

Chicken emulsion products. Several products have been developed using chicken meat emulsions, including chicken franks, chicken bologna, and chick-a-lona (an uncured bologna). These products have good commercial acceptance.

Poulet supreme, Chicken chunk roll, and Chunk-a-lona. These products are made from an emulsion similar to chick-a-lona with added pieces of poultry meat. Poulet supreme contains 80% pieces of meat; chunk roll is 50% meat, and chunk-a-lona contains 20% meat pieces. These products were the forebears of present-day products such as chicken or turkey roll, loaves, and similar types of cold cuts now available to foodservices. Some other products include chicken chili, chick-a-links (a chicken breakfast sausage), chicken steaks, smoked chicken, chicken hash, and bake-and-serve chicken loaf.

SUMMARY

One might seek answers to the following questions when considering the development of a new product.

Is the product new, or is it an improved version of an existing product?
Does a need exist for the product?
What would be the market potential of the product?
Can both the research and market testing budgets sustain the development of the product?

Are the raw materials and equipment needed to produce the product economically available?

Within what time frame can the development be completed?

How could the product meet competitive pressures?

Will the product fit into the production and sales areas as they now exist?

What possible effect could the new product have on products now being manufactured and sold?

Would growth in customer demand with time be expected when marketing this product?

Could new markets and products result from the development and marketing of this new product?

Might the internal and external images and reputation of the firm benefit as a result of the development of the product?

Could government regulations have a negative influence on the success of the product?

Is the technology sound or could other technologies threaten it?

How energy-efficient and convenient is the product?

Does the product have significant nutritional value?

Will the shelf-life guarantee safe, economical distribution and storage life prior to the use of the product?

REFERENCES

ANON. 1981. The barriers to irradiated foods are falling. Business Week p. 96. (28 September).

ESCOFFIER, A. 1969. The Escoffier Cook Book. Crown Publishers, Inc., New York.

GOURMET BOOKS Cookbooks and Menu Cook Book. Gourmet Books, Inc., New York.

NRA. 1981. NRA News, NRA Washington Report and NRA Foodservice Trends. National Restaurant Association, Washington, D.C. and Chicago, Ill.

PAUL, P.C. and PALMER, H.H. 1972. Food Theory and Applications. Chapters 14, 15, and 16. John Wiley and Sons, Inc., New York.

8 Laboratory Guide for Food Flavor Evaluation: Theory

This book has emphasized that the foodservices industry will be developed by and is dependent on the managers of tomorrow. It is imperative, then, that the students of today receive effective education and training in the principles of food science so that their efforts as foodservice leaders will enable them to attain and, perhaps, surpass the food science standards expressed in this book.

Materials that complete this chapter are taken from laboratory and class-developed materials used successfully to teach food flavor evaluation at Michigan State University from 1965 to 1981. They may be helpful to others charged with the responsibility of providing professional growth and development information to college and university foodservice students. The text used is Carl A. Rietz, *A Guide to the Selection, Combination, and Cooking of Foods, Volume 1, Selection and Combination of Foods*, published by the AVI Publishing Company, Inc., Westport, Connecticut, 1961.

FLAVOR SENSITIVITY REVIEW

Flavor increases the acceptability of nearly everything whether it be food, beverage, tobacco, medicine, or toothpaste (Crocker 1945). Whatever is pleasant is preferred over that which is least pleasant and is sure to be used more willingly and freely. Thus flavor and odor become the most important criteria of food quality and largely determine whether or not food is eaten with pleasure. In the foodservice industry this is of particular interest because, if the flavor or odor is so poor that the food is not appealing, it may mean ruin for the business.

The most primitive animal develops likes and dislikes for food with many species displaying well-known preferences for one food over another (Amerine *et al.* 1965). A study of Paleolithic man reveals that, despite the scarcity of food, he rejected certain foods completely and consumed others only when necessary for survival. As society differentiated and leisure time grew, flavor characteristics and food preferences developed rapidly. Dietary history does influence various food preferences.

It is interesting to note that many of our present day food habits undoubtedly developed during the Neolithic period. The prejudice of nomadic peoples against pork is one example. Although Mohammed preached that pork was dangerous to eat, there was also an economic reason for rejection—the conflict between the nomadic tribes that could not raise pork and the settled communities that could. Because one tribe did not want the other to have an advantage, pork was banned.

The Egyptians, Jews, Arabians, and Chinese all had distinct spices and aromatic foods. The very discovery of America is indirectly related to the demand of Europeans for Oriental odorous material for flavoring and cosmetics. The Western Hemisphere generously contributed allspice and chocolate to the world of flavor (Bienfang 1946).

Since the fate of a food product rests on the consuming public, it is crucial that the food manager be sensitive to quality in regard to flavor and odor. Consumer reactions are difficult to measure, but the necessity for such studies will continue to grow as competition for the food dollar increases (Amerine *et al.* 1965).

The customer expects to be favorably impressed and will express displeasure when the product does not measure up to that anticipation. By spreading adverse impressions, a customer can do much harm to a business.

There are many factors that influence acceptance, preference, and selection. Appearance, although it is the greatest initial influence, becomes secondary to color and texture as soon as the food has been tasted. Flavor in the final analysis brings repeat business.

Scent and taste are two stimuli that are repeatedly joined. The two organs of perception are a matter of inches apart in the body. This helps to account for the general confusion regarding the two senses and for the fact that many olfactory experiences are referred to as tastes.

ODOR STUDIES

Odor has been discussed since 1599, although the olfactory cells and their supporting cells were first described by von Brunn in 1892 (Amerine *et al.* 1965). One of the earliest measurements was made for mercaptan by Fischer and Pennzolt (1886).

Man has so little appreciation of olfaction that the English language is atrophied in that connection (Bienfang 1946). It is impossible to make the simple declarative statement, "he smells," without the risk of double entendre, for the common verb is both transitive and intransitive. We have a fast accumulation of systematic and artistic data for the other four senses. While a smattering is known about odor perception, the science of odors and the aesthetics of olfactory enjoyments have scarcely been explored. There yet remain vast areas to be explored by research workers in the field.

The Definition of Odor

Odor is the property of a substance or substances that is perceived in human and higher vertebrates by inhalation in the nasal or oral cavity and results in a sensory stimulus that is different from hearing, tasting, or feeling. Odor as a volatile substance has to be in the air to stimulate olfaction (Merory 1960). Without the pressure of air, odor bounces off the receptors and causes no change in stimulus.

Some odors are indistinct and insipid, as are some tastes, while some have a distinct character. However, the various kinds of odors, good and evil, although they exhibit considerable differences, have not received further distinguishing names. We speak of odor as pungent, faint, sweet, or heavy, though some of these descriptions apply to evil-smelling things as well as those which have a good odor. Sensations of smell are relatively homogeneous and untranslatable into the form of language (Bedichek 1960).

The Olfactory Mechanism

The olfactory region is about 1 in.^{2} in each nasal chamber. The cellular tissue covering the nerve area of the olfactory region consists of ordinary cells and delicate olfactory cells. Attached to each olfactory cell are five, six, or perhaps eight olfactory cells and delicate olfactory hairs, which are fragile protoplasmic filaments. These filaments protect the membrane covering the area. It is generally believed that the hairs are affected by odorous particles and set off the train of events culminating in our perception of odor.

The information gathered by the olfactory region in the nose is carried to the brain by the olfactory nerve. The olfactory nerve travels from the olfactory cleft, high up in the nose, to the olfactory bulb of the brain to which it transmits its messages.

ODOR THEORIES

There are numerous theories of odor of varying degrees of complexity. A few of the basic theories are presented here in summary form.

The Crocker–Henderson Theory

By the Crocker–Henderson system, an odor may be represented as a four-digit number (Crocker 1945). The first digit is the measure of relative fragrance, the second of acidity, the third of burntness, and the fourth of caprylic character.

Every odor has some value of each of the four components. Its distinctiveness is in the relative values of each. Sweet floral odors are high in fragrance, whereas vinegar is high in acid. Burnt is prominent in the odor of many substances that result from chemical changes and is also conspicuous in the odor of a skunk. Caprylic is another world for "goaty" and denotes the unpleasant odor associated with a billy goat.

The Amoore Theory

The Amoore theory (Amoore 1963) stipulates that the odorous properties of any compound depends on its volatility and on the size and shape and electronic status of its molecule. Amoore postulates that the olfactory receptor site corresponding to that molecule possesses complementary properties. Empirically, Amoore named seven olfactory sites: ethereal, camphoraceous, musky, floral, pepperminty, pungent, and repulsive. From these seven primaries every known odor could be made by mixing them in certain proportions. In this respect, the primary odors are like the primary colors of red, yellow, and blue.

To match these seven primary odors, Amoore postulated that there are seven different kinds of olfactory receptors in the nose. We can picture the receptor sites as ultramicroscopic. Each will accept a molecule of the appropriate configuration just as a socket takes a plug.

Henning Theory

The Henning smell prism depicts his theory of odor. He postulates six fundamental odor sensations: spicy (cloves, cinnamon), flowery (heliotrope), fruity (apple, orange), resinous (turpentine), foul (hydrogen sulfide), and burnt (tarry, scorched) (Henning 1924).

ODOR DETERMINATION

Experiments concerned with the sense of smell have provided more diversity and apparent contradiction than those concerning taste. For this reason it is almost impossible to set up a definite laboratory procedure. It will explain a few of the procedures most commonly used.

The Method of Zwaardemaker

The best-known name in this connection is that of Zwaardemaker, who first described an olfactometer. His instrument consisted of a tube whose inner surface was coated with odorous material into which was placed a second, closely fitting tube (Zwaardemaker 1895). One end of the smaller tube was shaped to fit the nostril, and the relative position between the tubes could be altered. The amount of odorous material exposed to the air—which formed the stimulus—could be controlled by setting the tubes to calibrated marks showing their relative positions. The length of exposed material that gave the threshold reaction (a detectable odor) was called an olfactive (Kalmus and Hubbard 1960). This word is still used as a threshold unit. However, it now denotes the number of molecules per milliliter of the stimulus at the threshold.

The Blast Injection Method

Another popular method is the blast injection technique whereby breathing is voluntarily stopped for a brief span and an odorous material is introduced into the nose at a known pressure and volume.

Sniffing

A simple technique and probably the most popular for odor determination is sniffing. This technique is adequate for threshold studies. Bags made of odorless plastic and filled with an odor have been used for sniffing in odor intensity studies (Reese and Stevens 1960). One difficulty associated with these methods is the preparation of a test series in some stable, inodorous, nonreactive solvent of low viscosity.

The Bottle Method

Another simple method that may be easily used in a classroom situation is a method described by Guadagni *et al.* (1963). Polyethylene bottles are filled with an aqueous solution of odorous material. A rubber tube connected to the bottle was placed into the nostril. Manual squeezing of the bottle forces the substance through the nasal passage. Teflon bottles are suggested rather than plastic because plastic may have an odor of its own.

The Odor Room Method

A method that is quite costly but effective is to use an odor test room. This room, in contrast to the smaller containers, provides an enclosed space suitable for study of a great diversity of odor situations. The test room is composed of two rooms, an antechamber and an examination room. The 200 ft^3 anteroom is not odorized and provides an odorless assembly and conditioning area for the panel prior to entrance into the room. The actual room measures about 500 ft^3. The walls, floor, and ceiling are lined with heavy gauge polished aluminum. This material is used for ease of cleaning and does not tend to pick up odors. The odorants are introduced into the room through a small opening in one wall. Fans flush the air out after each odor examination (Little 1958).

For a substance to be smelled, it must first be volatile. The second requirement for an odorous substance is that it should be soluble in water. It is also common for the material to be soluble in lipids. This enables it to penetrate the nerve endings through the lipid layer that forms part of the surface membrane of every cell (Amoore 1963).

An important point to remember in odor evaluation is that the threshold is about 10,000 times lower than the lowest taste threshold.

Although these techniques have been carefully developed for the determination of odor intensity and olfactory sensitivity, many have failed because they lack: an understanding of the dimensions of the stimulus or the sensation, control of temperature and humidity during testing, precise control of air-flow pressure and velocity, supply of odor-free air and stable and pure test substances, quantitative control of odor concentration, and use of odorless construction materials. In conducting the actual tests a few essential things must be kept in mind:

1. Compounds must be pure.
2. It is necessary to have a certain constant flow rate to obtain response; after a certain rate is obtained, increased rate does not give increased response.
3. Noise apparently reduces olfactory acuity.
4. Method of presentation may greatly influence the results.
5. Hunger and satiety may influence results, and chemicals that have odors may affect odor judgments.

A Laboratory Method

A laboratory procedure can be set up by making up various concentrations of odorous compounds in Teflon bottles. The most basic odors seem to be those postulated by Amoore (1963):

Primary odor	*Chemical example*	*Familiar substance*
Camphoraceous	Camphor	Moth repellant
Musky	Pentadecanolactone	Angelica root oil
Floral	Phenylethyl methyl ethyl carbinol	Roses
Pepperminty	Menthone	Mint candy
Ethereal	Ethyl dichloride	Dry-cleaning fluid
Pungent	Formic acid	Vinegar
Repulsive	Butyl mercaptan	Bad egg

A table of concentrations of some basic solutions (Amerine *et al.* 1965) follows:

Threshold Concentrations from International Critical Tables

Compound	*Nature of odor*	*Threshold (mg/l)*
Methyl salicylate	Wintergreen	0.100
Amyl acetate	Banana oil	0.039
Oil of peppermint	Minty	0.024
Benzene	Kerosene-like	0.0088
Ethyl acetate	Fruity	0.0036
Pyridine	Burned	0.0074
Hydrogen sulfide	Rotten egg	0.00018
Coumarin	New-mown hay	0.00002
Citral	Lemon	0.000003
Trinitro tertiary butyl xylene	Musk	0.000000075
Ethyl mercaptan	Decayed cabbage	0.00000005

Best and Taylor (1943) give the following threshold data:

Substance	*mg/liter of air*
Ethyl ether	5.83
Chloroform	3.30
Iodoform	0.018
Butyric acid	0.009
Propyl mercaptan	0.006
Artificial musk	0.00006

Research on odor is incomplete and in an infant stage, compared to research on taste evaluation, our next topic.

TASTE EVALUATION

It is estimated that there are about 9000 taste buds in man. They occur in the middle of the upper side of the tongue, on the inside of the cheek, on the lips and tonsils, and on the small piece of flesh hanging down from the soft palate in the back of the mouth (Dawson *et al.* 1963).

Within the taste bud area of the mouth are a number of elongated cells, each of which ends in a minute hairlike structure. The gustatory hair projects through a minute pore in the surface of the taste bud (which is called the gustatory pore) into the mouth cavity. Direct stimulation takes place on the hairs, and the impulse passes through the gustatory cells to the nerve fibers and then to the brain. Saliva plays an important role in taste by (1) altering the food consistency, (2) solvent action, (3) cleansing action, and (4) moistening and lubricating action (Nelson and Trout 1964).

The Tongue

The top surface of the tongue is divided into three distinct sections. The division is made by a V-shaped row of eight or nine large papillae.

The central surface of the tongue is comparatively insensitive to most tastes, but that area of insensitivity varies according to whether the substance is sweet, bitter, acid, or saline. The base of the tongue is most sensitive to bitter, and the principal sensitivity of the tip is to sweet.

Taste buds that respond to salt are mostly on the sides. The maximum sensitivity to acid has been found to occur about halfway down each side of the tongue with the sensitivity diminishing toward the tip and base. The tip and edge are most sensitive to saline, and the base is least sensitive (Crocker 1945).

Taste Thresholds

There is little doubt that different normal people have quite different tastes and that certain food preferences and aversions follow definite physiological, national, and social differences. It has sometimes been assumed that these differences are based on greatly different individual taste thresholds. A wide range of thresholds has indeed been found by many investigators, but no tangible connection between threshold values and food preferences has emerged (Kalmus and Hubbard 1960).

The role of the remarkable polymorphisms of taste thresholds for phenylthiocarbamide (PTC) in biology and pathology of man is still obscure, but a few interesting clues have been discovered that, in the opinion of some clinicians, promise to yield significant results (Kalmus and Trotter 1962). The nontasting of PTC has frequently been described as taste blindness. Nontasters have a perfectly normal ability to taste sweet, acid, salty, and bitterness. However, they differ from tasters by lacking all receptors that mediate a bitter sensation. The concentrations required by nontasters will differ, and their distinctions as to the quality of their sensations will be vague.

The influence of temperature on taste does not seem to be uniform. Optimums have been reported of 35°–50°C for sucrose and hydrochloric acid, 18°–35°C for saltiness, and 10°C for quinine. Increasing temperature appears to increase the response to sweet and decrease it to salty and bitter (Amerine *et al.* 1965).

Insufficient data to draw positive conclusions as to the effect of the medium used are available. It would appear that when the taste substance is mixed with other substances such as oil, agar, starch, or gelatin, the thresholds are increased, compared to water.

It is generally recognized that a foodservice operator should be able to identify the four taste factors—sourness, sweetness, saltiness, and bitterness—if he is to be able to properly evaluate the food he is serving in his establishment.

Taste Terminology

Evaluative Terms

Sweet: A quality of taste sensation of which the taste of sucrose is the typical example.

Sour: A quality of taste sensation of which the taste of acid is the typical example.

Salt: A quality of taste sensation of which the taste of sodium chloride is a typical example.

Bitter: A quality of taste sensation, the taste of quinine being a typical example.

Threshold Terms

Threshold of sensation, stimulus threshold, or absolute threshold: That magnitude of stimulus at which a transition occurs from no sensation to sensation. A detectable concentration without identification.

The difference threshold or recognition threshold: The least amount of change of a given stimulus necessary to produce a noticeable change in sensation. It is often designated as DL (difference level) and as jnd (just noticeable difference) and jnnd (just not noticeable difference). Here the specific taste can be recognized and identified when compared to a standard (Amerine *et al.* 1965).

Detectable concentration: Crocker and Henderson (1932) list average good tasters being sensitive to sweetness or cane sugar in a 0.68% solution, sourness or tartaric acid in a 0.019 solution, saltiness or sodium chloride in a 0.18 CP solution, and bitterness or caffeine in a 0.0090% solution USP (United States Pharmacopeia).

Best and Taylor (1943) give sweet as one part in 200 parts of water, acid (HCl) as one part in 1500 parts of water, salt as 1 part in 400 parts of water, and bitter or quinine as one part in 2,000,000 parts water.

Judging Taste

The taster should be in good condition, which implies good health, physical comfort, and mental poise. Never judge after having eaten a heavy meal, especially after having eaten foods of strong flavors such as cabbage, turnips, or onions.

The use of mild-flavored pepsin chewing gum prior to judging is considered beneficial to the flow of saliva, thus useful in preparing for judging.

Always taste an ample volume of food. Beginners or untrained people tend to pass judgement on a product without adequately tasting the item.

One must be alert to observe the sequence of flavors. Notice the first tastes that are sensed.

Cleansing the Tongue

The tongue must be treated before a stimulus is applied to it. Before the test stimulus is applied, it is necessary to rinse the tongue with a solution to reduce the spontaneous activity recorded from the nerve. Certain substances such as quinine and acids will often leave a residual effect: They will depress the neutral response for a period of time after application (Kare and Halpern 1961).

Each sample may be given to a subject at a 1 min interval; there should be a 5–10 min intermission between samples. It is suggested that 10 ml samples be presented to the subject.

Absolute Threshold

The first test procedure should be to determine the absolute threshold of the subject. This will be done with the single-sample test, using the series of solutions described hereafter. Each substance should be presented individually, progressing from dilute to high concentrations. The subject is asked to identify the taste sensation (e.g., same as water, very faint taste, weak taste, and the like).

Each series is presented three times. The first detectable taste will be the taste (absolute) threshold of the subject. The number of the item in the series at which the subject correctly identifies the taste is the recognition threshold.

Preparation

The subject will be given a series of six shuffled water solutions consisting of tap water and five different concentrations of a primary taste substance. The four substances and their concentrations are as follows:

Sucrose 0.17, 0.34, 0.51, 0.68, and 0.85%
Sodium chloride 0.010, 0.015, 0.030, 0.058, and 0.087%
Tartaric acid 0.008, 0.016, 0.032, 0.048, and 0.064%
Caffeine 0.005, 0.010, 0.019, 0.029%, and 0.040%

Recognition Threshold

The next test, the paired comparison, is designed to determine the recognition threshold. The judges are presented with two samples of different intensity at one time and are asked to indicate which sample is higher in intensity.

Tap water will be paired with each of the taste substances, as follows. The judge will be asked to indicate the sample of highest intensity and also to identify the basic taste.

Procedure

Series A	A1, A2	A3, A4	A5, A6	A7, A8	A9, A10	A11, A12
Series B	B1, B2	B3, B4	B5, B6	B7, B8	B9, B10	B11, B12
Series C	C1, C2	C3, C4	C5, C6	C7, C8	C9, C10	C11, C12
Series D	D1, D2	D3, D4	D5, D6	D7, D8	D9, D10	D11, D12

Series A

A1, A2	A1 = Water	A2 = 0.34 Sucrose
A3, A4	A3 = 0.85 Sucrose	A4 = Water
A5, A6	A5 = 0.17 Sucrose	A6 = Water
A7, A8	A7 = Water	A8 = 0.68 Sucrose
A9, A10	A9 = Water	A10 = Water
A11, A12	A11 = 0.51 Sucrose	A12 = Water

The other series will consist of like combinations of the other basic tastes.

Concentration

The next test is designed to determine how well the subject can detect concentration variability. The subject will be given samples of six shuffled solutions consisting of tap water and five different concentrations of a primary taste substance. The subject is told to arrange them in rank order from least to most concentrated.

Procedure

The following table gives five concentrations for each substance listed, to be presented in the order shown.

Sucrose	*NaCl*	*Tartaric Acid*	*Caffeine*
0.17—2	0.010—3	0.008—4	0.005—5
0.34—4	0.015—4	0.016—5	0.010—3
0.51—5	0.030—5	0.032—1	0.019—2
0.68—1	0.058—1	0.048—2	0.029—1
0.85—3	0.087—2	0.064—3	0.040—4

The preceding methods were primarily designed to determine the ability of the subject to taste. The tests described next—the paired-sample test, the duo–trio test, and the triangle test—are set up primarily to help the subject compare quality or preference between two products.

Interpreting Results

The One-Tailed Test

In analyzing the results of tests, care must be taken to establish what we are interested in so that the proper method of analysis is chosen. For example, tasters may be given two samples of juice, one sweetened and one unsweetened, and be asked to select the sample having the greatest sweetness. Here we are interested only in the probability that the frequency of correct choices will exceed that due to chance. This is properly a one-tailed test, since there is only one alternative. All of the values are on one side of the mean.

The Two-Tailed Test

In the second case, tasters are given two samples of juice, one sweetened and one unsweetened, and asked to select the sample that they prefer. Since they may choose either one, this is termed a two-tailed test.

The Paired-Sample Test

The procedure for the paired sample was described by Guilford (1954). The taster is given two samples, one containing 10% sugar and the other 12%. He is asked to pick the sweeter sample. The chi-square, χ^2, distribution to determine how well an observed frequency distribution compares with a theoretical distribution is defined as:

$$\chi^2 = \frac{[(X_1 - X_2) - 1]^2}{N}$$

where N = total number of tests, X_1 = tests favorable to sample 1, and X_2 = tests favorable to sample 2. With one degree of freedom χ^2 must equal or exceed 2.71 for significance at 5%, 5.41 at 1%, and 9.55 at 0.1%. Suppose the taster identifies 12 times out of 18 the samples containing 12% sugar. $\chi^2 = [(12 - 6) - 1]^2/18 = 1.39$. This is below 2.71; therefore the taster is unable significantly to identify the sweeter sample and would not be an acceptable judge.

In another test the taster asked to indicate which sample is preferred and has indicated the 12% sugar sample for 12 out of 18 times. This calls for a two-tailed test. The χ^2 values for the same levels of significance are now 3.84, 6.64, and 10.38 respectively, because the results can go both ways. It is found by analysis that he showed no significant preference.

The Duo–Trio Test

The duo–trio test is a paired test with the standard known. One of the paired samples is identified and presented first. The taster is then asked to select from two samples presented in random order the one that is different from the reference sample. The probability is 0.50, and the χ^2 test and tables of the paired-sample test are applicable. This test should be used only as a difference test.

The Triangular Test

Applications of the triangular test for brewery product control were described by Helm and Trolle (1946). It is the best-known form, most used in the past and most written about. Recent results have indicated that it is not so sensitive in selecting differences as the paired tests. It is considered useful for testing the ability of the judges.

In this method three samples are presented to the taster at one time. Two are known to be alike and one different. The taster is asked to select the different sample. The taster would be expected to identify the odd sample by chance in one-third of the trials. In this case, the suitable χ^2 is defined as:

$$\chi^2 = \frac{(4X_1 - 2X_2) - 3^2}{8N}$$

The triangular test should be used only as a difference test and should not be combined with quality.

Procedure

Fruit juice will be used. Identification of the sample (one-tailed) will be used for all three tests. Quality preference (two-tailed) will be used in the paired tests. Each of the tasters will be given the samples at least 4 times in each of the tests.

The coding of the samples for the paired-sample test and the duo–trio test will be similar to that used in the other paired tests. For the triangular tests, the following coding may be used: AAB, ABA, BAA, BAB, BBA, ABB.

The field of flavor sensitivity is still a new one. The facts that flavor components are present in very minute and elusive quantities and in many cases are very unstable make their characterization very difficult. Progress, however, is being made. These advances, in a large part, are due to the development of new and better isolation techniques, increased research effort made possible by financial support of flavor research, and the realization that the mysteries of flavor can be solved.

The Flavor Profile Method

Arthur D. Little, Inc., has provided the food industry with a valuable technique called the Flavor Profile method that yields qualitative and quantitative information. Sniffing and tasting result in the descriptive analysis of the flavor and odor of the food product. They have trained many food product development researchers in their laboratories, as a special service to the food companies, to become proficient in the application of the Flavor Profile. Since 1951 Arther D. Little has provided this training for some 300 groups in 120 companies (Cairncross 1977).

REFERENCES

AMERINE, M.A., PANGBORN, R.M. and ROESSLER, E.B. 1965. Principles of Sensory Evaluation of Food. Academic Press, New York.

AMOORE, J.E. 1963. Stereochemical theory of olfaction. Sci. Am. *21*, 42–49.

AMOORE, J.E. 1963. Stereochemical theory of olfaction. Nature *198*, 271–272.

BEDICHEK, R. 1960. The Sense of Smell. Doubleday and Co., Inc., Garden City, New York.

BEST, C.H. and TAYLOR, N.B. 1943. The Physiological Basis of Medical Practice, 3rd ed. Williams & Wilkins Co., Baltimore, Maryland.

BIENFANG, R. 1946. The Subtle Sense. University of Oklahoma Press, Norman, Oklahoma.

CAIRNCROSS, S.E. 1977. Flavor: Its Chemical Behavioral and Commercial Aspects. Proc. Arthur D. Little, Inc. Flavor Symp. Charles M. Apt (Editor). Westview Press, Boulder, Colo.

CAMPBELL SOUP COMPANY. 1961. Flavor Chemistry Symposium. Campbell Soup Co., Camden, New Jersey.

CLARKE, A. 1922. Flavoring Materials. H. Frowde and Hodder and Stoughton, London.

CROCKER, E.C. and HENDERSON, L.F. 1932. The Glutamate Taste. Am. Perfum. Essent. Oil Rev. *27*, 156–158.

CROCKER, E.C. 1945. Flavor. McGraw-Hill, New York.

DAWSON, E.H., BROGDON, J.L. and McMANUS, S. 1963. Sensory testing of differences in taste. I. Methods. II. Selection of panel members. Food Technol. *17*(9), 45–48, 51, (10), 39–41, 43–44.

FISCHER, E. and PENZOLT, F. 1886. Ueber die Empfindlickkeit des Geruchsinnes. Sitzber physik-med. Sozietat Erlanger *18*, 7–10.

GUADAGNI, D.G., BUTTERY, R.G., and OKANO, S. 1963. Odour thresholds of some organic compounds associated with food flavors. J. Sci. Food Agric. *10*, 161–165 (see also Nature *200*, 1288–1289).

HELM, E. and TROLLE, B. 1946. Selection of a taste panel. Wallerstein Lab Commun. *9*, 181–194.

HENNING, H. 1924. Der Geruch, 2nd ed. Verlag Barth, Leipzig.

KALMUS, H. and HUBBARD, S.J. 1960. The Chemical Senses in Health and Disease. Charles Thomas Publishers, Springfield, Illinois.

KALMUS, H. and TROTTER, W.R. 1962. Direct assessment of the effect of age on P.T.C. sensitivity. Ann. Human Genet. *20*, 145–149.

KARE, M.R. and HALPERN, B.P. 1961. Physiological and Behavioral Aspects of Taste. University of Chicago Press, Chicago, Illinois.

LITTLE, A.D. 1958. Flavor Research and Food Acceptance—From Symposium given in 1956–1957. Reinhold Publ. Co., New York.

MERORY, J. 1960. Food Flavoring Composition, Manufacture, and the Nose. AVI Publishing Co., Westport, Connecticut.

NELSON, J.A. and TROUT, M.G. 1964. Judging Dairy Products, 4th ed. The Olsen Printing Co., Milwaukee, Wisconsin.

REESE, T.S. and STEVENS, S.S. 1960. Subjective intensity of coffee odor. Am. J. Psychol. *73*, 424–428.

RIETZ, C.A. 1961. A Guide to the Selection, Combination and Cooking of Foods, Vol. 1. Selection and Combination of Foods. The AVI Publishing Co., Westport, Connecticut.

ZWAARDENMAKER, H. 1895. Die Physiologie des Geruchs. Englemann, Leipzig.

9 Laboratory Guide for Food Flavor Evaluation: Practice

Workbook used with *A Guide to the Selection, Combination, and Cooking of Foods, Volume 1*, by Carl A. Rietz, AVI Publishing Co., Westport, Connecticut, 1961.

EXPERIMENT 1: TASTE

Purpose:

To check your ability to recognize the basic tastes; namely, salty, sweet, sour and bitter at room temperature.

Materials:

Salt, sugar, tartaric acid (25 g), and caffeine (10 g)
1 volumetric flask, 2 liter
40 reagent bottles with caps, 2 liter
144 beakers, 150 ml
1 jug distilled H_2O and dispenser, 20 liter

Procedure:

a. Determination of recognition threshold. You will compare 5 paired samples in each series, as designated hereafter, at room temperature. Taste each solution by taking about 25 ml into your mouth, holding it for 5 sec. Do not talk. Taste again if necessary.

	Bitter	Sour	Salt	Sweet	Unidentified
Observer					
Correct Key					

b. Determination of concentration differences. Arrange each series in proper order from least to most concentrated, using numbers shown on reagent bottles in parentheses.

	Series A		Series B		Series C		Series D	
Relative concentration	Obs.	Key	Obs.	Key	Obs.	Key	Obs.	Key
Least								
Next								
Next								
Next								
Most								

c. Repeat step a by tasting a comparable series at refrigeration temperature.

	Bitter	Sour	Salt	Sweet	Unidentified
Observer					
Correct Key					

d. Repeat step b by tasting comparable series at refrigeration temperature.

	Series A		Series B		Series C		Series D	
Relative concentration	Obs.	Key	Obs.	Key	Obs.	Key	Obs.	Key
Least								
Next								
Next								
Next								
Most								

Questions

1. Diagram the tongue to indicate taste bud locations.
2. List the four major tastes and name a food characterized by each.

Significance in Triangular Tests ($p = 1/3$)

No. of tasters or tastings	Minimum correct results to establish significant differentiation			No. of tasters or tastings	Minimum correct results to establish significant differentiation		
	5%	1%	0.1%		5%	1%	0.1%
5	4	5	5	28	15	16	17
6	5	6	6	29	15	17	19
7	5	6	7	30	16	17	19
8	6	7	8	31	16	18	19
9	6	7	8	32	16	18	20
10	7	8	9	33	17	19	20
11	8	9	10	34	17	19	21
12	8	9	10	35	18	19	21
13	9	10	11	36	18	20	22
14	9	10	12	37	19	21	23
15	10	11	12	38	19	21	23
16	10	11	12	39	20	22	24
17	10	12	13	40	20	22	24
18	11	12	14	41	21	22	25
19	11	13	14	42	21	23	25
20	12	13	15	43	21	23	25
21	12	14	15	44	21	24	25
22	12	14	16	45	22	24	26
23	13	14	16	46	22	24	26
24	13	14	16	47	23	25	27
25	13	15	17	48	23	25	27
26	14	15	17	49	23	25	28
27	14	15	17	50	24	26	28

Significance in Paired Tests ($p = 1/3$)

No. of tasters or tastings	Minimum correct results to establish significant differentiation (one-tailed)			Minimum agreeing to establish significant preference (two-tailed)		
	5%	1%	0.1%	5%	1%	0.1%
7	7	7	—	7	—	—
8	8	8	—	7	8	—
9	8	9	—	8	9	—
10	9	10	10	9	10	—
11	9	10	11	10	11	11
12	10	11	12	10	11	12
13	10	12	13	11	12	13
14	11	12	13	12	13	14
15	12	13	14	12	13	14
16	12	14	15	13	14	15
17	13	14	16	13	15	16
18	13	15	16	14	15	17
19	14	15	17	15	16	17
20	15	16	18	15	17	18
21	15	17	18	16	17	18
22	16	17	19	17	18	19
23	16	18	20	17	19	20
24	17	19	20	18	19	21
25	18	19	21	18	20	21
30	20	22	24	21	23	25
35	23	25	27	24	26	26
40	26	28	31	27	29	31
45	29	31	34	30	32	34
50	32	34	37	33	35	37

EXPERIMENT 2: ODOR

Purpose:

To familiarize you with the odors of common organic chemicals and the 7 primary odors (odor spectrum) of Amoore. The great chef, Escoffier, always smelled the food before he tasted it.

Materials:

1. One-half ounce of each of the following organic compounds put into 28 1 oz bottles fitted with stoppers and sealed with wax: camphor, ethyl dichloride, formic acid, butyl mercaptan (if available in sealed vial), sodium sulfide, methyl salicylate, benzaldehyde, amyl lactate, benzene, pyridine, coumarin, citral, chloroform, carbon tetrachloride, ethyl ether, iodoform, butyric acid, cinnamaldehyde, eugenol, anethole, pinene, oil of peppermint, 2-methyl thiopropion-aldehyde, ethyl butyrate, 2-hexenal, amyl iso valerate, amyl butyrate, diacetyl, methone, menthol oil of eucalyptol, geraniol, and maraniol.
2. A box of cotton-covered swabbing sticks used by doctors for dipping into solutions.
3. 10 reagent bottles with caps, 2 liter.

Procedure:

1. Smell each solution. Make up a table describing the odor of each chemical.
2. The 7 primary odors of Amoore are (1) Camphoraceous (camphor), (2) Musky (pentadecanolactone), (3) Floral (phenylethyl methyl ethyl carbinol). (4) Pepperminty (menthone), (5) Ethereal (ethylene dichloride), (6) Pungent (formic acid), and (7) Repulsive (butyl mercaptan).
Examine these primary odor substances. Make a table listing (1) the primary odor, (2) the chemical example, and (3) a familiar substance resembling that odor.
3. Ten basic solutions representing threshold concentrations of each compound are in the refrigerator and numbered 1 to 10. Identify each one and tabulate your results.

Questions

1. Why is the sense of smell called the chemical warning system of man?
2. State the Amoore's stereochemical theory of olfaction by Amoore.

EXPERIMENT 3: TEMPERATURE EFFECTS

Purpose:

To determine your ability to interpret correctly the effects of sourness and saltiness on sweetness; the effects of sweetness on saltiness, sourness, and bitterness; and temperature's effects on taste.

Materials:

26 2-liter reagent bottles with caps. Salt, sugar, caffeine, citric acid.
30 water glasses
12 sets measuring spoons
12 spatulas
150 ml beakers (from Experiment 2)

Procedure:

a. Effect of acid on sweetness: Taste solution A containing 50 g sucrose and B containing 50 g sucrose plus 0.3 g citric acid per liter at RT (21°C) and the corresponding solutions A and B at 50°F (10°C). Tabulate the effect of acid on sweetness at the two temperatures.

Identification	Less Sweet	More Sweet	No Difference
At RT: Observer Correct key			
At 50°F: Observer Correct key			

b. Effect of salt on sweetness: Do the same steps as in A for solutions C containing 50 g sucrose/liter, D containing 70 g sucrose plus 0.5 g salt/liter, and E containing 50 g sugar and 0.5 g salt/liter at RT, and do for C, D, and E at 50°F (10°C). Tabulate the effect of salt on sweetness at the two temperatures.

Identification	Less Sweet	More Sweet	No Difference
At RT: Observer Correct key			
At 50°F: Observer Correct key			

c. Effect of sugar on saltiness: Taste solutions F containing 4.5 g salt/liter, and G containing 4.5 g salt/liter plus 7 g sugar/liter at RT (21°C) and taste F and G at 50°F (10°C).

Identification	Less Sweet	More Sweet	No Difference
At RT: Observer Correct key			
At 50°F: Observer Correct key			

d. Effect of sugar on sourness (acidity): Taste solutions H containing 2 g citric acid/liter, and I containing 2 g citric acid plus 7 g sugar/liter at RT (21°C) and taste H and I at 50°F (10°C).

Identification	Less Sweet	More Sour	No Difference
At RT: Observer Correct key			
At 50°F: Observer Correct key			

e. Effect of sugar on bitterness: Taste solutions J containing 0.02 g caffeine/liter, and K containing 0.02 g caffeine plus 7 g sugar/liter at RT (21°C) and taste J and K at 50°F (10°C).

Identification	Less Sweet	More Sour	No Difference
At RT: Observer Correct key			
At 50°F: Observer Correct key			

f. Effect of temperature on sweetness: Taste solution containing 50 g sucrose/liter, at RT (21°C) and 50°F (10°C) respectively.

	Less Sweet	More Sweet	No Difference
L (RT)			
L (50°F)			

Questions

1. What effect does acid have on the sweetness of solutions in step a at the two temperatures?
2. What effect has salt on the sweetness of solutions in step b at the two temperatures?
3. What effect has sugar on the saltiness of solutions in step c at the two temperatures?
4. What effect has sugar on sourness in step d?
5. What effect has sugar on bitterness in step e?
6. What effect has temperature on sweetness in step f?

EXPERIMENT 4: BLENDING

Purpose:

To prepare a satisfactory blend of seasonings, flavorings, and colorings to produce a vegetable bouillon, evaluate the blend, and change its character by means of additives.

Materials:

Salt, dextrose, monosodium glutamate, 5′ nucleotide, citric acid, ammonium chloride, vegetable protein derivative (HVP), toasted onion powder, white onion powder, seasoning (soluble celery and pepper), starch derivative, brown sauce coloring, corn oil, and bouillon cubes. 48 dry water glasses.

Note: These materials are hygroscopic. Keep everything dry.

Procedure:

a. Taste each substance and describe its physical characteristics (appearance, taste and odor, and solubility).
b. Smell and taste 2 kinds of onion powder and give a word description of the difference between them.
c. Prepare bouillon control (5 steps):

1. Place 1 Tbsp salt in a water glass, add ¼ tsp brown sauce coloring—blend thoroughly. Now add and blend 1 Tbsp salt at a time—do this 3 times.
2. Pre-mix 1½ Tbsp dextrose, 1 tsp corn oil, 2 tsp starch derivative, 1 tsp toasted onion powder, and 1 Tbsp of HVP in a separate water glass.
3. Combine ½ tsp seasoning and 1½ tsp MSG.
4. Then add blend (1), 1 Tbsp at a time, until all of (1) and (3) are thoroughly blended together.
5. Finish by blending 2 and 4 together.

d. Taste the prepared bouillon by dissolving 1 tsp in 1 cup of lukewarm water (100°F). Compare taste with that of commercial cube. Describe taste and score each product on evaluation chart.
e. (1) Add very small amounts (a few grains at a time) of 5′ nucleotide to your bouillon solution and describe the effect. (2) Do the same using citric acid and (3) using ammonium chloride. Score the results on the same product evaluation sheet you used in step d.
f. Save the remainder of your bouillon preparation for future experiments by placing it in a plastic bag.

Questions

1. Describe the taste of MSG and of 5′ nucleotide.
2. Describe the flavor of HVP.
3. Why is MSG called a taste and HVP called a flavor?
4. What effect did ammonium chloride have?
5. Describe the taste of corn oil.
6. In your opinion which of the additives improved the product? Explain.

EXPERIMENT 5: TIME AND TEMPERATURE

Purpose:

To show the effects of time and temperature in tasting.

Part I

Materials:

6 oranges and 6 small 6 oz cans tomato juice per student. Orange juice concentrate at RT (21°C) and 50°F (10°C). 48 plates.

Procedure:

a. Peel one RT orange and one 50°F (10°C) orange, and put on separate plates. Slice into 6 equally thick slices.
b. Repeat, this time preparing 12 thin slices from each orange.
c. Section the remaining 2 oranges.
d. Taste and compare oranges prepared in steps a, b, and c. Note the effects of time and temperature due to thickness. Score each variable on evaluation charts.
e. Taste orange juice prepared from concentrate at RT (21°C) and at 50°F (10°C). Score the results.
f. Taste tomato juice at RT (21°C) and at 50°F (10°C). Score the results.
g. Using the remainder of the two tomato juice samples from (f) as controls, prepare seasoned samples at each temperature by adding ¼ tsp vegetable bouillon (yours). Stir thoroughly, then taste and score results.

Questions

1. Based on the experiment, what method do you prefer for preparing and serving fresh oranges?
2. What relationship did you find between time exposure and flavor preference?
3. What difference did serving temperature make? On which product(s) was it most pronounced?
4. Which product, fresh or frozen, had the best intrinsic flavor, based on a comparison of orange juice concentrate and the fresh juice?
5. Do you think that juice flavor is inferior to whole fruit flavor? To what degree?
6. How did added seasoning affect tomato juice? At what temperature was the seasoning effect most pronounced? Why?

Part II

Materials:

Add orange juice in canned, concentrate, fresh, and bottled varieties. All at RT (21°C) and 50°F (10°C). 48 plates. Small disposable cups.

Procedure:

After you follow steps a through g in Part I, evaluate and compare these various juices on the score sheets as well.

Questions

1.–6. As in Part I.

7. Which orange-flavored beverage do you prefer? Why?

8. What differences do you note between the tomato juice samples (seasoned versus plain)?

EXPERIMENT 6: FLAVOR FATIGUE

Purpose:

To determine the effect of sensory perception fatigue on flavor.

Part I

Materials:

Cherry and strawberry gelatin at RT (21°C) and 50°F (10°C). Vanilla and chocolate ice cream at RT (21°C) and 20°F (−7.0°C). Watch or clock.

Procedure:

a. Taste cherry gelatin at each temperature, noting the time required for flavor fatigue to occur.
b. Do the same for strawberry gelatin.
c. Do the same for vanilla ice cream.
d. Do the same for chocolate ice cream.

Questions

1. What conclusions do you draw concerning the relative time of flavor enjoyment versus flavor fatigue for each product?
2. How do you think flavor fatigue might affect the pleasure of wine drinking?
3. What do we do to overcome taste bud anesthesia while eating?
4. How important is flavor fatigue with regard to food and beverage appreciation?

Part II

Materials:

Cherry, strawberry and lemon gelatin. Day-old raspberry gelatin. Commercially prepared gelatin. Gelatin with fresh pineapple. Pudding—two brands in regular and instant varieties of chocolate and vanilla. Cool and creamy vanilla and chocolate pudding. All at RT and at 50°F. Vanilla and chocolate ice cream in 12% butterfat and 8% butterfat and ice milk. All at RT and 20°F.

Procedure:

Follow steps a through d in Part I. Then compare and evaluate all other samples at the two temperatures.

Questions

1.–4. As in Part I.
5. Which products do you prefer? At which temperature?

EXPERIMENT 7: FLAVOR VARIANTS DUE TO FOOD STRUCTURE

Purpose:

To recognize the importance of structure or form in foods and how food acceptance may be affected by variation of the structural factor(s).

Materials:

Two small (6 oz) cans tomato juice per student, celery, tomatoes, carrots, onions, beets, lemons, oranges, grapefruit, and tomatoes and their filtered or pulp–juices. Filter set up. Juicer. (Note: Juices to be pre-filtered for class use. Fresh filtered fruit and vegetable juices may be obtainable from a local health food store by special arrangement.)

Procedure:

a. Compare the flavor of each vegetable and fruit and its filtered–and pulp–juices.
Note the differences and score the results.

b. Take a can (6 oz) of tomato juice and blend ¼ tsp of each pulp–juice into it.
Compare (b) with the tomato juice control and score results.

Questions

1. Which did you prefer, the vegetable or the juice?
2. How do the senses of sight and hearing affect kinesthetic values in foods?
3. Based on this experiment, how would you anticipate that hash as stew made from the same ingredients would score?
4. How did the blend of pulp juices and tomato juice score as compared with the tomato juice control?

EXPERIMENT 8: FLAVOR PERCEPTION FATIGUE FACTORS

Purpose:

To show that flavor fatigue factors probably vary inversely with temperature.

Part I

Materials:

Coffee at 50°F (10°C) and 125°F (52°C); cola at RT (21°C) and 50°F (10°C). Baked potato and boiled potato at 100°F (38°C).

Procedure:

a. Determine which you taste longer and can drink more of: coffee at 50°F or coffee at 125°F?

b. Do the same for cola at RT (21°C) and 50°F (10°C).

c. Which has more taste, a baked or a boiled potato? Score the potatoes on a product evaluation chart.

d. Remove the baked potato from the skin and add water to moisten it. Now taste the moistened baked potato and the boiled potato and score them on the same chart.

Questions

1. Explain your results in terms of flavor perception factors (FPF).
2. What variables affect flavor perception factors (FPF) of gases, liquids, and solids?
3. Why is brandy warmed and tasted in a snifter?
4. Explain why the flavor perception factor (FPF) of frozen ice cream is zero.

Part II

Materials:

Instant coffee. Freeze-dried coffee. Percolated coffee. Vacuum coffee. Creamer. Sugar. Honey. Liquors. Whipped cream. Silver coffee pots. Taste cups. Spoons. Cola at RT and 50°F (10°C) and 125°F (52°C).

Procedure:

Follow a–d in Part I.

e. Evaluate various coffees and score them.

f. Score flavor differences of one coffee w/cream; one with sugar; one w/honey.

g. Taste coffee liquor drinks.

Questions

1.–4. As in Part I.

5. Which coffee did you prefer? Why?

EXPERIMENT 9: KINESTHETICS AND "INSTANT" POTATOES

Purpose:

To demonstrate variations in potato flavor perception using instant potatoes and different liquid media.

Part I

Materials:

Instant potatoes, milk, vegetable bouillon (from Experiment 4), chicken base, butter, chives, and sauteed onion.

Procedure:

a. Prepare the mashed potato control, using instant potatoes and following directions on the package calling for half milk and half water.
b. Prepare another sample using vegetable bouillon broth in place of the milk–water mixture.
c. Prepare a third sample using chicken broth made from chicken base.
d. Score a, b, and c on a product evaluation chart.
e. Keep a small amount of a, b, and c for control references. Then to 3 measured samples add (1) a small amount of butter to one, (2) a small amount of chives to another, and (3) a small amount of sauteed onions to the third. Compare each of these preparations with the control samples and score the results on product evaluation charts.

Questions

1. Which tasted best to you?
2. How do you explain your result in terms of FPF?
3. What effect did butter have?

Part II

Materials:

See Part I. Add eggs for potato pancakes.

Procedure:

Follow steps a through e in Part I.
f. Make a potato pancake from flavored instant potatoes and eggs. Fry until brown. Sample and evaluate your product.

EXPERIMENT 10: TEMPERATURE EFFECTS ON WINES

Purpose:

To show the effect of temperature on white and red wines.

Material:

Chablis (white) wine; cabernet (red) wine; sugar, burgundy wine, sauterne wine, sherry wine, cinnamon.

Procedure:

a. Taste the chablis at 50°F (10°C), 98.6°F (37°C), and 125°F (52°C). Tabulate your results.

b. Taste the cabernet at 50°F (10°C), RT (21°C) and at 98.6°F (37°C). Tabulate the results for a and b together.

c. Mull some of the cabernet at 125°F (52°C) by adding ½ tsp of cinnamon sugar to a cup of wine.

d. Repeat (a) using sauterne.

e. Repeat (b) and (c) using burgundy and sherry.

f. Drive off all of the alcohol from a cup of sauterne and taste the end product.

g. Do the same for burgundy and sherry. Tabulate these results.

Questions

1. How does temperature influence the flavor of wines?
2. What are the reasons for using wine in cooking?
3. Explain your results in terms of FPF.

EXPERIMENT 11: CONCENTRATION AS A FLAVOR VARIANT

Purpose:

To determine the effect of concentration regarding active ingredient(s) on flavor.

Part I

Materials:

Mayonnaise (24 oz), blue cheese (10 oz), and malt vinegar.

Procedure:

a. Blend 3, 6, or 9 Tbsp finely divided blue cheese into 3 separate cups of mayonnaise.

Taste and enter scores on product evaluation charts. These blends approximate 10, 15, and 25% by weight of cheese in mayonnaise respectively.

b. Choose the best sample. Divide it into 2 equal portions, using one portion as a control. To the other portion add (1%) malt vinegar—about ½ tsp—and blend in carefully (into 1 Tbsp at a time) until thoroughly combined.

Score these samples.

c. Now add the amount of cheese required to bring the flavor level back to that of the control sample. Be sure that you blend the cheese in carefully and thoroughly, combining 1 tsp of cheese with 1 Tbsp dressing at a time and then blending that into the remaining dressing. About 5% of cheese—or 2 tsp—should suffice.

Questions

1. Prepare a bar graph relating the 3 concentrations of cheese in mayonnaise to low, medium, and high levels of flavor.
2. What are the principal taste, odor, and kinesthetic properties?
3. What are they in cheese?
4. Name 3 other prepared food products that are affected by concentration of active ingredient(s) and name the flavor factor(s) responsible for the characteristic flavor of each.
5. Give an example of how too high a concentration is undesirable.
6. Draw a hypothetical curve by plotting concentration vs. score for the food product named in (5).

Part II

Materials:

Mayonnaise. Blue cheese. Malt vinegar. Tarragon vinegar. Mushroom, chicken, ham bases. Cream Cheese. Oil. Spices. 1 small jar w/lid per student. Crackers.

Procedure:

Follow steps a through c in Part I.

d. Blend cream cheese with each base separately. Taste on crackers. Score on sheets.

e. Make a salad dressing with bases, oil, vinegar, and spices.

Questions

1.–6. in Part I.

7. Give your recipe for the salad dressing combination you prepared.

EXPERIMENT 12: SELF-DETERMINATION OF FLAVOR RATING I

Purpose:

To combine vegetable and animal foods, and estimate the resultant flavor levels. Note: Work independently on this.

Part I

Materials:

White and whole wheat breads. Butter and margarine, 8% butter-fat ice cream. 12% butter-fat ice cream enriched with eggs and ice milk.

Procedure:

a. Compare the white breads and score them.
b. Do the same for the whole wheat breads.
c. Select one kind of white bread and one kind of whole wheat bread as controls. Butter a half slice of each and compare their scores with those for the unbuttered controls.
d. Repeat step c, using margarine.
e. Toast the different breads to light, medium, and dark (not burned) and score their individual flavors at 98.6°F (37°C) serving temperature.
f. Lightly butter one-fourth slice of each kind of toast, taste, and enter scores.
g. Repeat step f using margarine.
h. Score the ice cream and ice milk samples at 30°F (−1°C) and RT (21°C).

Questions

1. How do the kinesthetic factors of the breads and toasts compare?
2. What effects did buttering have on the flavor of (a) bread and (b) toast?
3. How did margarine flavor compare with butter on (a) bread and (b) toast?
4. From your results what combination(s) of breads and spreads did you choose?
5. How did you react to assuming responsibility for self-determination of a flavor rating for these foods?
6. In choosing the best ice cream, what flavor perception factors were involved?
7. What kinesthetic differences were apparent between the different ice cream samples?

Part II

Materials:

Delete ice cream products from the experiment. Three brands fresh whole wheat and white breads. Store and fresh bakery Italian-type breads. Crescent rolls—frozen and heat-and-serve. Bisquick. Refrigerated doughnut dough. Strawberries. Whipping cream (48%). Bases (chicken and ham). Margarine—salted and unsalted. Butter—salted and unsalted. Frying fat.

Procedure:

Follow steps a through g in Part I. Omit H.

i. Taste Italian breads and crescent rolls and note flavor differences between products.

j. Make biscuits according to package directions, adding ½ tsp each base separately. Sample.

k. Make doughnuts and evaluate products.

l. Taste strawberry shortcake made from plain biscuits, fresh ripe strawberries, and whipped cream.

EXPERIMENT 13: SELF-DETERMINATION OF FLAVOR RATING II

Purpose:

To season and flavor beef patties in different ways and evaluate the results.

Materials:

Ground beef (1 lb), salt, pepper, bases (consomme, mushroom, chicken, and beef).

a. Form a control patty (4 oz) by hand—blending ¼ tsp salt dissolved in 1 tsp hot water into the meat. Broil slowly to medium-rare.

b. Do the same,–but season and flavor the 4 oz patty with ¾ tsp consomme base dissolved in ½ tsp hot water hand-blended into the meat. Broil.

c. Season and flavor a 4 oz patty by combining ⅛ tsp chicken base, 1/16 tsp mushroom base, ½ tsp consomme liquid, and 1 tsp hot water and hand-blending this into the meat. Broil.

d. Use ¼ tsp beef base dissolved in 1 tsp hot water to flavor another 4 oz patty. Broil. When all of the patties are done to medium-rare, remove them from the oven, taste, and score on product evaluation charts.

Questions

1. Make a list of the ingredients contained in each of the food bases.
2. Are any preservatives or chemicals used in the bases?
3. How did blending the bases offset meat flavor?
4. Could you detect mushroom in the patty that contained it?
5. Which patty did you score highest?
6. Why should pepper be added last?

EXPERIMENT 14: SELF-DETERMINATION OF FLAVOR RATING III

Purpose:

To demonstrate the effect of onion and garlic on beef flavor.

Part I

Materials:

Ground beef (1 lb), salt, pepper (black), bases (onion and garlic).

Procedure:

a. *Control:* Prepare the patty you preferred in Experiment 13 and use it as a control in this experiment.

b. Season a 4 oz beef patty by hand-blending in a mixture of ⅛ tsp garlic base and ⅛ tsp salt dissolved in 1 tsp hot water, into the meat.

c. Repeat (b) using onion base.

d. Repeat (b) using ⅛ tsp garlic base and ⅛ tsp onion base.

e. Smell and taste the onion and garlic bases by disolving ¼ tsps each in separate cups of hot water.

Score your results on product evaluation charts.

Questions

1. What effect did garlic have on beef flavor? Did you like it?
2. What effect did onion have on beef flavor? Did you like it?
3. Which did you prefer?
4. How did scores compare with those given to patties in Experiment 13?
5. Nineteenth century chefs and gourmets despised garlic flavor. Why do we use it?
6. How do garlic and onion odors compare?
7. Name 3 typical garlic-containing foods.
8. What chemicals are responsible for garlic and onion odors?

Part II

Materials:

Ground beef. Carrots. Onions. Potatoes. Bases. Aluminum foil. Butter.

Procedure:

a. Slice potatoes, carrots, onions. Mix ground beef with choice of bases. Place all ingredients on square of aluminum foil. Follow directions to wrap dinner:

1. Slice a peeled Idaho potato into paper-thin slices. Peel and slice a carrot paper-thin. Peel and chop an onion.
2. Blend onion or garlic base into 5 oz coarsely ground beef and form into patty ⅜ in. thick.
3. Tear off 10-inch piece of oven-wrap aluminum foil.
4. Spread butter on shiny side of foil in thin coating to prevent sticking and add flavor.
5. Place seasoned ⅜ in. thick ground beef patty on center of butter foil.
6. Next, spread desired amount of chopped onion on top of ground beef patty.
7. Then, put a ⅛ in. layer of carrot slices over the onion.
8. Finally, add ⅛ in. layer of the potato slices.
9. Seal the foil in the form of a package using a drugstore wrap. Bring the long edges of the foil together centered above the prepared food. Then fold the edges into a prepared food. Then fold the edges into a half-inch crease clear across. Double this fold over again and again until it is snug to the food. Treat each end of the foil that remains unsealed in a like manner.

b. Bake at 350°F (177°C) for 45 minutes to 1 hour. Evaluate product.

EXPERIMENT 15: SELF-DETERMINATION OF FLAVOR RATING IV

Purpose:

To compare and judge hot beverages.

Materials:

Instant coffee (spray-dried) and freeze-dried restaurant coffee, fresh-ground and brewed coffee, instant tea, fresh-brewed green tea and/or black tea, instant cocoa and/or fresh-blended and brewed cocoa, Sanka, Postum, consomme base, milk, sugar, and salt.

Procedure:

a. Prepare and compare the four kinds of coffee—with and without sugar, cream, and milk.
Note and describe flavor differences due to adding cream or milk with and without sugar. Taste full strength, then diluted one-half, at 125°F (52°C).

b. Do the same for tea.

c. Do the same for cocoa.

d. Do the same for Sanka, Postum, and consomme.
Score each product on an evaluation chart or charts.

Questions

1. What differences did you observe in the aromas and flavors of the coffees?
2. Of the teas?
3. Of the cocoas?
4. How does Sanka compare with coffee? How does it differ (chemically) from coffee?
5. How does Postum rate as a hot beverage?
6. How does consomme rate? When would you choose it in preference to coffee? Why?

EXPERIMENT 16: SELF-DETERMINATION OF FLAVOR RATING V

Purpose:

To compare and judge canned, dehydrated, and fresh-made (from bases) soup flavors.

Materials:

Canned consomme base, chicken food base, chicken broth (canned), chicken-style base (dehydrated), chicken-style bouillon cubes, beef-style bouillon cubes, clam base, whipping cream.

Procedure:

a. Prepare and heat consomme and beef-style bouillon cube samples; taste at 120°F and RT.
Score on product evaluation charts. Now dilute samples by one-half and score.

b. Compare canned chicken broth with broths made from chicken food base, chicken-style base (dehydrated), and chicken-style bouillon cubes. Score on product evaluation charts. Then dilute each sample one-half with water and taste again and smell. Score these dilute samples.

c. Prepare Clam Bellevue by blending one cup clam broth with one cup of chicken broth made from the bases. Garnish each serving with a dollop of freshly whipped cream.

Questions

1. What difference did you notice in judging flavor when broth samples were diluted?
2. Which of all the samples did you prefer?
3. Which sample had the most chicken meat flavor? Was it hard to tell the difference between chicken samples?
4. Was it easier to tell using full-strength samples or when diluted samples were tasted?
5. Do you like Clam Bellevue? When could this be served advantageously?

PRODUCT EVALUATION CHART

Score System

Points		*Quality*	*Points*		*Quality*
7	-----	Excellent	3	-----	Fair
6	-----	Very Good	2	-----	Poor
5	-----	Good	1	-----	Very Poor
4	-----	Medium			

DIRECTIONS:

1. Place the numerical score in the box in the upper left-hand corner.
2. Comments should justify the numerical score. Comments must be brief.
3. Evaluation of the food products must be done on an *INDIVIDUAL* basis.

PRODUCTS

Quality Characteristic	Score	Score	Score	Score	Score
Appearance					
Consistency					
Tenderness					
Flavor					
Overall Eating Quality					

Index